Perennial Gardening Guide

Perhaps this book should come with a warning "Contents may cause compulsive behaviour," or "This book may affect your use of free time." For with over 1,300 different plants described there is enough for a lifetime of plant collecting and gardening.

Although I can trace my interest in flowers back to my childhood, it has been since my wife Kelly and I started growing perennials commercially on our nursery that this compulsive behavior has manifested itself. Between the nursery and our gardens, there is always room to try just another new plant. Weekends and holidays may find us scouting botanical gardens or nurseries, always looking for something new and different to photograph or acquire.

After scouting the world for plants to grow, our next responsibility is to describe these plants. Drawing on many years of experience with perennials and gardens, John Valleau has written a thorough, accurate and entertaining reference book for beginning gardeners and enthusiastic collectors alike. This book is a descriptive catalogue of the plants we grow. As a reference for perennial gardening, it is doubly useful since it describes plants cultivated and offered for sale in North America.

Please use this book to guide you to the pleasure inherent in growing plants and flowers. And if you find that you are experiencing a compulsive need to add just one more perennial to your garden, don't say I didn't warn you!

John Schroeder, President
Valleybrook Gardens Ltd.

*I*n the early days of European settlement, perennial flowers were grown in almost every North American garden. After World War II, however, perennials gradually fell out of favour; foundation evergreen plantings, flowering trees and shrubs, masses of annuals and groundcovers swept us off our feet for a few decades. In the last ten years or so, many home gardeners have had a craving for something more. More than a carpet of petunias or impatiens, more than another spreading juniper, even more than a bed of hybrid tea roses. And for many, perennials have become the perfect answer.

Because there is such a vast array of perennials to choose from, it would be difficult for any gardener to become bored of using them. For the addicted perennial gardener, the possibilities become endless. Planning, arranging, planting, taking notes, rearranging again and again, these are the joys and challenges of perennial gardening. Indeed, most perennial fanatics would agree that the border is never truly finished; there is always a new idea waiting to be tried.

Beginning gardeners, please don't be scared off! One of the best things about perennial gardening is that it can be tailored to suit your needs, experience, and even your budget. No need to convert your whole lawn into an English-style border. Start with your current landscaping as a base, and try to figure out a way of integrating perennials into what is already there.

A few basics

Let's do a little review of a few gardening basics:

ANNUALS are plants that complete their life cycle within one year. Examples: marigolds, petunias, impatiens, zinnias.

BIENNIALS usually need two years to bloom, set seed and die. Sometimes they get mixed up and take one year or even three years to do this. Examples: sweet william, forget-me-not, foxglove, canterbury bells.

PERENNIALS generally live for several years, though some are longer-lived than others. This varies a lot, depending on your climate, soil conditions, insects or diseases, and the plant in question. Herbaceous is a word used to describe plants that do not develop woody stems. Most of our garden perennials therefore fall into the

category of herbaceous perennials. This is to distinguish them from trees and shrubs.

Perennial benefits

No matter what your garden situation, there are a number of perennials available that will adapt to the conditions you already have. There are perennials for sun, shade, clay, sand, wet or dry soil, hot or cold climates, and everything in between.

Perennials flowers appear in every colour of the rainbow, as well as black, white and brown! No matter what colour scheme you can think up, there will be a perennial available to match. Just as important, the range of form and texture among perennials is quite diverse. Low, spreading carpets, medium rounded bushes and tall spiky spires are all available from among the ranks. Texture ranges from fine and feathery to bold and glossy.

Perennials can provide you with a much broader selection of plant material to choose from when planning your landscape. Not using perennials in our gardens would be like not decorating the walls of a room. We would be ignoring the endless possibilities of colour, texture, and the changing seasons.

And they are a good investment. Not only do they provide you with most of the same benefits as annuals, they even come back! And they get bigger. Within a few years many varieties will need to be lifted and divided, and what an excellent opportunity that is to share or trade with friends and neighbours. One healthy, large clump of Summer Phlox can be divided into ten or more pieces, so you can easily see an increase in value right there in your own garden.

For people with a limited amount of time available to garden, some of the more rugged and carefree perennials will fit very nicely into a low-maintenance scheme.

Perennial misconceptions

One misconception about perennials is that they will somehow magically take care of themselves. In most cases this is not true. They will still need

help both in getting established, and in staying healthy and vigorous.

This regular watering, weeding, trimming back or pruning, dividing, transplanting, fertilizing, and sometimes dealing with pests or diseases. This might sound like a lot of work, but compared to growing and maintaining a healthy lawn it can actually amount to much less.

Creative gardening with perennials

Back at the turn of the century, the British developed the perennial garden concept, borrowing ideas from the quaint country cottage gardens and refining them into the herbaceous border, an impressive thing indeed! Twenty feet deep by two hundred feet long would have been an average-sized border in that age of cheap labour and wealthy estate owners. The English-style border, with its grand scale and lavish use of colour, is more or less relegated to large parks and botanical gardens in modern times.

Few of us have the space, energy, time, or money necessary to recreate this effect successfully in our own gardens. So instead, we must figure out a way of incorporating perennials into the smaller gardens of today.

There are several other ways of using perennials besides the classic perennial border. Renowned British plantsman Alan Bloom pioneered the concept of island beds, which can be viewed from all sides. By putting taller plants in the centre, and gradually shorter ones towards the outside edge, this sort of bed provides its own backdrop. Maintenance is fairly easy, as the bed can be reached from all sides.

A shaded site with lots of deciduous trees is the perfect spot for a woodland garden, combining shade-loving perennials with spring-blooming bulbs, and low shade-tolerant flowering shrubs. Ferns, hostas and daffodils would all do very nicely here.

Container gardening with perennials is a relatively new idea. In milder areas perennials may be left in the pots for the winter, and in colder areas either sink the pots in the ground, or remove plants to the garden in late fall.

Mass plantings of perennials are very effective around large office buildings and other public areas. They create a large block of colour and texture, and are especially good flowing around or among trees and shrubs. This groundcover effect can be easily adapted to the low-maintenance residential garden.

Many people like to enjoy their flowers indoors, and most perennials will last at least a few days when cut, some for well over a week! A special garden for cut flowers might be worth considering if you don't like to pick the flowers from other areas of your garden.

Perhaps the best way of using perennials though, is in a more integrated kind of scheme, one that mixes them together with flowering bulbs, shrubs, trees, evergreens, ornamental grasses, herbs, annuals, and perhaps even vegetables! The resulting pot-pourri of plants is often referred to as the mixed border. By mixing in woody plants with perennials, the garden has a real backbone or shape all year round, something that might otherwise be lacking in a garden that uses only perennials.

Getting started

Look at the basic landscape that you already have, and try to determine what the good and bad elements are. Removing any diseased trees or shrubs might be a good place to start. Changing the line of a sidewalk or the shape of

Contents

Hardiness Zones

Use this table to help determine which plants are suitable for your winter conditions. Any plant with your zone number or lower should be suitable. **If you are in doubt be sure to ask your local garden centre staff.**

Zone	Minimum Winter Temp.	
	°F	°C
1	Below -50	Below -46
2	-50 to -40	-46 to -40
3	-40 to -30	-40 to -34
4	-30 to -20	-34 to -29
5	-20 to -10	-29 to -23
6	-10 to 0	-23 to -18
7	0 to 10	-18 to -12
8	10 to 20	-12 to -7
9	20 to 30	-7 to -1
10	30 to 40	-1 to 4

Use this information as a general guide for selecting suitable plants for your area. Many other factors affect overwintering of perennials. Some of these factors include: reliability and depth of snow cover, soil moisture levels, and site-specific micro-climates.

a planting might be all that is required. A basic book on landscaping will come in very handy at this point.

Rather than look at your entire yard, try to focus in on just a few spots that could use some improvement. If you re-work a few areas each year, it won't take very long at all to see a marked difference in your whole garden.

Look for spots that seem to need brightening up at certain times of the year. For example, maybe you have an area with a lot of tulips or daffodils already planted, and the dying foliage is an eyesore in May and June. Consider planting summer-blooming perennials among the bulbs; Coreopsis 'Moonbeam', Babies breath (Gypsophila), or Monkshood (Aconitum) would all be effective.

Maybe you have a narrow area beside the house that gets hot and dries out quickly. This sounds like a good spot for Hens-and-chicks (Sempervivum) or dwarf Stonecrops (Sedum) of various kinds. Either will look much better than bare dirt, and will actually thrive in that hot, harsh environment.

Think ahead

The hardest part about designing with perennials is planning for colour over an extended season. Although certain varieties will bloom for many weeks on end, most perennials bloom for three to four weeks at the most. If all the varieties in your garden begin blooming in early June, there won't likely be much colour left by September.

Check the blooming information under each plant listing, or check plant tags at your garden centre. This will help you to choose combinations that bloom at the same or different times, depending on the design you have in mind.

Ideally, a good selection of different perennials will give you colour somewhere in the garden from early April to late October. Learning which varieties bloom at what time is part of the challenge of perennial gardening. Take a good look around your neighbourhood this year. Try to take notes about when plants that appeal to you put on their best display. It is only one step further to begin combining different varieties together in clever ways that perhaps nobody ever thought of before!

Plan in threes

When looking for an attractive combination of plants, one of the most successful methods is to think in threes. For example, maybe you have a nice big clump of old-fashioned pink

Bleedingheart (Dicentra); let's try to combine two other plants with it that will look attractive at the same time. Perhaps you might add a nice clump of blue Siberian Iris, which has tall, grassy leaves, and maybe a clump or two of white-edged Hosta down at the front. Notice that the Hosta does not bloom at the same time, but still adds interest with its variegated leaves.

Planting a combination of three plants together can easily lend itself to all sorts of interesting designs. Try to imagine combinations of herbs, perennials and annuals, for example; no need to just stick to perennials alone. This little trick can easily be adapted to container gardening as well.

So, before digging up that chunk of lawn to install an English herbaceous border, just ask yourself if that commitment of time, energy, and money is what you really want. If perennials are new to you, we recommend starting out in a small way first, and slowly adding to your perennial display. After all, you can always dig up the lawn next year.

Selecting and planting perennials

When buying perennials, look for fresh, healthy-looking plants that appear vigorous and ready to grow. Avoid overgrown, rootbound plants and any that have insects or diseases.

When to Plant

Spring is the ideal time to plant container-grown perennials. They have a chance to get well established before the heat of summer arrives. Spring is also a good time to divide or transplant most types of perennials that you may already have in your garden. Peonies, Iris and Oriental Poppies should not be divided in the spring. However they can be planted from containers all season long.

Summer planting can be very successful, as long as plants are not allowed to dry out. Watering is especially important if the weather is hot and dry. Transplanting or dividing perennials already established in your garden is not recommended during the summer, except for Bearded Iris, which should be divided only in July or August.

Fall planting is highly recommended in most areas. Early-blooming varieties will put on a colourful display in spring if planted in the fall. Dividing or moving established perennials in the fall is usually very successful.

Winter frosts may "heave" fall planted perennials. Check them in late winter, and if any have popped out of the ground, gently press them back in place.

How to plant perennials

1 Prepare soil, dig hole large enough to accomodate the root ball.

2 Remove pot, break up the rootball if plant is root bound.

3 Fill hole with water, place plant in hole and fill in around roots with soil.

4 Continue filling with soil. Top of root ball must be at or slightly below soil surface.

Preparing your soil

Most perennials grow best in a deep, rich, well-drained soil. Check the tag for specific soil or site requirements. Properly preparing your soil is the single most important step to having healthy, successful gardens.

Dry, sandy soils can be improved by adding plenty of organic matter, such as compost, moistened peat moss or composted manure. Dig the area to a depth of at least 8 inches, preferably with a fork or spade.

Heavy clay soils need to be opened by adding plenty of organic matter, along with perlite or coarse sand.

Few perennials do well in wet, poorly drained soils. Consider building raised beds or installing drainage tubing if you have a soggy garden area. If you are not prepared to do this, choose perennials which do well under these conditions.

Weeds

The planting area must be free of perennial weeds, especially spreading types like Canada Thistle and Couch or Quack Grass. Ask your garden centre how these can be eliminated. Annual weeds are easily controlled by hand weeding.

Mulching around your plants will help to control weeds, and will keep roots cool and moist. Choose a mulching material that is organic and weed free, such as bark, cocoa beans or shredded leaves.

Watering

If these planting instructions are followed, no more watering should be required for a week or so. This will of course depend on temperature, rainfall etc. Otherwise, water plants immediately after planting and once a week or so for the first two weeks, unless the weather is rainy.

Hold the pot upside-down and shake or tap to loosen the plant. If lots of roots are visible and all jumbled together, the plant may be rootbound. If so, the root ball must be disturbed to force new, healthy root growth. Using a sharp knife, slice up the bottom 2cm (1") of roots and rough up the sides of the ball with your fingers. Make sure the soil in the pot is moist. Planting a dry root ball makes it very difficult to provide sufficient water.

With a spade or trowel, open up a hole deep enough to accommodate the root ball. For best planting results, use the "puddling method." Fill the hole with water, place the plant upright in the hole and fill in around the roots with soil. Pat the soil to thoroughly mix the soil and water. This helps to eliminate any air pockets around the roots and ensures sufficient moisture for growth. Be sure the root ball surface is at or just slightly below the garden soil surface. After planting, spread a mulch to a depth of 2–5cm (1–2").

Summer plantings may require more frequent watering, especially during periods of drought.

Fertilizing

Perennials may be fertilized with either a liquid or a slow-release granular-type fertilizer. Ask your garden centre to recommend a good product. If your soil is fertile and well-prepared to begin with, no additional fertilizing should be necessary the first year, although incorporating some bone meal at planting is often helpful.

Established perennial beds benefit from a yearly spring application of slow-release fertilizer or compost.

Maintaining perennials

This guide on perennials will help you to learn about some of the special things that should be done to your plants, such as staking, cutting back and controlling any diseases or pests. Ask your garden centre which other books they recommend for additional information you may require.

Here are some general guidelines for maintaining perennials:

· Prune off any dead tops in late winter or early spring.
· Remove dead flowers to encourage repeat blooming.
· Water during drought if possible; early

morning is best.
· Clip back scruffy looking plants to promote fresh, attractive growth.
· Control pests and diseases as soon as noticed to avoid spreading the problem to other plants.
· Stake Peony, Delphinium, Summer Phlox and other tall plants early to avoid wind damage later.
· Divide perennials when the centre of the plant begins to die out with age.

Symbols Key

☀ **Full Sun**

☼ **Part Shade**

● **Full Shade**

△ **Alpine**

✄ **Good Cut Flower**

▲ **Evergreen**

〰 **Groundcover**

🦋 **Attracts Butterflies**

➤ **Attracts Hummingbirds**

▼ **Suitable for Containers**

🕱 **Drought Tolerant**

Acaena microphylla

Acanthus mollis

Achillea millefolium 'Red Beauty'

Achillea × 'Hoffnung'

ACAENA
(New Zealand Burr) ☀ ◑

A unique and under-used group of low-growing groundcovers from the southern Hemisphere, valued for their dense, spreading carpet of evergreen foliage, and colourful burr-shaped seed heads which appear in late summer. Although these are usually planted in rock gardens, they grow quickly and can sometimes smother out choicer alpines. Good cover plants in combination with early spring flowering bulbs. All are drought tolerant once established, and don't mind poor soils.

'Blue Haze'   ZONES 6–9
Attractive blue-green leaves, a little larger than *A. microphylla*. Many stems of brown burrs in the fall.

> "One that I have most often met…has quite tiny glaucous pinnate foliage borne on longish scrambling stems that can rise into and intermingle with any foot- or 18-inch-tall plant or shrub they happen to be near." —Christopher Lloyd, *Foliage Plants*

HEIGHT/SPREAD:	10cm (4")/30–60cm (1–2')
LOCATION:	Well-drained soil. Tolerates poor soil. Dislikes wet soil.
BLOOMS:	June–August
USES:	△⋀▲🏵 Fast spreaders

caesiiglauca   ZONES 5–9
(Silver-leaf New Zealand Burr) Silvery-blue leaves with a soft, downy texture. Reddish burrs. One of the best forms, and reported to be less invasive. Not widely tested yet for hardiness but worth a try to Zone 4.

HEIGHT/SPREAD:	10cm (4")/30–60cm (1–2')
LOCATION:	Well-drained soil. Tolerates poor soil. Dislikes wet soil.
BLOOMS:	June–August
USES:	△⋀▲🏵 Fast spreaders

microphylla   ZONES 3–9
(Bronze-leaf New Zealand Burr) Good low carpeter. Unusual bronzy-green foliage and showy copper-red burrs. The toughest species, great for between paving stones! Spreads quickly.

HEIGHT/SPREAD:	10cm (4")/30–60cm (1–2')
LOCATION:	Well-drained soil. Tolerates poor soil. Dislikes wet soil.
BLOOMS:	June–August
USES:	△⋀▲🏵 Fast spreaders

ACANTHUS
(Bear's-Breech) ☀ ◑

Bold specimen plants, very popular with landscape designers. When grown in borders or containers these form large leafy clumps with a tropical flair. Exotic upright spikes of light pink flowers appear throughout the summer months. Choose a well-protected area as they can be damaged by late spring frosts. In colder areas plant in tubs for easy overwintering indoors. Where hardy, these can spread to form a large patch.

> "Bear's breeches,…with its thick mounds of long, jagged leaves, easily dominates a borderful of smaller foliage, even without its head-high stems of tubular, mauvy flowers." —Ann Lovejoy, *The American Mixed Border*

mollis latifolius   ZONES 6–9
The hardiest variety, with large, glossy and deeply-lobed leaves. Mauve-pink flowers, vigorous habit. Excellent cut flower. Use a winter mulch in Zones 5–6.

HEIGHT/SPREAD:	90–150cm (3–5')/90cm (3')
LOCATION:	Well-drained soil. Dislikes winter wet
BLOOMS:	July–August
USES:	✂❦ Dried Flower, Specimen, Borders

ACHILLEA
(Yarrow) ☀

The Yarrows are among the best perennials for hot and dry locations, providing good colour throughout the summer months, and even tolerating poor soils. All varieties are superb for cutting, used fresh or dried. Divide and replant clumps every two years.

× 'Anthea'   ZONES 2–9
A newer hybrid, bred by Alan Bloom of Bressingham Gardens, an offspring of a cross with 'Moonshine'. Plants are upright with intensely silver foliage on a bushy, non-spreading clump. The large flower clusters open primrose yellow fading to cream, blooming continually all season if faded flowers are removed. Excellent for cutting. Moderately drought-tolerant.

HEIGHT/SPREAD:	30–45cm (12–18")/30cm (12")
LOCATION:	Average well-drained soil.
BLOOMS:	June–September
USES:	✂▲❦🏵 Dried Flower, Borders, Massing

filipendulina   ZONES 2–9
(Fern-Leaf Yarrow) Forms an upright clump of ferny green leaves with large clusters of golden-yellow flowers on tall stems. Good for massing. Flowers are superb for drying. Very drought-tolerant.

HEIGHT/SPREAD:	90–120cm (3–4')/45cm (18")
LOCATION:	Well-drained soil. Heat tolerant.
BLOOMS:	June–September
USES	✂🏵 Dried Flower, Borders

× Galaxy Hybrids   ZONES 2–9
This group of German hybrid *Achillea* offers a remarkable range of new colours, a welcome addition to the summer border. With strong stems and good-sized flower clusters, they are excellent for cutting, fresh or dried. Deadhead faded flowers to encourage continual blooming.

HEIGHT/SPREAD:	60–90cm (24–36")/60cm (24")
LOCATION:	Well-drained soil. Heat tolerant.
BLOOMS:	June–September
USES:	✂❦🏵 Dried Flower, Borders

'Apple Blossom' ('Apfelblute') Large clusters of lilac-pink flowers. To 90cm (3').

'Heidi' Clear pink flowers, compact form.

'Hoffnung' ('Great Expectations') Primrose yellow flowers tinged with peach. Compact habit.

'Paprika' Cherry-red, gold centered flowers, fading to light pink and creamy yellow.

'Summer Pastels' A seed-grown mix of the various Galaxy colours, including also some beautiful shades of wine, salmon and creamy white. An All America Award winner.

millefolium   ZONES 1–9
(Common Yarrow) Old-fashioned cut flowers, so useful for summer bloom. Medium-sized clusters are held above ferny green foliage. Inclined to spread, but may be useful as a groundcover on slopes. Clip back hard after blooming to force a second flush. Very drought-tolerant.

HEIGHT/SPREAD:	45–70cm (18–30")/60cm (24")
LOCATION:	Well-drained soil. Heat tolerant.
BLOOMS:	June–September
USES:	✂🏵 Dried Flower, Borders

'Lavender Beauty' Unusual pastel lavender-pink flowers.

'Red Beauty' Deep crimson-red clusters. Still the best red!

× 'Moonshine'   ZONES 2–9

An outstanding early hybrid by Alan Bloom of Bressingham Gardens. Valued for its summer-long display of rich canary-yellow flowers held in large clusters above silvery-grey leaves. Non-spreading habit. Combines well with ornamental grasses. Remove faded flowers for continual bloom. Still one of the best perennials of all time. Moderately drought-tolerant

HEIGHT/SPREAD:	45–60cm (18–24")/30cm (12")
LOCATION:	Average well-drained soil.
BLOOMS:	June–September
USES:	�◀▲▼⅗ Dried Flower, Massing, Borders

ptarmica 'Dwarf Ballerina'   ZONES 1–9

(Double White Yarrow) Airy sprays of fluffy white flowers similar to Baby's Breath. Compact form of an old-fashioned favorite. Inclined to spread.

HEIGHT/SPREAD:	30–45cm (12–18")/45–60cm (18–24")
LOCATION:	Average to moist soil. Heat tolerant.
BLOOMS:	June–September
USES:	✂⅗ Dried Flower, Massing, Borders

tomentosa 'Aurea'   ZONES 1–9

(Woolly Yarrow) Carpet-forming, with short stems of lemon-yellow flowers in early spring. Easy rock garden plant. Clip off the flowers after they fade. Very drought-tolerant.

HEIGHT/SPREAD:	20cm (8")/30cm (12")
LOCATION:	Well-drained soil.
BLOOMS:	May–July
USES:	△〰⅗ Edging. Borders

ACONITUM
(Monkshood) ☼ ◐

Tall, sturdy perennials, these look their best in larger borders. Showy spikes of flowers appear during the summer months and are beautiful for cutting. They prefer a cool, moisture-retentive soil. All Monkshood are extremely poisonous.

× cammarum 'Bicolor'   ZONES 2–9

Flowers are an attractive violet-blue and white combination.

HEIGHT/SPREAD:	90–120cm (3–4')/60cm (2')
LOCATION:	Cool, moist, well-drained soil.
BLOOMS:	June–August
USES:	✂ Borders

napellus   ZONES 2–9

(Blue Monkshood) Deep blue helmet-shaped flowers. Old-fashioned favorite.

HEIGHT/SPREAD:	120–150cm (4–5')/60cm (2')
LOCATION:	Cool, moist, well-drained soil.
BLOOMS:	June–August
USES:	✂ Borders

There are also some excellent selections available:

'Bressingham Spire' One of the best forms, hybridized and introduced by Alan Bloom of Bressingham Gardens. Compact stems don't require staking. Deep violet-blue flowers from midsummer through the fall. HEIGHT: 90cm (3')

'Carneum' A unique selection with pale rose-pink flowers. Similar in stature to the regular blue form, and a lovely contrast to it in the border. Flowers may fade during hot weather. HEIGHT: 120–150cm (4–5').

pyrenaicum   ZONES 2–9

(Yellow Monkshood) (= *A. lamarckii*) Unusual creamy-yellow flowers. Just as easy to grow as the blue-flowered forms.

HEIGHT/SPREAD:	60–90cm (2–3')/60cm (2')
LOCATION:	Cool, moist, well-drained soil.
BLOOMS:	June–August
USES:	✂ Borders

septentrionale 'Ivorine'   ZONES 2–9

Another Bressingham Gardens selection bred by Alan Bloom. Neat, compact variety. Ivory-white flowers in short spikes. Earlier blooming. The best of the white forms.

HEIGHT/SPREAD:	60–90cm (2–3')/60cm (2')
LOCATION:	Cool, moist, well-drained soil.
BLOOMS:	June–August
USES:	✂ Borders

AEGOPODIUM
(Goat's foot, Snow-on-the-Mountain) ◐●

podagraria 'Variegatum'   ZONES 1–9

Well-known groundcover, with green and white variegated foliage. Quickly forms a solid patch, even in poor soil. Difficult to eradicate once established. Dislikes hot sun. Recommended for pots and containers, or where it can spread without becoming a problem. Clip off the flower stems for best appearance. Extremely drought-tolerant.

HEIGHT/SPREAD:	30cm (12")/30–60cm (12–24")
LOCATION:	Tolerates most soils.
BLOOMS:	Flowers usually removed
USES:	〰▼⅗ Invasive! Use carefully

AGAPANTHUS
(African Lily) ☼ ◐

Magnificent, exotic plants from South Africa, valued for their large flower heads. Excellent container plants, especially in colder regions where plants may be easily overwintered indoors. May be hardy in Zones 6–7 with sufficient winter protection. Superb cut flower.

Hybrids   ZONES 8–9

The result of extensive breeding in England resulting in many good selections with increased hardiness and deeper colours.

SPREAD:	30–60cm (12–24")
LOCATION:	Well-drained soil.
BLOOMS:	July–September
USES:	✂▼ Borders, Massing

'Bressingham Blue' Alan Bloom selection. Probably the deepest blue available, vigorous plant. HEIGHT: 75cm (30")

'Bressingham White' Large growing plant with pure white flowers. Another Bressingham Gardens introduction. HEIGHT: 90cm (36")

'Headbourne Hybrids' A seed-grown strain noted for its improved hardiness, the gene pool for many of the modern named selections. Flowers vary in colour from pale through dark blue, with the occasional white. HEIGHT: 70–90cm (28–36").

'Lilliput' Excellent container plant. Dwarf, compact habit, bright blue trumpet flowers. HEIGHT: 45cm (18")

AGASTACHE
(Anise-Hyssop) ☼ ◐

foeniculum 'Fragrant Delight'   ZONES 2–9

Selection of a North American wildflower, native to sunny prairies and meadows. Tall wands of pale violet flowers appear summer through fall, and are a favorite of bees and butterflies. Good for cutting. Entire plant has a pleasant anise fragrance and can be used to make a soothing tea. (see also under Anise-Hyssop in the HERB chapter)

HEIGHT/SPREAD:	90–120cm (3–4')/45cm (18')
LOCATION:	Average well-drained soil.
BLOOMS:	July–September
USES:	✂🐛🦋 Wildflower, Dried Flower, Borders, Herb gardens

AJANIA see CHRYSANTHEMUM

Aconitum × *cammarum* 'Bicolor'

Aconitum napellus

Aegopodium podagraria 'Variegatum'

Agapanthus 'Lilliput'

Ajuga reptans 'Burgundy Glow'

Ajuga p. 'Metallica Crispa Purpurea'

Alchemilla mollis

Alcea 'Chater's Double Scarlet'

AJUGA
(Bugleweed) ☼☀●

Widely used as a groundcover for part-shade or sun. Most types are fast-spreading but easy to control, forming a low mat of rounded leaves. Showy spikes of flowers appear in late spring. There are a great number of varieties available.

genevensis   ZONES 2–9

(Geneva Bugle) Spikes of bright blue flowers, thick mat of green foliage, the hardiest form.

HEIGHT/SPREAD:	15–20cm (6–8")/30–45cm (12–18")
LOCATION:	Prefers moist soil.
BLOOMS:	May–June
USES	⋗▲♥ Edging

'Pink Beauty' Soft-pink flowers, held on more upright spikes. Long blooming season. Not as hardy as the blue form, Zone 5.

pyramidalis 'Metallica
Crispa Purpurea'   ZONES 3–9

(also known as 'Mini Crisp Red') A most unusual form, the deep-red leaves are crimped and crinkled like spinach, very compact and congested. This form is extremely slow compared to the other varieties. Can be used in a rockery with no fear of invasion. Almost black winter colour. Short spikes of blue flowers. Choice.

HEIGHT/SPREAD:	5–10cm (2–4")/20–30cm (8–12")
LOCATION:	Prefers moist soil.
BLOOMS:	May–June
USES	⋰⋗▲♥ Edging

reptans   ZONES 3–9

(Common Bugle) Fast-spreading mats, bright blue flowers in spring. Among the many selections are some outstanding forms with unusual foliage colouring. The deep red types are especially dramatic when massed below green or gold-leaved shrubs.

HEIGHT/SPREAD:	15cm (6")/30–45cm (12–18")
LOCATION:	Prefers moist soil.
BLOOMS:	May–June
USES	⋗▲♥ Edging

'Braunherz' (Brownheart) Newer German variety. Glossy deep purple-bronze leaves, contrasting deep blue flowers. The best dark leaved form.

'Bronze Beauty' Popular older bronze-leaved variety. Bright blue flowers.

'Burgundy Glow' Brightly-coloured leaves, variegated with scarlet, cream, and green. Bright blue flowers. Good fall colour. Rogue out any reverting shoots regularly.

'Catlin's Giant' Unusually tall spikes of blue flowers, huge bronzy leaves. Inclined to clump at first, later forming a solid patch. Excellent for edging! HEIGHT: 15–30cm (6–12")

'Silver Carpet' Newer variety with metallic silver foliage, blue flowers.

ALCEA
(Hollyhock) ☼

rosea   ZONES 2–9

These tall spikes of crepe-textured flowers have been grown in gardens for centuries. Best at the back of a sunny border with medium-sized plants in front to hide the bare lower stems. Usually biennial, the plants will readily self-seed if allowed. Leaf rust may be a problem, particularly with the double types; either ignore it or try using a systemic fungicide. Cutting plants back immediately after flowering may encourage them to return for another year. Said to attract hummingbirds.

> "For many years, I preferred the fat doubles but now find them congested and graceless next to the simple singles, perhaps because of the comment that doubles look 'like those toilet paper decorations on wedding cars'—enough to put one off any flower." —Patrick Lima, *The Harrowsmith Perennial Garden*

HEIGHT/SPREAD:	1.5–2.1m (5–7')/30cm (12")
LOCATION:	Average well-drained soil.
BLOOMS:	July–August
USES	⋗✂➤ Borders

'Chater's Doubles' Large double ruffled blooms, like Kleenex™ flowers. Generally available in mixed colours or sometimes separately in shades of maroon, rose, pink, scarlet, white, and yellow.

'Nigra' Unique single maroon-black flowers.

'Powderpuff Mix' More compact in habit, with fully double blooms in a complete range of mixed colours. Sometimes treated as an annual. HEIGHT: 1.2–1.5m (4–5')

'Single Mix' (*A. ficifolia* hybrids) The single-flowered forms of Hollyhock have a certain grace and charm that is totally lacking in the double types. They are generally not as badly affected by leaf rust, with an overall tougher constitution. Said to be the easiest to establish, with more of a perennial habit. Flowers are available in a whole range of pastel shades.

ALCHEMILLA
(Lady's Mantle) ☼☀

Popular plants for edging, these form a mound of rounded leaves with billowing sprays of yellow-green flowers. Sometimes mass planted as a groundcover. They adapt to most garden conditions.

alpina   ZONES 2–9

(Alpine Lady's Mantle) Compact grower. Silvery leaves, buff-coloured flowers.

HEIGHT/SPREAD:	15cm (6")/30cm (12")
LOCATION:	Well-drained soil.
BLOOMS:	June–August
USES	⋰⋗✂♥ Edging, Borders

mollis   ZONES 2–9

Scalloped green leaves, covered in a soft down. Flowers and foliage are good for cutting. Self-seeds readily.

> "It makes a fine cover for species crocus and minor bulbs, which bloom outside the circle of its crown, then ripen and wither in the shelter of its extensive arms." —Ann Lovejoy, *The American Mixed Border*

> "Its leaves are like an umbrella turned inside out and they are hairy, holding raindrops in their centre, but with a light-reflecting air bubble trapped underneath, that winks and sparkles with contagious glee." —Christopher Lloyd, *Foliage Plants*

HEIGHT/SPREAD:	30–45cm (12–18")/45–60cm (18–24")
LOCATION:	Well-drained soil.
BLOOMS:	June–August
USES	⋰⋗✂♥ Edging, Borders

ALLIUM
(Flowering Onion) ☼☀

A useful and under-used group of flowering perennials, offering a wide range of heights and colours for the sunny border. Flowers are arranged in a ball-shaped cluster, the taller varieties making excellent cut flowers.

caeruleum ZONES 2–9
(Blue Globe Onion) Good-size balls of deep blue flowers. This species appreciates a warm site. Greyish grassy leaves may stay evergreen in mild areas. Flowers are good for drying.

HEIGHT/SPREAD:	30–60cm (12–24")/30cm (12")
LOCATION:	Average to dry well-drained soil.
BLOOMS:	June–July
USES:	✂▲🌷 Dried Flower, Borders

cernuum ZONES 2–9
(Nodding Onion) Delicate nodding umbels of mauve to pale lilac flowers in summer. One of the best onions for the front of a border or rock garden. Will tolerate both shade and sun. A North American native wildflower.

HEIGHT/SPREAD:	30cm (12")/30cm (12")
LOCATION:	Average well-drained soil.
BLOOMS:	June–July
USES:	▲✂🌷 Borders, Woodland

schoenoprasum 'Forescate' ZONES 1–9
(Giant Chives) A select form of common chives, with extra large rose-purple balls of flowers. Doubles as a culinary herb, use as you would regular chives.

HEIGHT/SPREAD:	30cm (12")/30cm (12")
LOCATION:	Well-drained soil.
BLOOMS:	May–July
USES:	✂🌷🦋 Borders, Herb gardens

senescens 'Glaucum' ZONES 3–9
(Pink Curly Onion) Unique blue-green leaves twisting out from the base in a spiral. Small clusters of pink flowers in late summer. Nice edging or rockery variety.

HEIGHT/SPREAD:	15–30cm (6–12")/30cm (12")
LOCATION:	Well-drained soil.
BLOOMS:	July–September
USES	▲🌷 Edging, Borders

ALYSSUM
(Gold Dust, Basket-of-Gold) ☀
Extremely popular plants for the spring-blooming rock garden. Yellow flowers smother the cascading silvery foliage. Ideal for tumbling over walls and slopes or for edging.

montanum ZONES 2–9
(Mountain Alyssum) Low, compact form with small silvery leaves. Fragrant lemon-yellow flowers. Very hardy species.

HEIGHT/SPREAD:	10–15cm (4–6")/30cm (12")
LOCATION:	Lean, well-drained soil.
BLOOMS:	April–June
USES	▲▲🌿 Edging, Walls

saxatile ZONES 3–9
(= *Aurinia saxatilis*) The more common species, forming fairly large mounds of good silver-grey foliage. Especially nice on slopes or walls. Fairly drought-tolerant. There are several selections.

HEIGHT/SPREAD:	20–30cm (8–12")/30–60cm (12–24")
LOCATION:	Lean, well-drained soil.
BLOOMS:	April–June
USES	▲〰▲🌿 Edging, Walls

'Compactum' (Basket-of-Gold) Profuse, bright yellow flowers. The most popular variety.

'Citrinum' Like Basket-of-Gold but in a pale sulphur-yellow shade, an easier colour to design with.

'Dudley Neville Variegated' Primrose-yellow flowers, beautiful green and cream variegated leaves. Remove any all-green shoots. This variety seems to require perfect drainage. Grown from cuttings.

'Sunny Border Apricot' Pale apricot-yellow flowers.

AMSONIA
(Blue Star) ☀◑

tabernaemontana ZONES 3–9
An interesting native North American wildflower, forming an arching clump of green leaves, with clusters of light blue starry flowers in late spring and early summer. Especially recommended for moist sunny areas, but adapts well to border conditions. Good golden-yellow fall colour. Useful for cutting. Long lived.

HEIGHT/SPREAD:	60–90cm (2–3')/60–90cm (2–3')
LOCATION:	Average to moist, rich soil.
BLOOMS:	May–July
USES	✂ Wildflower, Borders

ANACYCLUS
(Mt. Atlas Daisy) ☀

depressus ZONES 4–9
Unique daisy flowers, white on the front, red on the back. Forms a low clump of ferny foliage. Good rock garden plant, blooming over a long season. Fairly drought-tolerant.

HEIGHT/SPREAD:	10cm (4")/20–30cm (8–12")
LOCATION:	Well-drained soil. Dislikes winter wet.
BLOOMS:	May–July
USES	▲🌿 Walls, Slopes

ANAPHALIS
(Pearly Everlasting) ☀

margaritacea ZONES 2–9
A native wildflower, often gathered and dried as an everlasting. Flowers are clusters of white buttons, contrasting nicely with the grey foliage. Good border plant, although somewhat invasive. Moderately drought-tolerant.

HEIGHT/SPREAD:	30–90cm (12–36")/30cm (12")
LOCATION:	Well-drained soil. Drought tolerant.
BLOOMS:	July–September
USES	✂🌿 Borders, Edging

ANEMONE
(Windflower) ◑☀

A large group of hardy perennials, many of easy garden culture. By far the most widely known are the fall-blooming hybrid Japanese Anemones, but there are also other species that flower in spring or summer.

blanda ZONES 4–9
(Grecian Windflower) One of the first spring flowers to appear, forming carpets of starry flowers under trees and shrubs. Plants are very low, the flowers nestling just above green ferny leaves. A good species for naturalizing, with a tendency to self-seed. Several forms are usually available with blue, pink or white flowers, and can often be bought as tubers in the fall.

HEIGHT/SPREAD:	15–20cm (6–8")/15cm (6")
LOCATION:	Rich, moist woodland soil.
BLOOMS:	March–April
USES	▲ Woodland gardens

× hybrida ZONES 5–9
(Japanese Anemone) Outstanding plants for the late summer and fall garden. The branching stems of poppy-like flowers are superb for cutting. These will spread to form a solid patch. Good low-maintenance perennial. Mulch well for the first winter.

Allium schoenoprasum 'Forescate'

Alyssum saxatile 'Compactum'

Amsonia tabernaemontana

Anacyclus depressus

Anemone × 'September Charm'

Anemone pulsatilla

Anemone sylvestris

Aquilegia alpina

"No plant of autumn brings more joy than Japanese anemones. They look wonderful if given a spot all to themselves in front of shrubbery, but they also associate very well with ferns growing at their feet." —Allen Lacy, *The Garden in Autumn*

HEIGHT/SPREAD: 60–150cm (2–5')/60cm (24")
LOCATION: Rich, moist to damp soil.
BLOOMS: August–October
USES: Massing, Borders

'Bressingham Glow' Raised by Alan Bloom at Bressingham Gardens. Deep magenta-rose flowers, semi-double. Compact. HEIGHT: 60cm (24")

'Honorine Jobert' Large, single white flowers, an excellent old variety. HEIGHT: 90–120cm (36–48")

'Lady Gilmour' Very large semi-double flowers, rose-pink. HEIGHT: 90cm (36")

'Pamina' Deep rose-red flowers, one of the darkest. HEIGHT: 60–90cm (24–36")

'Prince Henry' Small, deep rose semidouble flowers. HEIGHT: 90cm (36")

'Queen Charlotte' Pink, semidouble flowers. HEIGHT: 90cm (36")

'September Charm' Large silvery-pink, single flowers. HEIGHT: 60–90cm (24–36")

'Whirlwind' Semidouble white flowers. HEIGHT: 90–120cm (3–4')

× lesseri   ZONES 5–9
A spring-blooming hybrid with glowing rose-red flowers, glossy foliage. Often reblooms in the fall if cut back. This is a slower growing, non-invasive form.

HEIGHT/SPREAD: 45cm (18")/30cm (12")
LOCATION: Deep, well-drained soil.
BLOOMS: May–June
USES: Woodland gardens, Borders

nemerosa   ZONES 2–9
(Wood Anemone) A carefree little species for shaded deciduous woodland situations, where it will thrive for many years, spreading slowly. Needs a good moisture-retentive soil with plenty of leafmould or compost. Starry single flowers are in shades of white, blue or pink.

HEIGHT/SPREAD: 10–15cm (4–6")/15cm (6")
LOCATION: Rich, moist woodland soil.
BLOOMS: March–April
USES: Woodland gardens

pulsatilla   ZONES 2–9
(Pasque-Flower) (now correctly *Pulsatilla vulgaris*) A favorite early spring bloomer with violet-purple flowers like a Prairie Crocus. Showy in the rock garden or border, good for naturalizing. Occasionally there are other colour forms of this available in red, pink or white. Moderately drought-tolerant.

HEIGHT/SPREAD: 15–30cm (6–12")/30cm (12")
LOCATION: Well-drained soil.
BLOOMS: March–May
USES: Borders, Meadows

sylvestris   ZONES 2–9
(Snowdrop Anemone) Delicate nodding white flowers in late spring and intermittently throughout the summer. Quickly spreads to form a dense patch, suitable for use as a groundcover. Good cover for spring bulbs.

HEIGHT/SPREAD: 30–45cm (12–18")/30–60cm (12–24")
LOCATION: Average to moist soil.
BLOOMS: May–June
USES: Massing, Borders

tomentosa 'Robustissima'   ZONES 4–9
Similar to a pink Japanese Anemone, but even more vigorous and hardier. Upright clumps of deep green foliage remain attractive from spring to late fall. Light pink single flowers are held on branching stalks well above the leaves. One of the showiest perennials for the late summer and fall garden. Plants will quickly spread to form a large patch.

HEIGHT/SPREAD: 90–120cm (3–4')/60cm (2')
LOCATION: Average to moist well-drained soil.
BLOOMS: August–September
USES: Massing, Borders

ANTENNARIA
(Cat's-Paw, Pussytoes)

dioica 'Rosea'   ZONES 1–9
(Pink Pussy-Toes) Forms a dense carpet of silver-grey foliage. Clusters of rosy-pink flowers appear in late spring. An extremely drought-tolerant groundcover deserving wider use. Trim flower stems off after blooming. Native North American wildflower.

HEIGHT/SPREAD: 10–15cm (4–6")/30cm (12")
LOCATION: Well-drained soil. Withstands drought.
BLOOMS: May–June
USES: Between paving stones

ANTHEMIS
(Marguerite)

Hardy, showy members of the Daisy family. Best used as filler plants in hot sunny perennial borders. Though short-lived they will usually self-seed to form a large patch. Excellent for cutting. Trim plants back hard after the first flush of flowers.

tinctoria 'Kelwayi'   ZONES 2–9
(Golden Marguerite) A profusion of yellow flowers all summer long.

HEIGHT/SPREAD: 60–90cm (24–36")/30–45cm (12–18")
LOCATION: Well-drained soil. Moderately drought-tolerant.
BLOOMS: June–August
USES: Borders, Meadows

sancti-johannis   ZONES 2–9
(Orange Marguerite) Bright orange daisies with yellow centres.

HEIGHT/SPREAD: 60cm (24")/30–45cm (12–18")
LOCATION: Well-drained soil. Moderately drought-tolerant.
BLOOMS: June–August
USES: Borders, Meadows

AQUILEGIA
(Columbine)

Popular, old-fashioned perennials, available in a variety of sizes and colours. Both the flowers and ferny foliage are good for cutting. In many regions the Columbine Leaf Miner will spoil the appearance of the leaves in June; simply cut the plants back to encourage clean new growth.

alpina   ZONES 2–9
(Alpine Columbine) Bright blue flowers, nice compact form. Good choice for rock gardens.

HEIGHT/SPREAD: 30–45cm (12–18")/30cm (12")
LOCATION: Average to moist soil.
BLOOMS: May–June
USES: Borders, Woodland gardens

canadensis   ZONES 2–9
(Wild Red Columbine) Delicate brick-red flowers with yellow centres. Excellent in a woodland setting. A North American native wildflower.

HEIGHT/SPREAD: 60–75cm (24–30")/30cm (12")
LOCATION: Average to moist soil.
BLOOMS: May–June
USES: Borders, Woodland gardens

chrysantha ZONES 2–9

(Golden Columbine) Large golden-yellow flowers with long spurs, long blooming season. Mildew-resistant. Said to rebloom if dead-headed. A North American native wildflower.

HEIGHT/SPREAD: 75–105cm (30–42")/30cm (12")
LOCATION: Average to moist soil.
BLOOMS: May–June
USES ✂⚘ Borders, Woodland gardens

flabellata ZONES 2–9

(Japanese Fan Columbine) A truly dwarf Columbine with large, waxy flowers in blue or white. Beautiful in rockeries. Especially beautiful blue-green leaves.

HEIGHT/SPREAD: 20–30cm (8–12")/20cm (8")
LOCATION: Average to moist soil.
BLOOMS: May–June
USES △⚘⚘ Walls, Edging

Hybrid Strains ZONES 2–9

By far these are the most widely grown Columbines, their large pastel flowers usually have long tails or spurs that create an effect like a flying bird. Plants are vigorous and, although fairly short-lived, these will no doubt seed themselves around a bit. They will readily cross with any other Columbine species resulting in surprise colours and forms.

"In their numerous colours they blend or contrast well with Bearded Irises, Catmint, Lupins and Oriental Poppies."
—Graham Stuart Thomas,
Perennial Garden Plants

SPREAD: 30cm (12")
LOCATION: Average to moist soil.
BLOOMS: May–June
USES ✂⚘ Borders, Woodland gardens

'Crimson Star' Bright crimson flowers with a white corolla, long spurs. HEIGHT: 60–90cm (24–36")

'Dragonfly Hybrids' Full colour range in a mixture of blue, yellow, white, pink and red. Compact plants. HEIGHT: 45–60cm (18–24")

'McKana's Giants' Large, showy flowers in a wide mixture of pastel shades. Long spurs, widely flaring trumpets. HEIGHT: 75cm (30")

vulgaris ZONES 2–9

(Granny's Bonnet) An old cottage-garden form with small, frilly rounded flowers in a range of colours. Especially nice are the dark maroon, blue and violet shades that always seem to appear. These self-seed quite nicely.

SPREAD: 30cm (12")
LOCATION: Average to moist soil.
BLOOMS: May–June
USES ✂⚘ Borders, Woodland gardens

'Nora Barlow' Wide-open, fully double quilled flowers in a unique combination of red, pink, and green. Totally unlike any other variety, looking more like a miniature dahlia! This is a seed strain originally introduced by Bressingham Gardens. HEIGHT: 70cm (28")

'Plena' Mixture of double forms. Eventually singles may also appear among them. HEIGHT: 50–60cm (20–24")

ARABIS
(Wall Cress, Rock Cress) ☀

Popular spring-flowering perennials, often seen cascading over rock gardens and walls. Plants form a dense carpet of leaves, smothered with flowers for several weeks. All are evergreen. Said to attract butterflies.

× arendsii 'Spring Charm' ZONES 5–9

(= *A. blepharophylla*) Carmine-red flower spikes on a compact clump. Very bright and showy. A short-lived variety, will sometimes self-seed. Needs excellent drainage. Fairly drought-tolerant.

HEIGHT/SPREAD: 15cm (6")/15–20cm (6–8")
LOCATION: Well-drained soil.
BLOOMS: April–June
USES △⚘⚘ Walls, Slopes

caucasica ZONES 3–9

The old-fashioned type, so widely planted in rockeries. Prune back immediately after blooming to keep plants compact and attractive. Several forms of this are widely available. Fairly drought-tolerant.

HEIGHT/SPREAD: 20cm (8")/30–60cm (12–24")
LOCATION: Well-drained soil.
BLOOMS: April–June
USES △〰⚘⚘ Walls, Slopes, Edging

'Compinkie' Rosy-pink flowers, non-fading. Try it with blue Hyacinths!

'Snow Ball' Very dwarf, compact strain. Flowers pure white.

'Plena' Fully double sterile white flowers, blooming much longer than other forms. Outstanding!

'Variegata' Green leaves are strongly edged with creamy-white. Looks attractive throughout the year. White flowers. Rogue out any plain green shoots before they take over. Needs excellent drainage.

ferdinandi-coburgi ZONES 3–9

Very low alpine variety, slowly forming a low mat of attractively variegated leaves with white flowers in spring. There is more than one colour form of this available. An excellent and easy alpine! Fairly drought-tolerant.

HEIGHT/SPREAD: 10cm (4")/15–20cm (6–8")
LOCATION: Well-drained soil.
BLOOMS: April–June
USES △〰⚘⚘ Walls, Slopes

'Old Gold' A newer yellow and green variegated form, especially bright in spring.

'Variegata' Reliable white and green variegation, with hints of pink in the winter.

× sturii ZONES 3–9

(Hybrid Creeping Wall Cress) Makes a very tight low mat of glossy green leaves, studded with large white flowers. One of the best varieties available. Especially useful as a groundcover for a smaller areas. Fairly drought-tolerant.

HEIGHT/SPREAD: 10cm (4")/30cm (12")
LOCATION: Well-drained soil.
BLOOMS: April–June
USES △〰⚘⚘ Walls, Slopes

ARENARIA
(Sandwort) ☀

montana ZONES 2–9

(Mountain Sandwort) Very classy alpine, like a refined *Cerastium*. Large white flowers cover the compact green mat of leaves. Not at all invasive. Needs good drainage.

HEIGHT/SPREAD: 10cm (4")/30cm (12")
LOCATION: Well-drained soil.
BLOOMS: May–June
USES △ Walls, Slopes

ARMERIA
(Thrift, Sea Pink) ☀

These ball-shaped flower clusters make for a showy display, complimented by narrow grassy foliage. Shorter varieties have long been used to edge perennial beds, and in the rockery. Flowers eventually fade into papery everlastings.

juniperifolia ZONES 2–9

(Spanish Thrift) A true alpine species. Forms a very dense tuft or bun of needle-like green leaves. Soft pink flowers are held just above the leaves. Best planted in a scree or trough garden where it can easily be seen and admired.

Aquilegia chrysantha

Aquilegia 'Dragonfly Hybrids'

Arabis ferdinandi-coburgi 'Variegata'

Armeria juniperifolia

Armeria maritima 'Dusseldorf Pride'

Artemisia lactiflora

Artemisia × 'Valerie Finnis'

Artemisia ludoviciana 'Silver King'

HEIGHT/SPREAD:	5–10cm (2–4")/15cm (6")
LOCATION:	Well-drained soil, scree.
BLOOMS:	May–June
USES	△▲♥ Walls, Troughs

maritima   ZONES 2–9

(Common Thrift) Easy and rewarding rock garden plants. Flowers are showy over a long period. Low grassy tufts of evergreen leaves. Tolerant of seaside conditions. Very drought-tolerant.

HEIGHT/SPREAD:	10–15cm (4–6")/30cm (12")
LOCATION:	Well-drained soil.
BLOOMS:	April–June
USES	△▲♥ℱ Walls, Edging

'**Alba**' Pure white pompom flowers.

'**Dusseldorf Pride**' Rosy-red balls, remove faded flowers for continued blooming.

pseudarmeria 'Formosa Hybrids'   ZONES 2–9

(Large Thrift) A taller border strain, large balls of flowers in shades of carmine, pink or white. Useful for cutting, fresh or dried.

HEIGHT/SPREAD:	30–60cm (12–24")/30cm (12")
LOCATION:	Well-drained soil.
BLOOMS:	June–August
USES	✂ Dried Flower, Borders

ARTEMISIA
(Wormwood, Sage) ☀ ◐

These are valued for their silvery-grey foliage, which can be most effective in the landscape. A surprisingly wide range of heights and textures are displayed among the various types, making them suitable for many different purposes. With a couple of exceptions they are all drought and heat tolerant, preferring a well-drained site. The flowers are insignificant unless otherwise noted.

abrotanum   ZONES 2–9

(Southernwood) Spicy-fragrant, bright green ferny foliage forming a bushy, upright clump. Plant this near a gate or entranceway so the fruity scent can be enjoyed each time someone brushes by. Will slowly spread to form a patch, but not invasive. Attractive foliage for the border, and excellent for cutting. Often benefits from a mid-summer clip.

HEIGHT/SPREAD:	60–120cm (2–4')/60–90cm (2–3')
LOCATION:	Well-drained soil.
USES	✂ℱ Borders, Herb gardens

× 'Huntingdon'   ZONES 5–9

A near-shrubby hybrid. Similar foliage to 'Powis Castle' but easily twice the size, forming a loose upright bush of silvery-grey. Hardiness of this form is not yet widely determined. Grows fabulously well at the West coast and likely over a much wider area. Plants should be cut back to 15cm (6") in early spring to encourage fresh growth. Very drought-tolerant.

HEIGHT/SPREAD:	90–120cm (3–4')/90–120cm (3–4'")
LOCATION:	Well-drained soil.
USES:	✂ℱ Specimen, Borders

lactiflora   ZONES 4–9

(White Mugwort) Outstanding for its showy plumes of creamy-white flowers that appear in late summer. Highly recommended as a cut flower! An excellent background plant for a late season display. Definitely prefers a moist site.

HEIGHT/SPREAD:	1.2–1.5m (4–6')/60–90cm (24–36")
BLOOMS:	August–October
USES	✂ Dried Flower, Borders, Specimen

'**Guizho**' A unique new selection, with red-brown stems and ferny black-green leaves, pleasantly musk-scented. The showy sprays of creamy-white flowers are

a lovely contrast. Introduced by Bressingham Gardens. This cultivar may possibly be a hybrid or different species.

ludoviciana   ZONES 4–9

(Silver Sage) A species native to the plains of North America. The foliage is exceptionally effective, the leaves entire rather than ferny, and strongly silver-grey in colour. Plants are bushy and upright, spreading at the roots to form a patch or large clump, and doing so rather quickly in light sandy soils. Good drought and heat tolerance, generally remaining attractive throughout the season. The species itself is seldom available but there are several excellent selections, all useful for cutting fresh or drying. Extremely drought-tolerant.

> "An effective contrast for crimson roses, and any varieties of [summer] phlox, particularly the pink ones." —Graham Stuart Thomas, *Perennial Garden Plants*

SPREAD:	60–75cm (24–30")
LOCATION:	Well-drained soil.
BLOOMS:	August–September
USES:	⋔✂♥ℱ Massing, Borders.

'**Silver King**' Intensely grey leaves and stems, followed by a mist of fine-textured silver-white flowers that give a cloud-like effect. A vigorous selection hardy to Zone 2. HEIGHT: 75–90cm (30–36")

'**Silver Queen**' Leaves are slightly wider, and more jagged in appearance than 'Silver King' Flowers are fairly insignificant. HEIGHT: 75–90cm (30–36")

'**Valerie Finnis**' Like a compact version of 'Silver King', with very wide silvery leaves, and a less invasive habit. Some say this is the best grey foliage plant available. HEIGHT: 45–60cm (18–24")

pontica   ZONES 4–9

(Roman Wormwood) A ground-covering species, with grey-green filigree leaves. Very feathery in appearance. Good choice for containers. Can be fairly invasive, particularly on lighter soils. Site carefully. Very drought-tolerant.

HEIGHT/SPREAD:	30cm (12")/30–60cm (12–24")
LOCATION:	Well-drained soil.
USES	⋔♥ℱ Borders, Massing

× 'Powis Castle'   ZONES 5–9

Makes a bushy, upright clump of feathery, silver-grey leaves. An excellent non-invasive variety for the border, sometimes clipped to form a low hedge. Plants should be cut back to 15cm (6") in early spring to encourage fresh growth. Non-blooming. This selection is proving to be hardier than we first expected. Very drought-tolerant.

> "The arrival of *Artemisia* 'Powis Castle' on the scene a few decades ago was a great event." —Christopher Lloyd, *Christopher Lloyd's Flower Garden*

HEIGHT/SPREAD:	60–70cm (24–30")/60–70cm (24–30")
LOCATION:	Well-drained soil.
USES:	♥ℱ Massing, Borders.

schmidtiana 'Silver Mound'   ZONES 1–9

Perhaps the most popular grey-leaved perennial of all time. The feathery silver-grey leaves form a beautiful compact dome. Valuable as a rock garden plant, accent, or edging. Plants should be ruthlessly clipped back hard (to 2 inches!) when they begin to flower (mid to late June), otherwise they will melt out, get floppy and generally look like the dog slept on them. Fresh new growth will appear in about two weeks. Very drought-tolerant.

HEIGHT/SPREAD:	30cm (12")/30–45cm (12–18")
LOCATION:	Well-drained soil.
USES	△▲♥ℱ Edging, Borders, Massing

stelleriana 'Silver Brocade'   ZONES 2–9

A low, compact selection, fairly similar in appearance to Dusty Miller, with scalloped silvery-white foliage. Excellent for edging, groundcover, pots and hanging baskets. Evergreen in milder regions. Trim plants back in early spring and again in midsummer to encourage fresh growth. Introduced by the University of British Columbia Botanical Garden. Registered with the Canadian Ornamental Plant Foundation. Extremely drought-tolerant.

HEIGHT/SPREAD: 15–30cm (6–12")/60–75cm (24–30")
USES   ⚹△◗▲▼🐝 Massing, Edging

ARUM
(Arum) ⚹●

italicum   ZONES 6–9
(Italian Arum) A unique and wonderful plant for the woodland garden. Large exotic arrow-head shaped leaves make an appearance in the fall, remaining throughout the winter only to disappear by late spring. Short spikes of creamy-white flowers push out of the ground in May, followed by clusters of bright orange berries in the summer. A plant for all seasons! Appreciates some shelter from winter winds.

HEIGHT/SPREAD: 30cm (12")/30cm (12")
LOCATION: Rich moist woodland soil.
BLOOMS: April–May
USES   △◗🐝 Woodland borders

ARUNCUS
(Goatsbeard) ⚹

Moisture-loving plants, well suited to waterside or woodland plantings. All have creamy-white plumes of flowers in summer, and attractive lacy foliage, somewhat resembling Astilbes.

aethusifolius   ZONES 2–9
(Dwarf Korean Goatsbeard) The miniature of the genus. A delicate mound of crispy green leaves, with short forked spikelets of creamy white flowers. Good rock garden plant.

HEIGHT/SPREAD: 20–30cm (8–12")/30cm (12")
LOCATION: Rich, moist soil.
BLOOMS: June–July
USES   △▼ Woodland borders

dioicus   ZONES 2–9
(Giant Goatsbeard) A rather monstrous border plant, spectacular in flower with its enormous creamy plumes the size of your head. Elegant lacy leaves form a very dense and bushy clump. This plant demands space. Inclined to sulk in hot summer areas unless planted at the waterside or in peaty, moist soil. Cut plants back in summer if they look untidy.

> "…flowers with the main flush of shrub roses and is a lovely companion for them." —Graham Stuart Thomas, *Perennial Garden Plants*

HEIGHT/SPREAD: 1.2–1.8m (4–6')/90cm (3')
LOCATION: Rich, moist soil.
BLOOMS: June–July
USES   Dried Flower, Waterside, Borders

'Kneiffii' Leaves are finely cut, resembling a green Japanese Maple, setting off the creamy-white flowers. A more reasonable size for the smaller garden. Beautiful beside a tiny pool. Increased by division only. HEIGHT: 90cm (3')

ASARUM
(Wild Ginger) ⚹●

europaeum   ZONES 2–9
(European Wild Ginger) A choice woodlander, much sought after by plant connoisseurs, but usually in limited worldwide supply. The rounded leaves are dark green and brightly polished. This is a texture plant, contrasting beautifully against lacy ferns. Will slowly form a first-

class groundcover for a small area and will even self-seed if you are very lucky! Evergreen in Zones 8–9.

HEIGHT/SPREAD: 15cm (6")/30cm (12")
LOCATION: Moist rich woodland soil.
USES   △◗▲ Woodland border, Edging

ASCLEPIAS
(Milkweed) ⚹

Not all the members of this Genus are weedy, and a few are excellent summer-blooming perennials for the sunny border. Flowers are extremely attractive to butterflies. The species in cultivation are mostly native North American wildflowers.

incarnata 'Cinderella'   ZONES 3–9
(Swamp Milkweed) A tall species, growing naturally in wet areas. This selection is grown commercially in Holland as a cut flower. Forms a dense, leafy bush with plenty of rose-pink heads of flowers in mid to late summer. Much easier to please than the species below, this will grow in average border conditions. Non-invasive.

HEIGHT/SPREAD: 90–120cm (3–4')/60cm (2')
LOCATION: Average to moist soil.
BLOOMS: June–August
USES   ✂🦋 Dried Flower, Borders, Waterside

tuberosa   ZONES 4–9
(Butterfly Weed) Native to eastern North America where the clusters of bright orange flowers appear in early summer. Modern seed strains often include red and yellow forms, as well. The Monarch butterfly depends entirely on this plant for its food source. Plants prefer a well-drained, sandy or gravelly site. Flowers are good for cutting, the immature seed pods are also cut and dried for floral arranging. Removing faded flowers will encourage continual blooming. Butterfly milkweed comes up very late in the spring. Very drought-tolerant.

HEIGHT/SPREAD: 60–90cm (2–3')/60cm (2')
LOCATION: Well-drained sandy soil.
BLOOMS: July–August
USES   ✂🦋▲🐝 Borders, Meadows

ASPERULA see GALIUM

ASPHODELINE
(King's Spear) ⚹⚹

lutea   ZONES 5–9
A little-known member of the Lily family. Grassy clumps of grey-green leaves give rise to stiff spikes of fragrant star-shaped yellow flowers. Both the flowers and dried seed-heads are good for cutting. Slowly forms a sizeable clump remaining in place for years. Evergreen in mild-winter areas.

HEIGHT/SPREAD: 90–120cm (3–4')/30cm (12")
LOCATION: Well-drained soil.
BLOOMS: June–August
USES   ✂◀▲🐝 Dried Flower, Borders

ASTER, SPRING
(Alpine Aster) ⚹

alpinus   ZONES 2–9
Low-growing plants, these put on a bright display of single golden-eyed daisies in late spring. Ideal for the border front or rock garden. They are not long-lived but often will self-seed if conditions are to their liking.

HEIGHT/SPREAD: 20–25cm (8–10")/20–30cm (8–12")
LOCATION: Well-drained soil.
BLOOMS: May–June
USES   △✂ Walls, Edging

'Dark Beauty' Dark violet-blue.

'Happy End' Rose-pink flowers, compact.

Aruncus dioicus

Asarum europaeum

Asphodeline lutea

Aster alpinus 'Dark Beauty'

Aster divaricatus

Aster × 'Professor Kippenburg'

Aster × 'Audrey'

Aster novi-belgii 'Royal Ruby'

ASTER, FALL
(Michaelmas Daisy) ☀

Reliable, showy plants for a late summer and fall display, with a wide range of flower colours and plant heights to choose from. The different varieties all have similar daisy-style flowers, and plenty of them! The modern varieties are mostly descended from common roadside species, selected over the years for improved form, colour and disease resistance.

In general, taller cultivars should be staked by mid-summer to prevent flopping. Pinching or pruning plants back by half (before July 1st) will encourage dense, compact growth and more flowers. Plants will grow best in a rich moist soil— too dry a location will invariably lead to problems with unsightly powdery mildew on the leaves. Early frosts may damage the flowers in Zones 2–4, but in years with a mild fall the display is so wonderful that it's usually worth chancing. All cultivars are excellent for cutting.

divaricatus   ZONES 4–9
(White Wood Aster) A wild North American species, widely grown in Europe. Medium-size starry white flowers are held on branching purple-black stems. Plants are shade-tolerant, attractive grouped among shrubs where they can spread. May require pinching. Tolerant of dry soil.

HEIGHT/SPREAD:	45–90cm (18–36")/45cm (18")
LOCATION:	Average to dry well-drained soil.
BLOOMS:	August–October
USES	✂ 🦋 Borders, Woodland gardens

Dumosus Hybrids   ZONES 3–9
A group of compact hybrid selections, ideal for the front of a sunny border. When well grown the plants form a dome or cushion of colour in the fall. As these are heavy feeders, fertilize in spring and midsummer and keep plants well watered. Divide every year or two, and watch for signs of powdery mildew.

SPREAD:	30cm (12")
LOCATION:	Rich, moist soil.
BLOOMS:	August–October
USES	✂ 🦋 Borders, Edging

'Audrey' Mauve-blue. Excellent. HEIGHT: 30cm (12")

'Diana' Good medium-size variety. Clear rose-pink flowers. HEIGHT: 45–60cm (18–24")

'Jenny' Double red. HEIGHT: 40cm (16")

'Lady-in-Blue' Semi-double, blue. HEIGHT: 25cm (10")

'Little Pink Beauty' Semi-double, bright pink. HEIGHT: 40cm (16")

'Nesthäkchen' Clear pink flowers, compact. HEIGHT: 30cm (12")

'Professor Kippenburg' Clear bright blue, semi-double. HEIGHT: 40cm (16")

'Violet Carpet' Deep violet-blue. HEIGHT: 30cm (12")

'White Opal' White flowers. HEIGHT: 30–40cm (12–16")

ericoides   ZONES 3–9
(Heath Aster) Bushy mounded habit, with tiny leaves and clouds of starry flowers, white in the species, but there are several colour forms as well. Nice filler flower for the garden or for cutting. Quite mildew resistant, tolerant of dryer sites.

HEIGHT/SPREAD:	75–90cm (30–36")/60cm (24")
LOCATION:	Average to moist well-drained soil.
BLOOMS:	August–October
USES	✂ 🦋 Borders, Meadow gardens

'Blue Cloud' Masses of tiny lilac-blue stars. Good for toning down strong magentas or purples.

'Pink Cloud' Flowers are pale pastel pink. Good blending colour, delicate as a pink Baby's-Breath.

× frikartii 'Mönch'   ZONES 5–9
Lavender-blue flowers, a strong bloomer over a very long season. An excellent taller variety, quite distinct from the other species. Mildew resistant. Planting before midsummer is recommended. Needs good drainage in winter.

> "Plant this softly colored aster near to silver-gray *Artemisia* 'Powis Castle', mix it with pastel pink and pale powder-blue flowers and edge the bed with gray felted leaves of *Stachys olympica* 'Silver Carpet'." —Penelope Hobhouse, *Colour in Your Garden*

HEIGHT/SPREAD:	75cm (30")/60–90cm (24–36")
LOCATION:	Average well-drained soil.
BLOOMS:	July–October
USES	✂ 🦋 Borders, Meadow gardens

novae-angliae   ZONES 2–9
(New England Aster) Some of the best cutting types are in this group. The taller growing cultivars form large clumps of upright branching stems that will require staking, and are best used behind other plants as the lower leaves may wither early. Tolerant of wet soils. Watch for mildew.

SPREAD:	45cm (18")
LOCATION:	Rich, moist soil.
BLOOMS:	August–October
USES	✂ 🦋 Wildflower, Borders, Meadow gardens

'Alma Potschke' Warm, glowing salmon-pink. One of the best asters. HEIGHT: 100cm (40")

'Hella Lacy' Outstanding violet-blue flowered selection. Very tall. May be inclined to self-seed. HEIGHT: 1.2–1.5m (4–5')

> "...starting in mid- to late September, it is the handsomest plant in town, not only for its intensity of color but also for the great numbers of monarch butterflies hovering over it and lighting on its flowers to sip nectar." —Allen Lacy, *The Garden in Autumn*

'Pink Winner' Medium pink, tall habit. HEIGHT: 90cm (36")

'Purple Dome' Compact habit. Masses of deep purple flowers. A recent introduction from the Mt. Cuba Centre in Delaware. HEIGHT: 45cm (18")

'September Ruby' Deep ruby red. HEIGHT: 120cm (4')

novi-belgii   ZONES 3–9
(New York Aster) This species in one of the parents of the dwarf Dumosus hybrids. Selections of the true New York Aster are medium to tall in habit, preferring moist, rich soils and a sunny exposure. Powdery mildew can be problematic. Divide every year or two.

SPREAD:	30–45cm (12–18")
LOCATION:	Rich, moist soil.
BLOOMS:	August–October
USES	✂ 🦋 Wildflower, Borders, Meadow gardens

'Alert' Deep crimson red. HEIGHT: 30cm (12")

'Coombe Rosemary' Outstanding double violet-purple flowers. HEIGHT: 90cm (36")

'Royal Ruby' Deep red, semi-double. A selection by Alan Bloom of Bressingham Gardens. HEIGHT: 50cm (20")

pringlei 'Monte Cassino'   ZONES 4–9
Widely grown and imported year-round for use by commercial florists. Only recently introduced to gardens however, but proving to be one of the best border forms in existence. The sturdy, upright clumps of tiny green leaves

have a delicate texture all season long, developing nice bronzy tones in late fall. Masses of small starry white flowers go on blooming for several weeks, well into late fall. Seems tolerant of average to moist conditions.

HEIGHT/SPREAD: 75–120cm (30–48″)/45cm (18″)
LOCATION: Rich, moist soil.
BLOOMS: September–October
USES ✁< 🦋 Borders, Meadow gardens

sedifolius 'Nanus'   ZONES 2–9
(Rhone Aster) Clouds of starry blue, yellow-centred flowers. Has a delicate billowing appearance in the border. Always a reliable bloomer on the prairies. Mildew resistant.

HEIGHT/SPREAD: 45–60cm (18–24″)/30cm (12″)
LOCATION: Average to moist soil.
BLOOMS: August–October
USES ✁< 🦋 Borders, Meadow gardens

thomsonii 'Nanus'   ZONES 4–9
Compact border selection flowering before the main flush of fall varieties. Bushy plants are covered by light blue starry flowers for several weeks. Foliage is greyish. One of the parents of *A. × frikartii*.

HEIGHT/SPREAD: 30–45cm (12–18″)/30cm (12″)
LOCATION: Average to moist soil.
BLOOMS: July–August
USES ✁< 🦋 Borders, Edging

tongolensis 'Berggarten'   ZONES 4–9
Very early-blooming form, the large violet-blue flowers appearing in early summer. This needs to be divided every other year or it will thin out. Flower stems are held up well above the low carpet of leaves. Excellent for cutting.

HEIGHT/SPREAD: 45–60cm (18–24″)/30cm (12″)
LOCATION: Average to moist soil.
BLOOMS: June–July
USES ✁< 🦋 Borders, Meadow gardens

ASTEROMOEA see KALIMERIS

ASTILBE
(False Spirea) ☼●
Considered the Queen of Flowers for shady areas, these fluffy plumes are a familiar sight in the summer garden. With the many new varieties available there is a much wider selection of flower and leaf colour, plant form, and blooming time than ever before. Astilbes will also tolerate full sun in cool summer regions.

× arendsii   ZONES 3–9
(Garden Astilbe) Large showy flower spikes appear over upright mounds of elegant, lacy foliage. Complex breeding has resulted in many modern varieties, offering flowers in the complete range from clear white to cream, rose, peach, pink, red and magenta. The Astilbe season can even be extended by choosing varieties that bloom at different times. All cultivars share the same need for a rich moist soil. Because these types are heavy feeders they should be lifted and divided every two to three years, also fertilized in early spring and again after blooming. Remove faded flowers spikes and any tired-looking leaves throughout the season.

SPREAD: 60–75cm (24–30″)
LOCATION: Moist, rich, well-prepared soil.
BLOOMS: June–August
USES ✁< Borders, Woodland gardens

'Amethyst' Violet-rose, erect habit. Green foliage. Mid-season. HEIGHT: 90cm (36″)

'Bressingham Beauty' Rich pink, long lasting. Green foliage. Raised by Alan Bloom. Mid-season. HEIGHT: 100cm (40″)

'Elizabeth Bloom' A new compact selection from Bressingham Gardens. Large plumes of rich pink flowers over vigorous green foliage. Mid-season. HEIGHT: 60cm (24″)

'Peach Blossom' Delicate pink, glossy green foliage. Early. HEIGHT: 50cm (20″)

'Snowdrift' Selected by Alan Bloom of Bressingham Gardens for the especially clear snow-white flowers. Green foliage. Good compact habit. Mid-season.

'William Buchanan' Dwarf hybrid with crimson-tinged leaves. Creamy-white flowers. Mid-season. HEIGHT: 20–30cm (8–12″)

chinensis   ZONES 3–9
(Chinese Astilbe) These have very dense, lacy foliage. Plants will spread to form a patch, and are excellent for massing as a groundcover. Because they bloom after most of the Garden Astilbes the dwarf Chinese selections are useful for extending the season into late summer.

SPREAD: 30cm (12″)
LOCATION: Average to moist well-drained soil.
BLOOMS: August–September
USES ▲∧∿✁< Woodland garden

'Finale' Bright pink flowers, held just above the leaves. HEIGHT: 40cm (16″)

'Intermezzo' Salmon pink flowers, more upright habit. HEIGHT: 50–60cm (20–24″)

'Pumila' Makes a low, vigorous spreading patch, the best type for general groundcover purposes. Rose-purple flowers in short spikes. Will tolerate a fair bit of sun or dry shade. Undemanding. HEIGHT: 25cm (10″)

× crispa   ZONES 4–9
A newer group of hybrids, all with unusual dark green, crispy foliage. Compact in habit, these are excellent for the border front, edging, and in the shady rock garden.

SPREAD: 30cm (12″)
LOCATION: Moist to average well-drained soil.
BLOOMS: July–August
USES ▲ Woodland garden, Edging

'Perkeo' Short spikes of light pink flowers. HEIGHT: 15–20cm (6–8″)

simplicifolia Hybrids   ZONES 3–9
Another distinct group of hybrid *Astilbe*, mostly developed in recent years by British and German breeders. Many of these have a compact habit, the foliage generally not as lacy as other types, but richer in colour. Well suited to massed plantings, providing colour in late summer when it is so often lacking in shade gardens.

LOCATION: Moist, rich well-drained soil.
BLOOMS: July–August
USES ▲∧∿✁< Edging, Woodland gardens

'Sprite' An excellent selection bred by Alan Bloom of Bressingham Gardens. Spikes of delicate shell-pink flowers held above the dark bronzy-green leaves. Clumps are dense and compact. Outstanding shade garden plant! A former *Perennial Plant of the Year*. HEIGHT: 25cm (10″)

taquetii   ZONES 3–9
(Fall Astilbe) (now correctly included in *A.chinensis*) Unusual magenta-purple plumes are held high above the foliage. These are usually the last *Astilbe* to finish blooming. Flowers are good for cutting. Plants are heat tolerant.

HEIGHT/SPREAD: 90–120cm (3–4′)/60–90cm (2–3′)
LOCATION: Prefers a rich moist soil.
BLOOMS: August–September
USES ✁< Massing, Borders, Woodland

'Purple Lance' ('Purpurlanze') An improved form with large spears of bright purple-red flowers.

'Superba' Lavender-magenta flowers, held in a long, narrow spike.

Astilbe × 'Elizabeth Bloom'

Astilbe taquetii

Astilbe simplicifolia × 'Sprite'

Astilbe taquetii 'Superba'

Astrantia major Pink Form

Astrantia maxima

Aubrieta × 'Red Carpet'

Bellis 'Pomponette Mix'

ASTRANTIA
(Masterwort) ☀ ☽

Adored by floral designers for their unique umbels of starry flowers, a bit like a refined Queen-Anne's-Lace in effect, but not at all weedy in habit. Especially nice as a filler in moist, shady borders.

carniolica 'Rubra'   ZONES 4–9
(Dwarf Red Masterwort) A compact species for the front of the border. This selection has rich maroon-red flowers, surrounded by green bracts. Lacy green foliage.

HEIGHT/SPREAD:	30–45cm (12–18")/45cm (18")
LOCATION:	Prefers a moist, rich soil.
BLOOMS:	June–August
USES:	✂ Borders, Woodland

major   ZONES 4–9
A variable species, with good-sized umbels of greenish-white flowers with a distinctive, showy collar or bract that ranges in colour from white through green to rose-red. Loose clumps of dark-green compound leaves. Likes to self-seed. Blooms over a long season.

HEIGHT/SPREAD:	75cm (30")/45cm (18")
LOCATION:	Prefers a moist, rich soil.
BLOOMS:	June–August
USES:	✂ Borders, Woodland

'Rubra' Flower bracts are various shades of red through pink. Showy!

maxima   ZONES 4–9
Large rose-pink or white flowers, surrounded by sharp pinkish-green bracts. Individual flowers look a bit like a *Scabiosa*. Considered by some to be the most beautiful species. Plants spread quickly underground, forming a patch.

HEIGHT/SPREAD:	45–60cm (18–24")/45cm (18")
LOCATION:	Prefers a moist, rich soil.
BLOOMS:	June–August
USES:	✂ Borders, Woodland

AUBRIETA
(Rock Cress) ☀ ☽

Hybrids   ZONES 4–8
(*A. × cultorum*) Popular rock garden plant, smothered with brightly coloured flowers in spring. The grey-green carpet of leaves will cascade over sunny banks or walls. Seed-grown colour forms will show some variation; buy plants in flower if you require a specific shade. Shear plants back lightly after flowering to keep them compact.

HEIGHT/SPREAD:	10–15cm (4–6")/30–60cm (12–24")
LOCATION:	Well-drained soil among cool rocks.
BLOOMS:	April–June
USES:	△ ∧∼▲ Walls, Slopes

'Blue Carpet' Various shades of blue.

'Dr. Mules' Especially good deep violet-purple form. May rebloom in fall. Cutting-grown.

'Red Carpet' Red to rose flowers.

'Purple Gem' ('Whitewell Gem') Velvety purple to violet.

AURINIA see ALYSSUM

BAPTISIA
(Wild Indigo) ☀ ☽

Cousins to the Lupines, with similar spikes of pea-like flowers in late spring. These are sturdy wildflowers native to the prairies of North America. Easy to grow in average sunny border conditions, the plants are long-lived but resent being disturbed once established. Consider these as a substitute if you have not succeeded in growing Lupines.

australis   ZONES 2–9
(Blue Wild Indigo) Short spikes of deep blue flowers, followed by attractive curly black seed pods that are sometimes used for dried arrangements. Dark green foliage forms a dense bushy mound. Moderately drought-tolerant.

HEIGHT/SPREAD:	90–120cm (3–4')/90cm (3')
LOCATION:	Average well-drained soil.
BLOOMS:	May–June
USES:	✂ ⚘ Wildflower, Borders, Meadows

pendula   ZONES 3–9
(White False Indigo) A white-flowered counterpart to *B. australis* with a very similar habit. Upright spikes of white flowers are followed by drooping seed pods. Emerging foliage and stems are deep purple-blue. Moderately drought-tolerant. May be a form of *B. alba*.

HEIGHT/SPREAD:	90–120cm (3–4')/90cm (3')
LOCATION:	Average well-drained soil.
BLOOMS:	May–June
USES:	✂ ⚘ Dried Flower, Wildflower, Borders, Meadows

BEGONIA
(Hardy Begonia) ☽ ●

grandis   ZONES 6–9
A much sought-after rarity for the shade garden. This unusual and unlikely perennial has large, tuberous begonia-shaped green leaves, and light pink single flowers that are held above in summer. Reportedly hardy to –18°C when mulched.

HEIGHT/SPREAD:	30–45cm (12–18")/30cm (12")
LOCATION:	Moist, rich soil.
BLOOMS:	July–September
USES:	△ Borders, Woodland gardens

BELLIS
(English Daisy) ☀ ☽

perennis   ZONES 3–9
Widely used for bedding with spring-blooming bulbs, English Daisies are an old-fashioned favorite, usually treated as a biennial or short-lived perennial. They will sometimes self-seed. They perform best in coastal climates.

SPREAD:	15cm (6")
LOCATION:	Well-drained soil. Dislikes hot weather.
BLOOMS:	April–June
USES:	✂ Massing, Edging

'Monstrosa' Flowers are double and extra large, in shades of white, pink or red, with distinctive quilled petals. HEIGHT: 20cm (8")

'Pomponette' Smaller button-type flowers in profusion. Compact habit. Shades offered: rose and white. HEIGHT: 10cm (4")

BERGENIA
(Bergenia) ☀ ☽

cordifolia   ZONES 2–9
(Heartleaf Bergenia) Reliably evergreen in most climates, the large glossy leaves take on rich bronzy-red tones throughout the fall and winter months. Clusters of nodding pink flowers rise above in early spring, and both these and the leaves are valuable for cutting. At their best when mass planted. Tolerant of a wide range of soils and conditions, including dry shade. Many selections and hybrids of this species have been made.

> "The plant can look very presentable…sandwiched between the edge of a border and something taller than itself behind, under whose skirts the bergenia can investigate." — Christopher Lloyd, *Foliage Plants*

HEIGHT/SPREAD:	30–45cm (12–18″)/60cm (24″)
LOCATION:	Average to moist soil.
BLOOMS:	April–June
USES:	⬠◇◈◆✂ Massing, Edging, Borders

'Baby Doll' Baby-pink flowers, very freely flowering. HEIGHT: 30cm (12″)

'Bressingham Ruby' Winter colour is deep burnished maroon. Rose-red flowers. Green foliage in summer. An Alan Bloom selection. HEIGHT: 35cm (14″)

'Bressingham Salmon' Late flowering variety, salmon-pink flowers. Alan Bloom selection. HEIGHT: 30cm (12″)

'Bressingham White' Robust growth, snowy white flowers fading to pink. Early-blooming Alan Bloom selection. HEIGHT: 30cm (12″)

'Perfect' Lilac-red flowers, large bronze tinged leaves. HEIGHT: 30cm (12″)

'Silberlicht' ('Silver Light') Flowers are white flushed with pale pink, very free-flowering. Leaves lie flat. HEIGHT: 40cm (16″)

BLETILLA
(Hardy Orchid) ☼

striata   **ZONES 5–9**
(Chinese Ground Orchid) Arching sprays of magenta-pink flowers rise over slender, pleated leaves. This easy-to-grow deciduous orchid is a treasure for the shady rock garden. Also reported to tolerate sunny locations with regular moisture. May be overwintered indoors in colder regions.

HEIGHT/SPREAD:	30cm (12″)/20–30cm (8–12″)
LOCATION:	Prefers a cool, woodland soil.
BLOOMS:	May–June
USES:	△◈✂✿ Woodland gardens

BOLTONIA
(Boltonia) ☼ ◐

asteroides   **ZONES 4–9**
(Bolton's Aster) Similar in effect to a tall fall-blooming *Aster* or Michaelmas Daisy. Billowing clouds of small daisies appear in late summer and fall. Foliage remains disease free. Nice background plant for borders, growing especially big and tall in moist, rich soils. Good for cutting. North American wildflower. The selections below are more commonly grown over the species.

HEIGHT/SPREAD:	90–120cm (3–4′)/90cm (3′)
LOCATION:	Average well-drained soil.
BLOOMS:	August–October
USES:	◈✂ Borders, Meadows.

latisquama 'Nana' Rose-lilac flowers, compact habit. HEIGHT: 60–90cm (2–3′)

'Pink Beauty' Pale pink flowers, somewhat loose habit.

'Snowbank' Masses of white daisies, good bushy habit.

BRUNNERA
(Siberian Bugloss) ☼

macrophylla   **ZONES 2–9**
Low clumps of heart-shaped leaves produce upright stems of blue Forget-me-not flowers for many weeks. Lovely woodland plant for moist, shady sites. A true perennial. The form 'Variegata' is excellent, with cream and green foliage, but is rather difficult to obtain.

> "A drift of dark blue at the back of a
> shrubbery or under the canopy of a
> silver-leaf weeping pear is
> unforgettable." —Penelope Hobhouse,
> *Colour in Your Garden*

HEIGHT/SPREAD:	30–45cm (12–18″)/45cm (18″)
LOCATION:	Prefers a rich moist soil.

BLOOMS:	April–June
USES:	◈◈✂ Massing, Woodland gardens

BUDDLEIA
(Butterfly Bush) ☼

Truly these are shrubs, attaining a large size in mild winter areas. In colder regions the woody stems often die back severely, regrowing again from the base and flowering on new wood in late summer. Many gardeners just treat Buddleia like a perennial, cutting them back to 15cm (6″) every spring. By pruning them this way the flowers are on shorter stems where they can be easily seen at eye level, and associate nicely with other perennials in the fall border. The long wands of flowers are fragrant and attract butterflies and hummingbirds like crazy!

davidii   **ZONES 5–9**
This species has given rise to numerous modern selections, some of them naturally compact and well suited to border use. There is an excellent range of colours to choose from. Great for cutting. Moderately drought-tolerant.

HEIGHT/SPREAD:	.9–2.4m (3–8′)/.9–1.2m (3–4′)
LOCATION:	Average well-drained soil.
BLOOMS:	July–October
USES:	◈✂✿✿✿ Borders

'Black Knight' The deepest midnight blue flowers. Tall.

'Harlequin' Gorgeous variegated creamy-yellow and green leaves, magenta-red flowers. Fairly compact.

'Nanho Blue' Naturally compact. Silver foliage, deep blue flowers.

'Nanho Purple' Similar to above, dark purple spikes.

'Pink Delight' Good clear pink flowers, tall.

'Royal Red' Fairly compact habit, rich wine-red flower spikes.

'White Profusion' Silvery-white flowers, tall.

CALAMINTHA
(Calamint) ☼ ◐

nepeta subsp. nepeta   **ZONES 5–9**
(= *C. nepetoides*) Good choice for edging pathways, where the minty-fragrant foliage will be brushed on passing. Tiny pale lilac flowers are produced abundantly on upright stalks. Nice frontal plant for the late summer border. Long blooming season. Not at all invasive.

> "An imperturbable little plant with a
> long flowering season, and a delicious
> minty odour when crushed." —Graham
> Stuart Thomas, *Perennial Garden Plants*

HEIGHT/SPREAD:	30cm (12″)/30–45cm (12–18″)
LOCATION:	Well-drained soil.
BLOOMS:	August–October
USES:	◈ Massing, Edging.

CALCEOLARIA
(Pocket-Flower) ☼ ◐

biflora   **ZONES 4–9**
(Yellow Slipperflower) Delicate stems of yellow pouch-shaped flowers arise from a flat rosette of leaves. Reasonably easy alpine plant. Grows well in cracks, between rocks and will self-seed there if it's happy. Dislikes hot summers.

HEIGHT/SPREAD:	15–30cm (6–12″)/15cm (6″)
LOCATION:	Well-drained humus-rich soil.
BLOOMS:	June–July
USES:	△✿ Troughs, Screes.

Bergenia cordifolia

Bergenia cordifolia 'Bressingham Ruby'

Bletilla striata

Buddleia davidii 'Pink Delight'

Caltha palustris

Campanula carpatica 'Blue Moonlight'

Campanula garganica 'Dickson's Gold'

Campanula lactiflora 'Loddon Anna'

CALTHA
(Marsh Marigold) ☀☼

palustris   ZONES 2–9

Native wildflowers over most of the northern hemisphere, and much loved for their showy single buttercup flowers that grace streamsides and other wet places in early spring. They grow best in a rich moist soil that never dries out, but will adapt to moist border conditions. There are a couple of selections that are sometimes available.

HEIGHT/SPREAD:	15–30cm (6–12")/30cm (12")
LOCATION:	Rich constantly moist soil.
BLOOMS:	April–May
USES:	⚂☙ Waterside, Moist areas

'**Alba**' Compact mound, early pure white flowers.

'**Plena**' Perfectly double golden buttercups.

CAMPANULA
(Bellflower) ☀☼

One of the most popular groups of perennials, ranging in height from low creeping alpines to tall stately spikes for the back of a border. Their bell-shaped flowers seem to have a universal appeal, usually blue in colour, but sometimes ranging to lavender, violet, rose or white. Most of the taller varieties are excellent for cutting. All prefer a sunny exposure, although many types are tolerant of partial shade.

alliariifolia 'Ivory Bells'   ZONES 3–9

(Spurred Bellflower) Creamy-white bells hang from arching stems for several weeks. Medium-sized plant for the border or woodland edge. A true perennial. Introduced by Bressingham Gardens.

HEIGHT/SPREAD:	45–60cm (18–24")/45cm (18")
LOCATION:	Average well-drained soil.
BLOOMS:	June–August
USES:	✂ Border, Woodland garden

× 'Birch Hybrid'   ZONES 4–9

Outstanding variety, trailing stems are smothered with nodding purple-blue flowers. Choice rock garden plant, blooming all summer long. Not invasive.

HEIGHT/SPREAD:	10–15cm (4–6")/30cm (12")
LOCATION:	Well-drained soil.
BLOOMS:	June–September
USES	⚂☙ Walls, Slopes

carpatica   ZONES 2–9

(Carpathian Bellflower) Compact rounded clumps bearing large, upturned cup-shaped flowers in various shades, blooming over a long period. Excellent for edging, also happy growing among rocks.

HEIGHT/SPREAD:	15–20cm (6–9")/30cm (12")
LOCATION:	Average well-drained soil.
BLOOMS:	June–September
USES:	⚂☙ Edging, Borders

'**Blue Clips**' Medium blue shades.

'**White Clips**' White flowers.

'**Blue Moonlight**' Light azure-blue cups, compact. An Alan Bloom selection. HEIGHT: 10cm (4")

'**Bressingham White**' Outstanding clear white large-flowered form selected by Alan Bloom.

'**Chewton Joy**' Later blooming, pale dusky blue flowers.

turbinata '**Karl Foerster**' Deep cobalt-blue, compact habit to 15cm (6").

'**Wheatley Violet**' Very dwarf form, dark flowers.

cochleariifolia   ZONES 2–9

(Fairy Thimble) (formerly *C. pusilla*) Forms a low creeping mat with an abundant display of little nodding bells in summer. Very easy alpine plant, attractive growing in cracks and crevices or between patio stones.

HEIGHT/SPREAD:	10cm (4")/15–30cm (6–12")
LOCATION:	Well-drained soil.
BLOOMS:	June–August
USES:	⚂ᐱᘉ☙ Walls, Troughs

'**Blue Tit**' Especially deep blue flowers. Raised and named by Alan Bloom in the 1930's.

garganica 'Dickson's Gold'   ZONES 5–9

An exciting, unique form, similar to *C. poscharskyana*, but with bright golden-green leaves and loose clusters of bright blue flowers. A unique rock garden specimen, appreciating protection from hot sun. Nearly evergreen.

HEIGHT/SPREAD:	15cm (6")/15–30cm (6–12")
LOCATION:	Average well-drained soil.
BLOOMS:	June–August
USES:	⚂☙ Troughs, Edging.

glomerata 'Superba'   ZONES 2–9

(Clustered Bellflower) Rich violet-purple flowers in large clusters. Good choice for a lightly shaded border. Clumps should be divided frequently. Very popular for early summer colour. May need a trim after blooming.

HEIGHT/SPREAD:	45–60cm (18–24")/45–60cm (18–24")
LOCATION:	Average well-drained soil.
BLOOMS:	June–July
USES:	✂ Borders, Woodland, Meadows

lactiflora   ZONES 4–9

(Milky Bellflower) Generally this is a tall border plant, but some of the newer compact varieties are excellent for frontal positions. Their large clusters of starry flowers bloom for many weeks. Best in part shade.

SPREAD:	30cm (12")
LOCATION:	Prefers a cool, moist soil.
BLOOMS:	June–September
USES:	✂ Borders, Woodland

'**Loddon Anna**' Tall-growing selection with clusters of flesh-pink flowers in summer. Excellent for cutting. HEIGHT: 120–150cm (4–5')

'**Pouffe**' Bushy green mounds with clouds of lavender-blue flowers. An early Alan Bloom selection. HEIGHT: 25–45cm (10–18")

'**White Pouffe**' White counterpart to 'Pouffe' with the same compact habit. HEIGHT: 25–45cm (10–18")

medium   ZONES 2–9

(Canterbury Bells) Old-fashioned cottage-garden plants, valued for their showy display in early summer. Huge bell-shaped flowers are held on upright spikes, in shades of rose, pink, blue, lilac, through white. The regular single-flowered form is charming, but the double form has bizarre cup-and-saucer style flowers that are a hit with kids! Superb for cutting. Biennial, sometimes self-seeding.

HEIGHT/SPREAD:	60–90cm (24–36")/30cm (12")
LOCATION:	Well-drained soil.
BLOOMS:	June–July
USES:	✂ Bedding, Massing

persicifolia   ZONES 2–9

(Peach-leaved Bellflower) Flowers are large blue or white bells, arranged on strong stems that are excellent for cutting. Blooms over a long period. Old-fashioned cottage garden perennial. Often self-seeds. Still one of the easiest and most rewarding perennials.

HEIGHT/SPREAD:	60–90cm (24–36")/30–45cm (12–18")
LOCATION:	Average well-drained soil.
BLOOMS:	June–August
USES:	✂☙ Borders

'**Telham Beauty**' Especially good taller form. Large china-blue flowers. HEIGHT: 90–120cm (3–4')

poscharskyana   ZONES 2–9

(Serbian Bellflower) Trailing rockery plant, smothered with starry lavender-blue flowers. Spreads fairly quickly, so keep this away from delicate alpines. Useful as a ground-cover, or try it in containers. Grows well in part shade.

HEIGHT/SPREAD:	10–15cm (4–6")/30–45cm (12–18")
LOCATION:	Average well-drained soil.
BLOOMS:	May–July
USES:	△∿❦ Walls, Slopes

'E.H. Frost' Flowers are porcelain white with a pale blue eye. Long-blooming.

rotundifolia 'Olympica' ZONES 2–9
(Bluebell of Scotland) Airy masses of nodding lavender-blue flowers. Performs best in cool-summer areas. Delightful native North American wildflower. Terrific cut flower.

HEIGHT/SPREAD:	30cm (12")/30cm (12")
LOCATION:	Average to lean well-drained soil.
BLOOMS:	June–September
USES:	△✂ Borders, Meadows

takesimana ZONES 4–9
(Korean Bellflower) Forms a spreading clump, with arching stems of large dangling bells. Flowers are pale lilac, with dark maroon spots on the inside. Tolerant of dry shade.

HEIGHT/SPREAD:	45–60cm (18–24")/30cm (12")
LOCATION:	Average well-drained soil.
BLOOMS:	June–August
USES:	✂ Borders, Woodland garden

CARNATION see DIANTHUS

CARYOPTERIS
(Bluebeard) ☀ Home

× clandonensis ZONES 5–9
Also called Blue Spirea. Although actually a woody shrub, this is usually cut back each spring to 15cm (6") and treated more like a perennial, blooming in the fall on new wood. Upright stems hold clusters of fragrant blue flowers from late summer on. This colour is welcome in the fall border as a contrast to the many types of yellow daisies blooming at the end of the season. Several selections have been made. Planting before midsummer is recommended. Fairly drought-tolerant, also said to be a butterfly magnet.

HEIGHT/SPREAD:	60–90cm (2–3')/60–75cm (24–30")
LOCATION:	Well-drained soil.
BLOOMS:	August–October
USES:	✂❦❧ Borders, Massing

'Dark Knight' One of the darkest forms, rich deep-purple flowers.

'Heavenly Blue' Deep blue flowers. Good for cutting.

'Longwood Blue' Sky-blue flowers, silver-grey leaves. Floriferous.

'Worcester Gold' Bright blue flowers contrasting against golden-green foliage. Unusual!

CASSIA
(Wild Senna) ☀

hebecarpa ZONES 4–9
A sturdy upright-growing member of the pea family, native to eastern North America. The foliage is dark green, compound and lacy in appearance, forming a bushy mound topped with spikes of golden-yellow flowers in summer. A unique specimen or back-of-the-border subject. Drought-tolerant.

HEIGHT/SPREAD:	90–150cm (3–5')/90cm (3')
LOCATION:	Well-drained soil.
BLOOMS:	July–August
USES:	✂❦ Borders

CATANANCHE
(Cupid's Dart) ☀

caerulea ZONES 3–9
Papery lavender-blue flowers with a maroon eye. Plant forms a neat, slender clump of grey-green leaves. Moderately drought-tolerant. Short-lived, but will usually re-seed itself freely. Excellent for cutting, fresh or dried.

> "Mingled with some grey foliage to give them rather better furnishing— *Artemisia stelleriana*, for instance—they give a long-lasting summer picture." — Graham Stuart Thomas, *Perennial Garden Plants*

HEIGHT/SPREAD:	60cm (24")/30cm (12")
LOCATION:	Well-drained soil. Dislikes winter wet.
BLOOMS:	June–August
USES:	✂❦ Borders

CENTAUREA
(Perennial Cornflower) ☀
Sturdy, handsome perennials for planting in the border. Brightly coloured thistle-shaped blooms are long-lasting cut flowers. All types benefit from a hard shearing back after blooming. Reliable and long-lived.

dealbata ZONES 3–9
(Persian Cornflower) Rosy-purple flowers in early summer. Foliage is grey-green, handsomely lobed.

HEIGHT/SPREAD:	45–75cm (18–30")/60cm (24")
LOCATION:	Average well-drained soil.
BLOOMS:	June–July
USES:	✂ Borders

hypoleuca 'John Coutts' ZONES 3–9
An especially attractive form with finely-lobed greyish foliage and masses of clear pink flowers over a long season. This will usually rebloom in the fall if deadheaded. Excellent for massing in the border.

HEIGHT/SPREAD:	60–75cm (24–30")/60cm (24")
LOCATION:	Average well-drained soil.
BLOOMS:	June–August
USES:	✂ Borders, Massing

macrocephala ZONES 2–9
(Globe Centaurea) Showy, golden-yellow flowers on stiffly upright stems. Nice at the back of a border. Superb for cutting, fresh or dried.

HEIGHT/SPREAD:	90–120cm (3–4')/60cm (24")
LOCATION:	Average well-drained soil.
BLOOMS:	June–August
USES:	✂ Borders

montana ZONES 2–9
(Perennial Bachelor's Button) Cornflower-blue blossoms are an old-fashioned favorite. Nice filler plant towards the front of a border. Will usually rebloom in the fall if cut back. Very drought-tolerant.

HEIGHT/SPREAD:	30–60cm (12–24")/60cm (24")
LOCATION:	Average well-drained soil.
BLOOMS:	May–June
USES:	✂❦ Borders

CENTRANTHUS
(Red Valerian) ☀

ruber ZONES 4–9
An old-fashioned cut flower, back by popular demand. Large rounded clusters of rosy-red, fragrant flowers for many weeks. Plants are upright and bushy. Short-lived, but will self-seed. Moderately drought-tolerant.

HEIGHT/SPREAD:	30–90cm (1–3')/30–45cm (12–18")
LOCATION:	Average to poor well-drained soil.
BLOOMS:	June–September
USES:	✂❦ Borders, Slopes, Walls

Campanula takesimana

Catanache caerulea

Centaurea macrocephala

Centranthus ruber

Ceratostigma plumbaginoides

Cheiranthus × 'Bowle's Mauve'

Cheiranthus linifolium 'Variegatum'

Chelone obliqua

CEPHALARIA
(Giant Scabious) ☀

gigantea   ZONES 3–9
Pale yellow pincushion flowers, similar in shape to *Scabiosa* but on a very tall, open upright bush. Nice subject for the back of a moist border. Plants will be more bushy and compact if pinched in May or June. May need staking. Good for cutting.

HEIGHT/SPREAD:	1.5–1.8m (5–6')/60–90cm (2–3')
LOCATION:	Prefers a rich moist soil.
BLOOMS:	June–September
USES:	✄ Borders

CERASTIUM
(Snow-in-Summer) ☀

Low, mat-forming plants, popular for planting in rock gardens and walls, with handsome grey leaves and white flowers. Despite their reputation, not all types are invasive. Shear lightly after blooming to keep plants looking neat.

alpinum lanatum   ZONES 2–9
(Woolly Cerastium) Compact alpine, forming a low mound of fuzzy grey-green leaves, white flowers. Slow growing and not at all invasive. Excellent rock garden perennial, needs good drainage.

HEIGHT/SPREAD:	5–10cm (2–4")/15–30cm (6–12")
LOCATION:	Well-drained soil.
BLOOMS:	May–June
USES:	▲△▲� Scree, Trough

tomentosum   ZONES 1–9
(Snow-in-Summer) Vigorous, spreading mat of bright grey leaves, smothered with white flowers in early summer. Spreads quickly, often used as a groundcover on sunny slopes. Sometimes invasive. Not recommended for rock gardens! Very drought-tolerant.

HEIGHT/SPREAD:	15–30cm (6–12")/60cm (24")
LOCATION:	Well-drained soil.
BLOOMS:	May–June
USES:	⋎▲☖ Slopes, Walls

CERATOSTIGMA
(Blue Leadwort) ☀ ◐

plumbaginoides   ZONES 5–9
An unusual low perennial, valuable for fall display. Flowers are brilliant blue, foliage turns from green to maroon red in late fall. Nice as a ground cover or at the front of the border. Needs a winter mulch in colder areas. Planting before midsummer is strongly recommended.

> "Its coppery red leaves and lucid blue flowers make an excellent understory for bronzed chrysanthemums and rose or purple asters and sets off lavender colchicums attractively." —Ann Lovejoy,
> *The American Mixed Border*

HEIGHT/SPREAD:	20–30cm (8–12")/45cm (18")
LOCATION:	Well-drained soil. Dislikes winter wet.
BLOOMS:	August–October
USES:	▲△⋎ Massing, Edging, Borders

CHEIRANTHUS
(Wallflower) ☀

Since experts are having problems sorting out the correct nomenclature of *Cheiranthus* and *Erysimum*, we are treating them as one group for the time being. Best known are the spring-blooming Wallflowers, often used for massing with bulbs. All types have similar sweetly-fragrant flowers.

allionii   ZONES 3–9
(Siberian Wallflower) Often mass planted with tulips, these late-spring bloomers will hide that unsightly shrivelling bulb foliage. Usually treated as a biennial, they will freely self-seed in a favorable location, especially in well-drained gravelly soils. The loose spikes of flowers are typically yellow or orange.

HEIGHT/SPREAD:	30–60cm (12–24")/20cm (8")
LOCATION:	Well-drained soil.
BLOOMS:	May–July
USES:	✄❦ Bedding, Naturalizing

× 'Bowle's Mauve'   ZONES 6–9
Shrubby, upright plant, evergreen in milder regions. Handsome grey-green leaves nicely set off the profuse clusters of mauve flowers. This blooms over a long season, sometimes all winter at the West coast. Plants develop a woody base and should be sheared back to 15cm (6") in midsummer to promote fall flowering. In colder regions this performs well as a container plant.

HEIGHT/SPREAD:	60–75cm (24–30")/45cm (18")
LOCATION:	Well-drained soil.
BLOOMS:	May–October
USES:	✄⋎❦ Specimen, Borders

linifolium 'Variegatum'   ZONES 7–9
Similar to the shrubby 'Bowle's Mauve' in habit, this variety is valued for its handsome cream and green variegated foliage. Flowers are mauve and brown. Best used as a container plant in most areas. Shear back to 15cm (6") in midsummer where hardy.

HEIGHT/SPREAD:	30–60cm (12–24")/30cm (12")
LOCATION:	Well-drained soil.
BLOOMS:	May–October
USES:	✄⋎❦ Specimen, Borders

CHELONE
(Turtlehead) ☀ ◐

obliqua   ZONES 3–9
(Pink Turtlehead) Stiff spikes of rose-pink flowers, blooming over a long period. Excellent for cutting. Nice waterside plant, also does well in the border. A North American native wildflower. Outstanding for fall flower colour! There is also a beautiful white form known simply as 'Alba'.

HEIGHT/SPREAD:	60–90cm (24–36")/60cm (24")
LOCATION:	Moist to wet rich soil.
BLOOMS:	August–October
USES:	✄⋎ Borders, Waterside

CHIASTOPHYLLUM
(Cotyledon) ◐

oppositifolium   ZONES 5–9
Dangling chains of yellow flowers, succulent green leaves like a *Sedum*. Will cascade nicely over rocks and walls. An unusual, easy alpine plant for a shaded rock garden.

HEIGHT/SPREAD:	15cm (6")/30cm (12")
LOCATION:	Well-drained soil. Dislikes hot sun.
BLOOMS:	June–July
USES:	▲⋎ Edging, Walls

CHRYSANTHEMUM
(Daisy, Chrysanthemum) ☀ ◐

This large group of plants includes some of the best garden perennials available. Recently split by botanists into several genera, we are continuing to list them together here under *Chrysanthemum* for convenience sake, with the new currently correct name indicated in brackets.

Most selections are excellent for cutting. All prefer a sunny location, and an average to rich well-drained soil. Divide every 1–2 years to keep plants vigorous as they may become woody and begin to decline.

coccineum   ZONES 2–9

(Painted Daisy) (now *Tanecetum coccineum*) An old-fashioned cutting flower with large red, pink or white daisies on wiry stems. Plants form a clump of ferny green leaves. Deadhead regularly to encourage continued blooming. Short-lived unless divided every year or two. Although named selections exist in Europe, the forms grown here are mostly seed strains, but still excellent.

HEIGHT/SPREAD:	45–75cm (18–30")/45cm (18")
LOCATION:	Average well-drained soil.
BLOOMS:	June–July
USES:	✂❀ Borders

'Extra Double Mixture' High percentage of double and semi-double flowers in a mixture of colours.

'James Kelway' Deep vermilion-red single flowers.

'Robinson Rose' Bright rose-pink, single flowers.

'Robinson Single Hybrids' Mixture of colours, large single flowers.

× morifolium   ZONES 5–9

(Hybrid Garden Mum) (now *Dendranthema indica*) Unlike the typical modern garden mums, these are vigorous old varieties that have stood the test of time, only recently making it back into commercial production. Plants spread to form a clump, and should be divided every year or two to maintain vigour. Pinch as for regular garden mums.

SPREAD:	60cm (24")
LOCATION:	Well-drained soil.
BLOOMS:	September–November
USES:	✂ Borders

'Mei-Kyo' Small deep-rose double flowers with a yellow centre. Late. HEIGHT: 60cm (2')

'Hillside Pink' (a.k.a. 'Sheffield') Pale pink single daisy flowers. HEIGHT: 70cm (28")

nipponicum   ZONES 5–9

(Nippon Daisy, Montauk Daisy) (now *Nipponicanthemum nipponicum*) A nearly shrubby type of daisy, with thick leathery green leaves. Plants grow fairly tall, and can be used to good specimen effect. Shasta-type white flowers appear in fall. Prune plants back to 10cm (4") in spring, and pinch in midsummer if you want compact growth. Tolerant of ocean-side conditions.

HEIGHT/SPREAD:	60–90cm (2–3')/60cm (2')
LOCATION:	Well-drained soil.
BLOOMS:	September–October
USES:	✂❀ Specimen, Borders

pacificum   ZONES 5–9

(Silver and Gold) (now *Ajania pacifica*) Recently arrived from Japan. Bushy mounds of toothed green foliage, attractively edged with silver. Yellow button flowers will appear very late fall if the season is long and warm, in some areas blooming into December. Also a superb container plant, either kept bushy or trained into a standard.

HEIGHT/SPREAD:	20–30 cm (8–12")/30cm (12")
LOCATION:	Average well-drained soil.
BLOOMS:	October–November
USES:	✂❀ Edging, Borders

parthenium   ZONES 3–9

(Feverfew) (now *Tanacetum parthenium*) Branching sprays of small daisies, like little button mums, blooming for many weeks. Flowers are excellent for cutting. Foliage is bushy and aromatic. Plants will stay nice and compact if pinched back by half in May or June. These are short-lived perennials but readily self-seed and can

then be moved to where you want them. Use a winter mulch in Zones 3–5. There are several selections. Also listed under HERBS.

SPREAD:	15–20cm (6–8")
LOCATION:	Average well-drained soil.
BLOOMS:	July–October
USES:	✂❀ Borders, Herb gardens

'Double White' Pure white button flowers. A taller form, the best for cutting. HEIGHT: 30–90cm (1–3')

'Golden Ball' Golden-yellow button flowers. Compact plants. HEIGHT: 30–45cm (12–18")

'Santana' Extremely compact form. White button flowers. Great for edging. HEIGHT: 20cm (8")

'White Stars' White daisies with yellow centres. HEIGHT: 30–45cm (12–18")

× rubellum   ZONES 4–9

(now *Dendranthema zawadskii*) Large, fragrant single daisies are held in loose sprays. Plants form a densely branching clump. Easy and reliable border plant, blooming several weeks ahead of fall mums. Plants will be more compact if pinched back by half in early June. Very few selections from this hybrid group are still in existence.

HEIGHT/SPREAD:	60–75cm (24–30")/60cm (24")
LOCATION:	Average well-drained soil.
BLOOMS:	July–September
USES:	✂❀ Borders

'Clara Curtis' Large, deep-pink single flowers.

'Mary Stoker' Golden-apricot flowers, fading to peach.

× superbum   ZONES 4–9

(Shasta Daisy) (now *Leucanthemum maximum*) No sunny border would seem complete without these familiar, sturdy white daisies. Recent breeding has resulted in a good selection of flower types and plant heights. All bloom June–September for many weeks, especially when dead flowers are removed. Good drainage in winter is essential.

SPREAD:	30–45cm (12–18")
LOCATION:	Average well-drained soil.
BLOOMS:	June–September
USES:	✂❀ Borders

'Aglaia' The true form has large, frilly double flowers with a crested white centre. Hardier than 'Esther Read'. Beware of single-flowered seed-grown impostors. HEIGHT: 60–75cm (24–30").

'Alaska' Classic single flowers. Hardy to Zone 3. HEIGHT: 60cm (24").

'Esther Read' Fully double flowers, almost like a florist's mum. Zones 5–9. HEIGHT: 30–60cm (12–24").

'Polaris' Very large single flowers. HEIGHT: 90cm (36").

'Sedgewick' (now *Leucanthemum vulgare*) Fully double flowers, spreading habit. This is likely a double form of Ox-eye Daisy. Zones 1–9. HEIGHT: 30–45cm (12–18").

'Silver Princess' Compact, mounded plants, the best compact seed-grown selection. Single flowers, long blooming. HEIGHT: 30cm (12").

'Snowcap' Excellent, compact selection raised by Alan Bloom at Bressingham Gardens. Ideal for massing or edging along the front of the border. Large single white daisies all summer long. Must be vegetatively propagated. HEIGHT: 35cm (14").

'Snow Lady' Very dwarf habit, large single flowers. Award-winning, but noticeably lacking in vigour. HEIGHT: 25cm (10").

weyrichii   ZONES 4–9

(now *Dendranthema weyrichii*) A low, creeping species, in effect like a dwarf garden mum. Flowers are large yellow-centred single daisies. These usually bloom fairly late.

Chrysanthemum coccineum 'Robinson Rose'

Chrysanthemum parthenium 'White Stars'

Chrysanthemum × 'Esther Read'

Chrysanthemum × 'Polaris'

Chrysogonum virginianum

Clematis integrifolia

Cimicifuga ramosa 'Atropurpurea'

Codonopsis clematidea

SPREAD:	45cm (18")
LOCATION:	Well-drained soil
BLOOMS:	September–October
USES:	△⅊≺▼⤙ Edging, Massing

'Pink Bomb' Large rosy-pink flowers. HEIGHT: 25cm (9")
'White Bomb' Creamy-white flowers, fading to pale pink. HEIGHT: 30cm (12")

CHRYSOGONUM
(Golden Star) ☀☼ ●

virginianum   ZONES 5–9
This is a useful little groundcover, tolerating shady locations, and spreading to form a low patch of green foliage, studded with yellow star-shaped flowers for many weeks. A native North American wildflower. Appreciates a site sheltered from winds.

HEIGHT/SPREAD:	15–30cm (6–12")/30cm (12")
LOCATION:	Moist, well-drained soil.
BLOOMS:	May-July
USES:	⋀⋋ Borders, Woodland gardens

CIMICIFUGA
(Bugbane) ☀☼

Some of the more interesting and unusual forms of Bugbane are starting to become available here in North America, although will likely always be in short supply! The lacy clumps of foliage are not unlike Astilbe, but flowers are held on tall stems, in a bottle-brush spike. Good for late summer and fall interest. All types prefer a rich, moist humusy soil and a woodland setting. Avoid disturbing established clumps.

cordifolia   ZONES 3–9
(Heartleaf Bugbane) A variation on *C. racemosa*, from the southern states. This species has long white bottle-brush flowers on purple stems. Leaves are slightly broader.

HEIGHT/SPREAD:	90–120cm (3–4')/60cm (2')
LOCATION:	Likes a rich, moist soil.
BLOOMS:	August–September
USES:	⅊≺ Wildflower, Borders, Massing

racemosa   ZONES 3–9
(Black Snakeroot) Tall spikes of ivory-white flowers in late summer. Fruit capsules remain attractive into early winter. A wild flower native to eastern North America.

HEIGHT/SPREAD:	90–150cm (3–5')/60cm (2')
LOCATION:	Likes a rich, moist soil.
BLOOMS:	August–September
USES:	⅊≺ Wildflower, Borders, Massing

ramosa 'Atropurpurea'   ZONES 4–9
(Purple-leaf Bugbane) Unusual and exotic foliage, forming a medium-sized clump of dark purple, lacy leaves. An eye-catching contrast to the tall spikes of creamy-white flowers. Move this up to the front of the border for all to see! Chronically in short worldwide supply.

HEIGHT/SPREAD:	1.5–2.1m (5–7')/60cm (2')
LOCATION:	Likes a rich, moist soil.
BLOOMS:	August–September
USES:	⅊≺ Specimen, Borders

'Brunette' An even darker form, with black-purple leaves and fragrant pale pink flowers. Difficult to obtain.

simplex 'White Pearl'   ZONES 3–9
(Kamchatka Bugbane) Tall bottlebrush spikes of creamy-white flowers are held above light green, lacy leaves. Nice background plant for the fall border, and excellent for cutting.

HEIGHT/SPREAD:	90–120cm (3–4')/60cm (2')
LOCATION:	Likes a rich, moist soil.
BLOOMS:	September–October
USES:	⅊≺ Borders, Massing

CLEMATIS
(Clematis) ☀☼

Although the flashy, large-flowered hybrid types are great old favorites, the smaller flowered varieties listed here are valuable garden plants as well, and are deserving of wider use. Some of these are woody climbing vines, others sprawling perennials that die back to the ground each year, leaning on the nearest shrub or stake in the border for a little support.

integrifolia   ZONES 2–9
(Solitary Clematis) Not a climbing vine, but a border perennial that forms a sort of sprawling clump. Nodding, urn-shaped flowers are rich indigo blue, followed by fluffy seed heads. Plant this where it can sprawl up or over a shrub, or plan on staking it. Cut back to the ground in spring.

HEIGHT/SPREAD:	60–90cm (2–3')/60cm (2')
LOCATION:	Prefers a rich, moist soil.
BLOOMS:	July–August
USES:	≺ Borders

✕ 'Prairie Traveler's Joy'   ZONES 1–9
Very hardy hybrid developed by the late Dr. Frank Skinner in northern Manitoba. Sprays of starry white flowers bloom throughout the summer, followed by fluffy seed heads. Very vigorous to the point of being aggressive. Mow or prune back hard every two or three years. Use as either a hardy climber or sprawling groundcover. Very drought-tolerant.

HEIGHT/SPREAD:	30cm–5m (1–15')/90cm (3')
LOCATION:	Average well-drained soil.
BLOOMS:	June–September
USES:	⋀⋋▼⤙ Climbing vine

recta 'Purpurea'   ZONES 2–9
(Ground Clematis) Another herbaceous species, this requires some support to be at its best, though it is not really a climbing vine. Rich maroon-purple leaves are featured, with a good display of fragrant little white star flowers in summer. Silvery seed heads are attractive in fall.

> "The purple leaves are modest but give color and interest in a border planned primarily for flowers, and look particularly effective with a pink-flowered theme." —Penelope Hobhouse, *Colour in Your Garden*

HEIGHT/SPREAD:	90–120cm (3–4')/60cm (2')
LOCATION:	Prefers a rich, moist soil.
BLOOMS:	June–July
USES:	≺ Borders

tangutica   ZONES 2–9
(Golden Clematis) Bright yellow bell-shaped flowers through the summer and fall, followed by large feathery puffs. Excellent cover for difficult areas with poor soil, or trained as a climbing vine.

HEIGHT/SPREAD:	30cm–5m (1–15')/90cm (3')
LOCATION:	Average well-drained soil.
BLOOMS:	July–September
USES:	⋀⋋▼ Climbing vine

CODONOPSIS
(Bonnet Bellflower) ☀☼

clematidea   ZONES 3–9
A semi-sprawling plant that can be quite showy when planted on a bank or wall so the flowers can be viewed from below. Flowers are large light blue bells, with dramatic purple and orange patterns on the inside. Plants have a mysterious fragrance when in bloom.

HEIGHT/SPREAD: 30–45cm (12–18″)/60cm (24″)
LOCATION: Well-drained soil.
BLOOMS: June–August
USES: ⚊ Walls, Slopes

CONRADINA
(Cumberland Rosemary) ☀ ☽

verticillata   ZONES 5–9
An endangered species, native to the Cumberland mountains in the southeastern U.S. Plants have narrow green-grey foliage, similar to rosemary, with a strong mint fragrance. Flowers are lavender pink, appearing in late spring. Forms a nice little bush, excellent in the rock garden.

HEIGHT/SPREAD: 30–40cm (12–16″)/30cm (12″)
LOCATION: Prefers a sandy, well-drained soil.
BLOOMS: May–June
USES: ⚊✿ Wildflower, Troughs

CONVALLARIA
(Lily-of-the-Valley) ☽●

majalis   ZONES 1–9
Fragrant, white bell-shaped flowers. A sturdy groundcover for difficult shady sites, even under trees. Old-fashioned cut-flower. All parts of this plant are poisonous, especially the red berries.

> "Lily-of-the-valley must not be
> forgotten, for though we grow it in
> greater quantity in reserve ground for
> cutting and in woodland, yet its
> beautiful foliage and sweetest of sweet
> bloom must be near the front edge of
> this border also. " —Gertrude Jekyll,
> *Wood and Garden*

HEIGHT/SPREAD: 15cm (6″)/30cm (12″)
LOCATION: Average to moist soil.
BLOOMS: April–May
USES: ⋏✂ Woodland gardens

COREOPSIS
(Tickseed) ☀

Bright yellow daisy-like flowers characterize this popular group of plants. All bloom constantly from midsummer to frost, particularly when fading flowers are removed. Good for cutting. The original species are all native North American wildflowers.

auriculata 'Nana'   ZONES 4–9
(Maysville Daisy) A long-lived dwarf variety, ideal for edging or in the rock garden. Plants give a showy display of single orange-yellow flowers in late spring. May repeat bloom if deadheaded.

HEIGHT/SPREAD: 15–25cm (6–9″)/30cm (12″)
LOCATION: Average to moist well-drained soil.
BLOOMS: May–July
USES: ⚊⋏✿ Edging, Borders

grandiflora   ZONES 4–9
(Large-flowered Coreopsis) Large, golden-yellow flowers, blooming for many weeks in the summer. Both single and double flowered forms are available as well as a good range of heights. Hybrids between this species and *C. lanceolata* have produced many of the modern selections. These all have a tendency to bloom themselves to death; removing the flower stems from about early September on will encourage plants to form overwintering leaves rather than going to seed and wearing themselves out. Outstanding cut flowers.

SPREAD: 30cm (12″)
LOCATION: Prefers a rich, moist soil.
BLOOMS: June–September
USES   ⋏✿✿ Borders, Massing

'Baby Sun' Single flowers. HEIGHT: 30–50cm (12–20″)
'Double Sunburst' Fluffy double flowers. HEIGHT: 75–90cm (30–36″)
'Early Sunrise' Semi-double, award winner. HEIGHT: 45–60cm (18–24″)
'Goldfink' Miniature single flowers, true dwarf. Must be grown by vegetative means. HEIGHT: 20–25cm (8–10″).

rosea   ZONES 3–9
(Pink Flowered Coreopsis) Charming plant for edging or massing. Low, airy mounds of green leaves are studded with bright rose-pink daisies. The deep-pink form commonly grown in North America is known as 'American Dream' in Europe. Plants are vigorous and spreading, to be used with caution in the border. Prefers a moist soil.

HEIGHT/SPREAD: 30–45cm (12–18″)/30–45cm (12–18″)
LOCATION: Average to moist soil.
BLOOMS: June–September
USES   ✂⋏✿✿ Massing, Borders

verticillata   ZONES 3–9
(Thread-leaved Coreopsis) Truly among the best garden perennials available. Plants form an airy dome of narrow leaves, covered with starry flowers for many weeks. Can be mass planted as a groundcover. Excellent for combining with ornamental grasses. Generally long-lived and carefree. Very drought-tolerant.

> "For bright pure color a group of this
> fine daisy is hard to beat. Grow it next
> to dark reds, bright orange curtonis or
> crocosmia with sword-like leaf contrast,
> or associate it with a pale yellow×
> *Solidaster luteus*." —Penelope
> Hobhouse, *Colour in Your Garden*

SPREAD: 30–45cm (12–18″)
LOCATION: Average well-drained soil.
BLOOMS: June–September
USES: ✂✿🌱 Massing, Borders

'Golden Showers' (a.k.a. 'Grandiflora') Large golden-yellow flowers. Vigorous. HEIGHT: 60–75cm (24–30″)
'Moonbeam' Unusual pale yellow flowers. Deservedly popular, and perhaps one of the all-time best perennials, blending in nicely with pastel colour schemes. Not always long-lived, however, and very late to make an appearance in spring. A former *Perennial Plant of the Year*. HEIGHT: 45–60cm (18–24″)
'Zagreb' Especially compact form. Bright chrome-yellow flowers, similar to 'Golden Showers'. HEIGHT: 30cm (12″)

CORONILLA
(Crown Vetch) ☀

varia   ZONES 3–9
Widely used as a groundcover on roadsides and other difficult sunny sites, valued for its ability to fix nitrogen from the air, improving the soil. Rose-pink clover-like flowers bloom all summer. Very aggressive, unsuitable for most garden situations. Extremely drought-tolerant.

HEIGHT/SPREAD: 30–60cm (12–24″)/60cm (24″)
LOCATION: Very tolerant of poor soils.
BLOOMS: June–August
USES: ⋏🌱 Roadsides, Slopes

CORYDALIS
(Corydalis) ☀ ☽

Related to the familiar Bleedingheart, these have similar ferny foliage, and upright stems of delicate but showy flowers. They appreciate a cool, moisture-retentive but well-drained soil, perhaps at the edge of a woodland.

Coreopsis grandiflora 'Early Sunrise'

Coreopsis verticillata 'Golden Showers'

Coreopsis verticillata 'Moonbeam'

Coronilla varia

Corydalis flexuosa 'Blue Panda'

Cosmos atrosanguineus

Crocosmia × 'Jenny Bloom'

Crocosmia × 'Lucifer'

flexuosa 'Blue Panda'   ZONES 5–9

(Blue Corydalis) Lacy blue-green foliage with arching stems of the most incredible sky-blue, fragrant flowers over a long season. A recent arrival from China, and worth a try in any partly shaded rockery. Flowering is intermittent from spring to fall.

HEIGHT/SPREAD: 20–30cm (8–12″)/30cm (12″)
LOCATION: Rich, moist well-drained soil.
BLOOMS: May–October
USES: ⛰▲♣☕✂ Edging, Walls

lutea   ZONES 4–9

(Golden Corydalis) A charming little plant for a rock wall or slope, with pretty yellow locket-shaped flowers for months! The fresh green leaves make a low ferny mound. In a partly shaded cool site this will happily self-seed all over the place.

> "No better companion for Jacob's ladder [*Polemonium*] could be found than a foreground planting of *Corydalis luteus*." —Patrick Lima, *The Harrowsmith Perennial Garden*

HEIGHT/SPREAD: 20–30cm (8–12″)/30cm (12″)
LOCATION: Prefers a moist, well-drained soil.
BLOOMS: May–September
USES: ⛰▲♣ Walls, Borders

COSMOS
(Cosmos) ☀

atrosanguineus   ZONES 7–9

(Chocolate Cosmos) This plant has quickly become a hit. The large dark maroon-red flowers are distinctively chocolate-scented on warm days. Good for cutting. Plants form a tuberous root which can be lifted and stored indoors like a Dahlia, so this can even be grown in colder regions!

HEIGHT/SPREAD: 45–75cm (18–30″)/30cm (12″)
LOCATION: Well-drained soil.
BLOOMS: June–September
USES: ✂♣ Borders

COTULA
(Brass Buttons) ☀◑

potentillina   ZONES 5–9

(New Zealand brass Buttons) (now *Leptinella potentillina*) A flat, carpeting groundcover, the leaves are soft and feathery in texture. Green foliage develops some bronzy tones in cold weather. One of the best plants for between paving stones! Flowers are insignificant. Evergreen at the west coast.

HEIGHT/SPREAD: 5cm (2″)/30cm (12″)
LOCATION: Evenly moist, well-drained soil.
USES: ⛰▲〰▲ Between flagstones

COTYLEDON see CHIASTOPHYLLUM

CRAMBE
(Sea Kale) ☀

cordifolia   ZONES 5–9

(Heartleaf Seakale, Colewort) A most bizarre and unusual plant, something like a Baby's Breath crossed with a cabbage! Huge green leaves are deeply lobed and form a large mound. Clouds of tiny star-shaped flowers are held above on tall stalks in early summer. An interesting specimen plant for the larger border. Very long-lived.

> "…with its huge rough cabbage-shaped leaves and tall stems of cloud-like white flowers, is a wonderful perennial. It flowers early, needs no staking, and contributes architectural quality, so often lacking in flowering border plants." —Penelope Hobhouse, *Colour in Your Garden*

HEIGHT/SPREAD: 120–180cm (4–6′)/120cm (4′)
LOCATION: Well-drained soil.
BLOOMS: June–July
USES: ✂ Specimen, Borders

CROCOSMIA
(Crocosmia, Montbretia) ☀

Becoming popular both for gardens and as a cut flower. Recent breeding work has greatly increased the selection of heights and flower colours and generally improved hardiness. Upright clumps of sword-shaped leaves produce arching stems of brilliant nodding funnel flowers from midsummer on, the effect a bit like some kind of exotic gladiola. In Zones 1–4 the fleshy roots may be overwintered indoors like Canna lilies, and this is well worth the effort. Divide plants every 2–3 years for best blooming. A deep winter mulch is recommended in Zones 5–7, or wherever snowcover is unreliable. Superb cut flowers.

Hybrids: ZONES 5–9

Although our zoning may seem optimistic, there are gardeners in both Zones 5 and 6 that are succeeding with Crocosmia outside. Reliable snowcover and/or a deep mulch of leaves in winter appears to be the key to success in these regions. An addition, planting before the end of June would be well advised.

SPREAD: 30cm (12″)
LOCATION: Average well-drained soil.
BLOOMS: July–September
USES: ✂♣ Borders, Massing

'Bressingham Beacon' Beautiful orange and yellow bicolor raised by Alan Bloom. HEIGHT: 100cm (40″).

'Emberglow' Very large flowers, burnt orange-red. An older Alan Bloom selection. HEIGHT: 75cm (30″).

'Firebird' Rich flame-orange. An older Alan Bloom selection. HEIGHT: 80cm (32″)

'Jenny Bloom' A newer deep yellow hybrid by Alan Bloom. HEIGHT: 100cm (40″).

'Lucifer' Brilliant flame-red. The most famous of the older Alan Bloom hybrids. HEIGHT: 120cm (4′)

'Severn Sunrise' Glowing orange with a yellow eye. Compact. HEIGHT: 60cm (2′)

'Vulcan' Compact habit, flame-orange flowers. Another Alan Bloom hybrid. HEIGHT: 60cm (2′)

DARMERA see PELTIPHYLLUM

CYCLAMEN
(Hardy Cyclamen) ◐

hederifolium   ZONES 5–9

Suited to a shady rockery or woodland area, these form low clumps of ivy-shaped green leaves with intricate grey and bronzy patterning. The little pink or white rocket-shaped flowers appear in early fall, followed by the leaves. Clumps remain evergreen for the winter, going dormant during the heat of summer. Large corms develop underground. These resent overhead watering in the summer, so are best paired up with plants that are fairly drought tolerant. Excellent under trees and shrubs, these often begin to self-seed.

HEIGHT/SPREAD: 10–15cm (4–6″)/15–20cm (6–8″)
LOCATION: Very well-drained soil.
BLOOMS: September–October.
USES: ⚠▲▼ Woodland gardens

DELOSPERMA
(Hardy Ice plant) ☀

Spreading, succulent plants similar in effect to *Sedum*. Flowers are single stars, studding the evergreen mat of leaves. These require very good drainage, especially in wet winter regions. Best on a slope or gravelly rock garden. Drought-tolerant.

cooperi   ZONES 6–9
(Purple Ice Plant) Blooms all summer long with magenta-purple daisy-like flowers. Intolerant of wet soil, and often treated as an annual in the eastern part of the continent. Foliage develops good red fall and winter colour. Much used as a groundcover in the south-western U.S. Very drought-tolerant.
HEIGHT/SPREAD: 5–10cm (2–4″)/30–60cm (12–24″)
LOCATION: Very well-drained soil.
BLOOMS: June–September.
USES: ⚠Ⓜ▲▼ Slopes

nubigenum   ZONES 3–9
(Yellow Ice Plant) Low weed-proof mat of green foliage, turning bronze-red in cold weather. Flowers are bright yellow, mostly in late spring. Reliably hardy, much more tolerant of wet soils and extended cold than the Purple Ice Plant. Worth considering as a lawn substitute. Very drought-tolerant.
HEIGHT/SPREAD: 5–10cm (2–4″)/30–60cm (12–24″)
LOCATION: Average to very well-drained soil.
BLOOMS: May–June.
USES: ⚠Ⓜ▲▼ Slopes

DELPHINIUM
(Delphinium, Larkspur) ☀

One of the classic garden perennials, so important to the traditional English-style herbaceous summer border. We are all familiar with the taller types, with their stately spires of colour. However, the smaller-flowered larkspur-style varieties are also excellent border plants, so useful for cutting, and often succeeding in hot humid climates where the taller forms do not.

All types need a rich, moist but well-drained soil and full sun. Taller types are especially heavy feeders, so they should be fertilized regularly. Removing faded flowers will encourage repeat blooming; cut taller varieties back to 10cm (4″) after flowering, shorter types need only to be dead-headed. Staking of the larger forms in late May will help to prevent damage by strong winds at flowering time.

> "…we wind stout cord from stake to stake and tie the plant in at several ascending levels, but not so tightly as to give it a Scarlet O'Hara waist. Support is the goal, not strangulation." —Patrick Lima, *The Harrowsmith Perennial Garden*

Elatum Hybrids   ZONES 2–9
(Pacific Giant Hybrids) (*D.* × *cultorum*) These tall colourful spikes of double flowers can be the backbone for the early summer border. Flowers often have a contrasting centre or "bee". Plan to renew plantings every three years, otherwise the plants will get woody and begin to decline. Fall flowering is usually good if plants are trimmed back after the summer flush is over. Many seed strains have been developed in a wide range of separate colours.

HEIGHT/SPREAD: 120–180cm (4–6′)/60cm (2′)
LOCATION: Rich, average to moist soil.
BLOOMS: June–July, fall.
USES: ✄ Borders

'Astolat' Lavender pink, dark bee.
'Black Knight' Deep midnight violet, the darkest.
'Blue Bird' Clear medium blue, white bee.
'Blue Jay' Medium blue, dark bee.
'Camelliard' Lavender blue shades.
'Galahad' Pure white.
'Guinevere' Lavender-pink with white bee.
'King Arthur' Royal violet with white bee.
'Summer Skies' Light blue, white bee.
'Magic Fountains Mix' Compact, windproof strain in a good range of colours, including blue, lavender, rose and white. HEIGHT: 75–90cm (30–36″)

× belladonna   ZONES 2–9
Larkspur-style flowers held in a loosely-branching spikes, rather than in a solitary one. These are in various shades of blue and white, and are excellent for cutting. Good repeat bloomer if dead-headed. Not as long-lived as the Elatum hybrids.
HEIGHT/SPREAD: 90–120cm (3–4′)/45cm (18″)
LOCATION: Rich, average to moist soil.
BLOOMS: June–August.
USES: ✄ Borders

× 'Connecticut Yankee'   ZONES 3–9
Also with larkspur-type flowers on compact, bushy plants that require no staking. These are more suited to a smaller garden, with an extended season of bloom. Flowers are in mixed shades of white, blue, lavender and purple.
HEIGHT/SPREAD: 60–75cm (24–30″)/60cm (24″)
LOCATION: Rich, average to moist soil.
BLOOMS: July–September.
USES: ✄ Borders

grandiflorum 'Blue Elf'   ZONES 3–9
Totally unlike the taller forms already listed, these form dwarf bushy mounds, covered with large brilliant blue flowers all summer and fall. Excellent for edging or massing. Although short-lived, these put on such a spectacular show that they are worth using even as a bedding annual. Sometimes self-seeds.
HEIGHT/SPREAD: 30cm (12″)/30cm (12″)
LOCATION: Average to moist well-drained soil.
BLOOMS: June–September.
USES: ⚠▼✄ ⚘ Borders, Edging

nudicaule   ZONES 6–9
(Orange Larkspur) Unusual species native to California, with a nice display of bright orange-red flowers. Most effective when several are planted closely together in a group. Short-lived, best treated as an annual in wetter areas. Needs perfect drainage in winter. Drought-tolerant.
HEIGHT/SPREAD: 30–60cm (12–24″)/30cm (12″)
LOCATION: Very well-drained.
BLOOMS: June–August.
USES: ⚠✄▼ Wildflower, Borders

DENDRANTHEMA
see CHRYSANTHEMUM

DIANTHUS
(Pinks) ☀

A large and diverse group of plants, including Carnations and Sweet William. Many forms are low growing, well-suited to rock gardens or for edging. Divide all but the alpine types every two years to keep plants vigorous and young. Most are evergreen. Cushion-forming Dianthus will benefit

Delosperma cooperi

Delphinium 'Blue Fountain'

Delphinium elatum × 'Camelliard'

Delphinium grandiflorum 'Blue Elf'

Dianthus barbatus 'Dwarf Double'

Dianthus gratianopolitanus 'Tiny Ruby'

Dianthus gratianopolitanus 'Spotty'

Diascia cordata 'Ruby Field'

from a little cleanup after flowering, removing flower stems and giving a light trim to the foliage.

alpinus   ZONES 3–9
(Alpine Pink) Very dwarf rock-garden type. Grassy clumps of leaves and large, single hot-pink flowers. Appreciates a little afternoon shade.

HEIGHT/SPREAD:	5cm (2")/15cm (6")
LOCATION:	Well-drained, moist soil.
BLOOMS:	May–June.
USES:	▲△▲� Scree, Troughs

arenarius   ZONES 2–9
(Sand Pink) Fragrant, deeply-fringed white flowers over mounding green foliage. Forms a loose mat. An easy reliable groundcover for hot, dry locations.

HEIGHT/SPREAD:	20–30cm (8–12")/30cm (12")
LOCATION:	Average well-drained soil.
BLOOMS:	May–July.
USES:	△⋀⋅▲� Edging, Borders

barbatus   ZONES 2–9
(Sweet William) Classic cottage garden plant. Large showy clusters of flowers, blooming all summer if dead-headed regularly. A biennial or short-lived perennial, but will usually self-seed freely. Taller types make excellent cut flowers. There are several mixed seed strains available in both single and double-flowering forms, with varying heights and in colours ranging from shades of red, pink, and salmon, through to white.

HEIGHT/SPREAD:	15–60cm (6–24")/20–30cm (8–12")
LOCATION:	Average well-drained soil.
BLOOMS:	May–August.
USES:	△⋀⋅✂� Edging, Borders

caryophyllus 'Grenadin Series'   ZONES 4–9
(Hardy Carnation) Ever popular as cut-flowers. These are not long-lived and benefit from yearly division to keep the plants thriving. A thick mulch will help to bring them through cold winters. Their large, fragrant double flowers appear throughout the summer in a good range of colours, including shades of pink, red, white, and soft yellow. Blooms reliably as an annual in cold areas.

HEIGHT/SPREAD:	30–45cm (12–18")/30cm (12")
LOCATION:	Well-drained soil. Dislikes hot summers.
BLOOMS:	June–September
USES:	✂ Borders.

deltoides   ZONES 2–9
(Maiden Pinks) Low, spreading mats of foliage are smothered by small single flowers in summer. Good edging plants. Will often self-seed. Several colour strains are available.

HEIGHT/SPREAD:	15–20cm (6–8")/30–45cm (12–18")
LOCATION:	Average well-drained soil.
BLOOMS:	June–August.
USES:	△⋀⋅▲� Edging, Borders

'Albus' Green foliage, white flowers.

'Flashing Light' Ruby-red flowers, bronzy leaves.

'Zing' Deep rose-red flowers, green leaves, fairly upright habit. Repeat bloomer. Likely a hybrid.

gratianopolitanus   ZONES 2–9
(Cheddar Pinks) These have been grown in gardens for centuries, and a large number of named cultivars exist. All form a low cushion of grassy foliage, usually tinted grey or steel blue. Flowers are sweetly scented, the taller varieties excellent for cutting. Popular for edging and rock gardens, and outstanding growing in or over walls.

SPREAD:	20–30cm (8–12")
LOCATION:	Average well-drained soil.
BLOOMS:	May–July
USES:	✂△⋀⋅▲� Edging, Walls, Borders

'Bath's Pink' An especially vigorous new selection. Fringed soft-pink flowers in great numbers. Widely

reported to be tolerant of warm, humid conditions. Steel-blue leaves. HEIGHT: 15cm (6")

'Blue Hills' Silvery-blue foliage, single rose-pink flowers HEIGHT: 15cm (6")

'Dottie' Fringed single white flowers with a crimson eye. Compact green clump. An offspring of 'Spotty'. HEIGHT: 10cm (4")

'Frosty Fire' Deep ruby-red fringed flowers. Bright silver foliage. an outstanding form! Registered with the Canadian Ornamental Plant Foundation. HEIGHT: 15–20cm (6–8")

'Little Jock' Grassy grey cushion, semi-double pink flowers with a red eye. HEIGHT: 15cm (6")

'Spotty' Bluish leaves, unusual cerise-red flowers with white spots. HEIGHT: 15–20cm (6–8")

'Tiny Rubies' Tiny, double rose-pink flowers. Extremely compact mounds of olive-green leaves. Best in a rock garden. Very fragrant. HEIGHT: 10cm (4")

knappii   ZONES 3–9
(Yellow Pinks) Open, upright habit. Flowers are pale yellow, blooming over several weeks. Good for cutting. Short-lived but self-seeds prolifically.

HEIGHT/SPREAD:	45cm (18")/30cm (12")
LOCATION:	Average well-drained soil.
BLOOMS:	May–June
USES:	✂ Borders

'Laciniated White'   ZONES 2–9
(White Moss Pink) A hybrid of unknown origin with extremely tight moss-like cushions of grey-green leaves, studded with tiny white flowers. Needs very good drainage, best in a rockery or wall.

HEIGHT/SPREAD:	5–10cm (2–4")/30cm (12")
LOCATION:	Very well-drained soil.
BLOOMS:	May–June.
USES:	△⋀⋅▲� Walls, Troughs, Scree

plumarius   ZONES 4–9
(Cottage Pinks, Clove Pinks) Blue-grey, grassy foliage forms a wide, handsome clump. Flowers are like small carnations, strongly clove scented, with fringed petals. A true cottage garden perennial. Excellent for edging. Fairly drought-tolerant. There are many named forms of this.

HEIGHT/SPREAD:	30cm (12")/30cm (12")
LOCATION:	Average well-drained soil.
BLOOMS:	May–June
USES:	✂△⋀⋅▲� Edging, Walls, Borders

'Roseus Plenus' Very old form. Extremely fragrant rose-pink double flowers.

'Spring Beauty Mix' Double-flowering mix with many excellent forms. Colours include pink, rose, salmon and white shades.

DIASCIA
(Twinspur) ☼◑◔
These are widely grown in England, but relatively new to North American gardens. Plants will bloom all summer long, with a showy display of bright pink flowers. Worth a try in containers or hanging baskets. Best treated as half-hardy, even in mild West coast gardens.

> "Their small, spurred flowers of rose or coral or coppery salmon bring zest to an excess of pastels, and they have a knack for putting themselves into stunning combinations." —Ann Lovejoy, *The American Mixed Border*

cordata 'Ruby Field'   ZONES 7–9
A vigorous variety, forming a low, spreading clump of fresh green leaves, with clusters of bright salmon-pink

flowers all summer long. Reported to be slightly hardier than *D. rigescens*. Also performs well as an annual.

HEIGHT/SPREAD: 20cm (8")/30cm (12")
LOCATION: Well-drained soil. Dislikes winter wet.
BLOOMS: June–September
USES: ▲▼ Edging, Baskets, Borders

rigescens   ZONES 8–9

Introduced by the U.B.C. Botanical Garden. Short spikes of rose-pink flowers clothe the clumps all summer long. Best treated as a summer-blooming annual in all but the mildest regions. Dislikes hot, humid weather.

HEIGHT/SPREAD: 30cm (12")/30cm (12")
LOCATION: Well-drained soil. Dislikes winter wet.
BLOOMS: June–September
USES: ▲▼ Edging, Baskets, Borders

DICENTRA
(Bleedingheart) ☀◐

Much-loved shade garden plants, although most Dicentra will also tolerate full sun if they have adequate moisture. The various types all have the same classic heart-shaped flowers. Divide dwarf varieties every three years to maintain vigour. All are excellent for cutting.

eximia 'Alba'   ZONES 3–9

A selection of the Fringed Bleedingheart, native to eastern North America. Flowers are milky-white, over a ferny clump of light green leaves. Similar in effect to 'Luxuriant' but more delicate. A nice little woodlander but usually very slow to establish. Prefers bright shade.

HEIGHT/SPREAD: 30cm (12")/30cm (12")
LOCATION: Rich, moist well-drained soil.
BLOOMS: May–July
USES: ▲✂ Massing, Woodland garden

formosa oregona 'Pearl Drops'   ZONES 4–9

A vigorous dwarf fern-leaved variety with pure white flowers. Foliage is blue-green, flowers are held well above on arching stems. Long-blooming.

HEIGHT/SPREAD: 30cm (12")/30cm (12")
LOCATION: Well-drained soil.
BLOOMS: May–August
USES: ▲✂ Borders, Massing

× 'Luxuriant'   ZONES 2–9

Cherry-red flowers bloom continually above clumps of ferny green foliage. Compact mounds are great for edging. Also good in containers. Blooms best with at least some direct sun.

HEIGHT/SPREAD: 30–40cm (12–16")/30cm (12")
LOCATION: Rich, moist well-drained soil.
BLOOMS: June–October
USES: ▲✂▼ Massing, Edging

spectabilis   ZONES 2–9

(Old-fashioned Bleedingheart) An old favorite from everyone's childhood, with the familiar drooping chains of pink hearts on a large, bushy mound. Often goes dormant by late summer, especially in hot climates, so be sure to plant something in front that will get big later in the season. In cool-summer areas cut plants back to 10cm (4") after blooming to encourage fresh new growth. The white form 'Alba' is a refreshing change from the pink, and they look especially nice together.

> "I would rate the white bleeding heart as one of the loveliest and most elegant perennials we grow. If its foliage lasted until fall, it would be the perfect plant."
> —Patrick Lima, *The Harrowsmith Perennial Garden*

HEIGHT/SPREAD: 60–90cm (2–3')/60cm (24")
LOCATION: Rich, moist well-drained soil.

BLOOMS: May–June
USES: ✂ Borders, Woodland gardens.

DICTAMNUS
(Gas Plant) ☀

albus   ZONES 2–9

(formerly *D. fraxinella*) Truly a superb plant for the sunny border, where it will form a large green clump with spikes of white flowers in the early summer. The old tale about the flowers giving off a flammable gas is true; we tried lighting it on fire and it worked! Spectacular once established in the garden, these always look rather pathetic for the first year or two until they take hold, so be patient. Very long-lived. Resents being disturbed. The form 'Purpureus' has soft mauve-pink flowers with darker veins.

HEIGHT/SPREAD: 60–90cm (2–3')/60cm (2')
LOCATION: Average well-drained soil.
BLOOMS: June–July
USES: ✂ Borders

DIGITALIS
(Foxglove) ☀◐

These showy spikes of large, dangling tubular flowers are a classic sight in the early summer border. They grow best in a woodland setting but adapt well to border conditions. Dead-heading will encourage continual blooms. All types will self-seed.

grandiflora   ZONES 2–9

(Yellow Foxglove) (= *D. ambigua*) Short wind-proof spikes of pale butter-yellow flowers. Excellent for cutting. Good repeat blooms in the fall. A true perennial type, long-lived.

HEIGHT/SPREAD: 60–90cm (2–3')/30cm (12")
LOCATION: Moist, well-drained soil.
BLOOMS: June–August
USES: ✂ Borders, Woodland gardens

× mertonensis   ZONES 4–9

(Pink Foxglove) A perennial variety, compact in habit, with spikes of large deep-pink flowers. Excellent foliage. Divide plants every two years to maintain vigour.

HEIGHT/SPREAD: 90cm (3')/30–45cm (12–18")
LOCATION: Moist, well-drained soil.
BLOOMS: June–July
USES: ✂ Borders, Woodland gardens

purpurea   ZONES 4–9

(Common Foxglove) Very showy in bloom, with stately spikes of large bell flowers. Requires an evenly moist soil. Biennial, but usually self-seeding. Various seed strains are available; in the garden these will often revert back to magenta-purple after several years of self-seeding.

SPREAD: 30–45cm (12–18")
LOCATION: Moist, well-drained soil.
BLOOMS: May–July
USES: ✂ Borders, Woodland gardens

'Apricot Beauty' Unusual soft apricot-pink flowers. HEIGHT: 120cm (4')

'Excelsior Mixture' Mixed shades of white, rose, pink, and lavender. Very large flowers, very colourful. HEIGHT: 120–150cm (4–5')

'Foxy' Bright mix of colours, compact plants. HEIGHT: 90cm (36")

DODECATHEON
(Shooting Star) ☀◐

meadia   ZONES 2–9

Delicate umbels of flowers rise up from a flat rosette of leaves. Flowers are rose-pink with a yellow band, cyclamen-shaped. Plants usually go dormant by midsummer, so mark the area well to avoid digging them out! Nice

Dicentra × 'Luxuriant'

Dicentra spectabilis

Dictamnus albus 'Purpureus'

Digitalis × *mertonensis*

Doronicum cordatum

Echinacea purpurea

Echinops ritro

Epimedium grandiflorum

companions to various Primula. A native North American wildflower.

HEIGHT/SPREAD: 30cm (12")/15cm (6")
LOCATION: Likes a rich, moist soil.
BLOOMS: May–June
USES: ⚘⚘⚔ Woodland gardens

DORONICUM
(Leopard's Bane) ☀◐

cordatum   ZONES 2–9
(= *D. caucasicum*) These large perky yellow daisies bloom in early spring, combining so nicely with tulips or tall blue Forget-me-nots. Plants usually go dormant and leave a gap by midsummer. Great for cutting. Tolerant of woodland conditions.

> "A sparkling spring picture has golden alyssum (where it thrives) and candytuft in the foreground, a mass of soft orange tulips behind and, still farther back, leopard's bane, the first of the garden's daisies to bloom." —Patrick Lima, *The Harrowsmith Perennial Garden*

HEIGHT/SPREAD: 50cm (20")/30cm (12")
LOCATION: Average to moist well-drained soil.
BLOOMS: April–June
USES: ⚔ Borders, Woodland gardens.

DRABA
(Draba) ☀

aizoides   ZONES 2–9
Tiny alpine plant, forming a tight bun of grey-green, needle-like leaves. Clusters of lemon-yellow flowers appear in early spring and are always one of the first things to bloom. At its best in a gravelly rock garden or trough.

HEIGHT/SPREAD: 10cm (4")/15cm (6")
LOCATION: Well-drained gravelly soil.
BLOOMS: March–April
USES ⚘▲ Troughs, Scree

ECHINACEA
(Purple Coneflower) ☀
Similar to Rudbeckia, highly valued for their large brightly-coloured daisies. Each flower has a prominent central brown cone, the petals often drooping down attractively. These make a rich display in the border and are also excellent for cutting, the seed-heads used in dried arrangements. Plants bloom over a long season, standing up well to summer heat and humidity. A favorite of butterflies! All are native North American wildflowers.

angustifolia   ZONES 3–9
(Western Coneflower) Native to the prairies and plains, this species has narrow rose-purple petals and leaves. Currently being promoted in the health industry for its potential immune-system boosting medicinal properties. A useful addition to the cutting garden border. Very drought-tolerant.

HEIGHT/SPREAD: 60–75cm (24–30")/30cm (12")
LOCATION: Average well-drained soil.
BLOOMS: July–August
USES: ⚔🦋🐝 Borders, Wild gardens

purpurea   ZONES 3–9
The most common garden species. In recent years breeders have developed more compact strains that bloom over a longer season. Flowers are available not only in the regular purple, but also in a handsome white form with an unusual greenish-brown cone. Very drought-tolerant.

HEIGHT/SPREAD: 75–90cm (30–36")/45–60cm (18–24")
LOCATION: Average well-drained soil.
BLOOMS: July–September
USES: ⚘⚔🦋🐝 Borders, Meadows

ECHINOPS
(Globe Thistle) ☀

ritro   ZONES 2–9
Globular, metallic-blue flowers are excellent for cutting, fresh or dried. Tall, thistly-looking plants are dramatic at the back of the border. Not invasive. May require staking in rich soils.

> "Globe thistles…with their needle-studded flower balls poised on long stalks like so many vegetable maces, have a strong garden presence. Even when out of bloom, their great, toothed leaves, rich green backed with gray, rise powerfully amid shrubby looking peony foliage and grassy daylilies " —Ann Lovejoy, *The American Mixed Border*

HEIGHT/SPREAD: 90–120cm (3–4')/60cm (24")
LOCATION: Average to moist well-drained soil.
BLOOMS: June–September
USES: ⚘⚔🐝 Borders, Specimen.

'Taplow Blue' Freely blooming variety, large steel-blue heads. HEIGHT: 120cm (4')

EPIMEDIUM
(Barrenwort) ◐●

Hybrids   ZONES 4–9
Valued for their unusual semi-evergreen foliage. Leaves often become bronzy in cold weather. Superb as a slow-spreading groundcover for shady areas. Short sprays of starry flowers appear in spring, looking like tiny Columbines. Varieties are either clumping or spreading in habit, so choose according to the site requirements. Trim off any tired-looking foliage in early spring before the new growth begins. Slightly drought-tolerant.

HEIGHT/SPREAD: 20–30cm (8–12")/30cm (12")
LOCATION: Rich, moist woodland soil.
BLOOMS: April–May
USES: ⚘▲🦋🐝 Woodland garden, Borders

grandiflorum **'Rose Queen'** Compact variety. Dainty pink flowers, clumping habit.

× *perralchicum* **'Fröhnleiten'** Compact variety. Bright yellow flowers, bronzy marbled foliage. Spreading habit.

× *rubrum* Large red flowers. Showy. Clumping habit.

× *versicolor* **'Sulphureum'** Light yellow flowers. Slowly spreading.

× *youngianum* **'Niveum'** Ivory-white flowers. Clumping habit.

× *youngianum* **'Roseum'** Lilac-rose flowers. Clumping habit.

EREMURUS
(Foxtail Lily) ☀
These tall spires of lily-like flowers are a spectacular sight. Since the foliage dies back at flowering time, it is a good idea to plant something of medium height at the base to hide the fact. Try these in a sunny, very well-drained location. Protect from late-spring frosts.

robustus   ZONES 5–9
Very tall spikes of light pink flowers with brown speckles. Lasts well as a cut, if you dare!

HEIGHT/SPREAD: 1.8–2.4m (6–8')/60cm (2')
LOCATION: Must have well-drained soil.

BLOOMS: June–July
USES: ✂ Specimen, Borders

stenophyllus ZONES 5–9

A more reasonable height for the smaller garden. Flowers open dark yellow, fading to an attractive burnt orange, usually with multiple stems. Also good for cutting. Plants are long-lived and easier than the taller species.

HEIGHT/SPREAD: 90–150cm (3–5')/60cm (2')
LOCATION: Very well-drained soil.
BLOOMS: June–July
USES: ✂ Borders

ERIGERON
(Fleabane) ☀

Sprays of small daisies, quite similar to the fall-blooming Asters, but blooming through the summer months. Reliable, tough plants mostly for a sunny border or cutting garden.

compositus ZONES 1–9

(Alpine Fleabane) An exception to the taller types, with compact silvery filigree foliage, and pale lavender-blue flowers. An easy little alpine native to the Rocky Mountains. Will self-seed into cracks and walls. Very drought-tolerant.

HEIGHT/SPREAD: 10cm (4")/10–15cm (4–6")
LOCATION: Needs a well-drained soil.
BLOOMS: April–June
USES: △▲♥ Troughs

Border Varieties ZONES 2–9

Valuable cut flowers, good display of colour in the summer border. Divide clumps every 2–3 years or they will become woody. Inclined to be floppy if planted in too rich a soil. May need staking. Shear plants back after blooming to promote a second flush in the fall.

HEIGHT/SPREAD: 50–75cm (20–30")/30–60cm (12–24")
LOCATION: Average well-drained soil.
BLOOMS: June–August
USES: ✂ Borders, Cutting garden.

× **'Darkest of All'** Deep violet-blue flowers.

× **'Pink Jewel'** Bright pink to rose flowers. Compact.

speciosus macranthus Deep lilac blue flowers.

ERINUS
(Fairy-foxglove) ☀◐

alpinus ZONES 3–9

An easy little alpine, with short spikes of lavender to carmine-red flowers over a low tuft of evergreen leaves. Not long-lived but will often self-seed. Good choice for a brand new rock garden.

HEIGHT/SPREAD: 10cm (4")/10–15cm (4–6")
LOCATION: Well-drained rock garden or wall.
BLOOMS: May–July
USES: △▲♥ Troughs, Walls

ERODIUM
(Storksbill) ☀

Closely related to the hardy *Geraniums*, these are long-flowering plants for the alpine garden or trough. Plants seem to resent wet winters, and are not always reliably hardy, but worth a little extra effort to grow as they are so showy. In colder areas these are well worth trying as annuals for their constant colour.

reichardii 'Roseum' ZONES 7–9

Lovely pink flowers on a low mat of green leaves. Plants bloom constantly. Especially sensitive to winter wet. Perhaps best in the alpine house.

HEIGHT/SPREAD: 5cm (2")/15–30cm (6–12")
LOCATION: Well-drained gravelly soil.
BLOOMS: May–September
USES: △▲♥ Troughs, Edging

× variabile ZONES 7–9

Like a miniature hardy *Geranium*, with a show of dainty flowers all season long. Forms a low clump.

HEIGHT/SPREAD: 10cm (4")/15–30cm (6–12")
LOCATION: Well-drained gravelly soil.
BLOOMS: May–September
USES: △▲♥ Troughs, Edging

'Album' White flowers with a tiny pink stripe.

'Bishop's Form' Bright pink flowers, very cheery.

ERYNGIUM
(Sea Holly) ☀

Open umbels of steel-blue, prickly flowers are a favorite for cutting and drying. Tolerant of hot, dry sites and high salt soils. Attractive in the border and generally well-behaved. Most are very drought-tolerant.

alpinum ZONES 4–9

(Alpine Sea Holly) Extremely large heads of bright steel-blue flowers, each surrounded by prickly bracts. This is by far the showiest species in the border, excellent also for cutting and drying. This looks rather thistly but is well behaved in the garden.

HEIGHT/SPREAD: 45–60cm (18–24")/30cm (12")
LOCATION: Average to moist well-drained soil.
BLOOMS: July–August
USES: ✂ Dried Flower, Borders

amethystinum ZONES 2–9

(Amethyst Sea Holly) Branching stems of small metallic-blue flowers in profusion. Nice filler plant. Drought tolerant.

HEIGHT/SPREAD: 75–90cm (30–36")/45cm (18")
LOCATION: Poor to average well-drained soil.
BLOOMS: July–August
USES: ✂♥ Dried Flower, Borders

giganteum ZONES 4–9

(Miss Willmott's Ghost) Unique among Sea Hollies, this species has very large silvery-grey flower bracts, and is superb for drying. Plants generally behave as self-seeding biennials. British plantswoman Ellen Willmott, it is said, used to secretly scatter seeds of this whenever she went visiting other people's gardens.

HEIGHT/SPREAD: 75–90cm (30–36")/30–45cm (12–18")
LOCATION: Average well-drained soil.
BLOOMS: June–August
USES: ✂♥ Dried Flower, Specimen, Borders

planum ZONES 2–9

(Blue Sea Holly) One of the hardiest species, and a reliable long-lived plant for the border. Umbels of small steel-blue flowers are fine for drying. Will spread to form a small patch.

HEIGHT/SPREAD: 75–90cm (30–36")/30cm (12")
LOCATION: Average well-drained soil.
BLOOMS: July–August
USES: ✂♥ Dried Flower, Borders

× tripartitum ZONES 4–9

(Blue Sea Holly) Very similar in effect to *E. planum*, small heads of blue flowers on branching stems.

HEIGHT/SPREAD: 75–90cm (30–36")/30cm (12")
LOCATION: Average well-drained soil.
BLOOMS: July–August
USES: ✂♥ Dried Flower, Borders

yuccifolium ZONES 4–9

(Rattlesnake Master) A species native to North America, and quite different from the other Sea Hollies listed. Evergreen leaves are arranged at the base of the plant like

Erigeron × 'Pink Jewel'

Erodium × *variabile* 'Bishop's Form'

Eryngium giganteum

Eryngium alpinum

Eupatorium purpureum

Euphorbia characias wulfenii

Euphorbia griffithii 'Fireglow'

Euphorbia polychroma

a yucca plant, with tall stems of creamy-green golf-ball shaped flowers. Very unusual for cutting.

> "The stiff, spiky rosettes of our native rattlesnake master…do indeed mimic gray-blue yuccas, though the flowers that open in small sprays above their four-foot stems look more like frosted white thistles than the open, creamy bells of true yuccas." —Ann Lovejoy, *The American Mixed Border*

HEIGHT/SPREAD: 90–120cm (3–4')/30cm (12")
LOCATION: Average well-drained soil.
BLOOMS: July–September
USES: ✄ Dried Flower, Specimen, Borders

ERYSIMUM see CHEIRANTHUS

EUPATORIUM
(Boneset) ☼ ☽

With increasing frequency these hardy, reliable plants are showing up in perennial gardens from coast to coast. They can provide welcome colour and structure to late summer and fall schemes. All are selections of native North American wildflowers.

coelestinum   ZONES 5–9
(Hardy Ageratum) An unusual sky-blue shade for the autumn border! Plants look very much like a tall version of annual Ageratum. Benefits from a good pinching back in July to encourage bushiness. Does very well in wet, sunny areas. Planting before midsummer is recommended. Can be an aggressive spreader.

HEIGHT/SPREAD: 60–90cm (2–3')/60cm (2')
LOCATION: Moist to wet soil.
BLOOMS: September–October
USES: ✄ Borders, Waterside

fistulosum 'Selection'   ZONES 3–9
(Compact Joe-pye Weed) Very similar in effect to *E. purpureum* but of a more compact size, better suited to smaller gardens. Flowers are described as mauve-lilac in colour, on top of hollow purple stems.

HEIGHT/SPREAD: 1.2–1.5m (5–6')/90cm (3')
LOCATION: Rich, moist to wet soil.
BLOOMS: August–October
USES: ✄ Specimen, Borders

purpureum 'Atropurpureum'   ZONES 4–9
(Joe-pye Weed) Often described as an architectural plant. This forms a very large clump, with big umbrella-like heads of rosy-purple flowers in late summer and fall. Stems are solid, not hollow, purple in colour, with whorls of bold leaves. An excellent choice for a late-summer specimen plants! Long-lived.

> "I look forward as eagerly to the first appearance of Joe Pye weed in early August as I do to the first snowdrop in late winter. It too is a harbinger, but a harbinger of fall." —Allen Lacy, *The Garden in Autumn*

HEIGHT/SPREAD: 2.1–3m (7–10')/90cm (3')
LOCATION: Rich, moist to wet soil.
BLOOMS: August–October
USES: ✄ Specimen, Borders

rugosum   ZONES 3–9
(White Snakeroot, Boneset) Quite unlike the taller purple Joe-pye Weeds, this is a species of medium texture that forms a fairly large bushy mound. The clusters of pure white flowers look very much like annual ageratum. This is an easy border perennial, and the flowers are excellent for cutting. Reported to tolerate dry shade.

HEIGHT/SPREAD: 90–120cm (3–4')/75cm (30")
LOCATION: Moist to average well-drained soil.
BLOOMS: August–September.
USES: ✄ Borders

EUPHORBIA
(Spurge) ☼ ☽

This huge group of plants includes the well-known Poinsettia. These all have colourful flower heads (bracts) that sit on top of the foliage. Milky sap can irritate the skin. The varieties listed are not invasive.

amygdaloides 'Rubra'   ZONES 6–9
(Purple Wood Spurge) Mounding purple foliage, spreading to form a patch. Clusters of greenish-yellow flowers are an attractive contrast in the spring, produced on the previous years growth. Recommended as a groundcover for partial shade, especially among trees or shrubs. Evergreen in milder areas. Prune lightly after blooming.

HEIGHT/SPREAD: 30–45cm (12–18")/60cm (24")
LOCATION: Average well-drained soil.
BLOOMS: April–May
USES: ✄ Massing, Shady borders

characias wulfenii   ZONES 8–9
(Evergreen Spurge) Very bushy, upright growing variety for mild winter areas. The stems are surrounded with leathery blue-green leaves that remain evergreen. Huge clusters of greenish-yellow flowers open in very early spring. A unique, bold sculptural plant best used as a specimen. Also can be grown in a cool greenhouse.

HEIGHT/SPREAD: 120–150cm (4–5')/90cm (3')
LOCATION: Average well-drained soil.
BLOOMS: March–May
USES: ✄ Specimen, Borders

griffithii   ZONES 2–9
These make a large shrub-like mound of green leaves. Flame-orange bracts are showy over a long period. Superb plant. Fall foliage colour is often a good red.

HEIGHT/SPREAD: 50–90cm (20–36")/60cm (24")
LOCATION: Average well-drained soil.
BLOOMS: May–August
USES: ✄ Borders, Massing

'Dixter' Newer selection, similar to 'Fireglow', the foliage is dark bronzy green.

'Fireglow' The original Alan Bloom selection, fiery orange flowers.

myrsinites   ZONES 5–9
(Donkey-tail Spurge) A succulent, evergreen species with large steel-blue leaves arranged around the stem. This trails and flops in all directions, the ends of the stems producing clusters of sulphur-yellow flowers in spring. A unique rockery or wall plant. Extremely heat and drought-tolerant.

HEIGHT/SPREAD: 15–20cm (6–8")/45cm (18")
LOCATION: Average to very dry soil.
BLOOMS: May–June
USES: ✄ Edging, Walls

polychroma   ZONES 2–9
(Cushion Spurge) (= *E. epithymoides*) Forms a perfect dome of pale green leaves, covered by bright, chrome-yellow flower bracts in late spring. An unusual cut-flower. Foliage turns red in fall. Extremely drought-tolerant.

HEIGHT/SPREAD: 30–45cm (12–18")/45cm (18")
LOCATION: Average well-drained soil.
BLOOMS: May–June
USES: ✄ Borders, Massing

FALLOPIA see POLYGONUM

FILIPENDULA
(Meadowsweet) ☀◐

Mostly large, upright plants for moist to wet soils. Showy clusters of flowers are similar to Spirea. Foliage is jagged and bold.

palmata 'Nana'   ZONES 3–9
(Dwarf Pink Meadowsweet) A compact selection, perhaps a better choice for the smaller garden than the taller forms. Fluffy heads of bright pink flowers are held above the dark green lobed leaves. Likes a moist or wet site.

HEIGHT/SPREAD: 20–45cm (8–18")/30cm (12")
LOCATION: Rich moist to wet soil.
BLOOMS: June–July
USES: ✄ Borders, Waterside

purpurea 'Elegans'   ZONES 4–9
(Japanese Meadowsweet) Fragrant white flowers with showy red stamens. Excellent background plant or specimen, nice at the waterside.

HEIGHT/SPREAD: 90–120cm (3–4')/60cm (2')
LOCATION: Rich moist to wet soil.
BLOOMS: July–August
USES: ✄ Specimen, Borders

rubra 'Venusta'   ZONES 3–9
(Martha Washington's Plume) Bold accent plant, forms a sturdy bush. Large panicles of deep pink flowers. One of the showiest perennials for moist sites. This is a selection of a native North American wildflower.

HEIGHT/SPREAD: 120–180cm (4–6')/90–120cm (3–4')
LOCATION: Rich moist to wet soil.
BLOOMS: July–August
USES: ✄ Specimen, Borders

ulmaria   ZONES 3–9
(European Meadowsweet) A taller form with the usual ferny leaves, topped with fragrant clusters of creamy-white flowers in summer. The species itself is not often grown, but several interesting selections exist. These prefer average to moist soils, the coloured-leaf forms growing best in part shade, otherwise they are prone to sunburn and spider mites. Some gardeners prefer to remove the flower stems as they appear, to maintain the attractive leaves.

HEIGHT/SPREAD: 75–120cm (30–48")/45cm (18")
LOCATION: Average to moist soil.
BLOOMS: June–July
USES: ✄ Borders, Woodland gardens.

'Aurea' A bright, attractive gold-leaved form. Dislikes direct sun.

'Variegata' Dark green leaves with a large creamy yellow blotch in the centre. Unique!

vulgaris 'Flore-Pleno'   ZONES 2–9
(Double Dropwort) Preferring average to drier soils, unlike its taller cousins. Forms a low rosette of finely-cut ferny leaves that radiate out in a perfect circle. Long-lasting pure white flowers. Nice edging plant for the border.

HEIGHT/SPREAD: 30–45cm (12–18")/30cm (12")
LOCATION: Average well-drained soil.
BLOOMS: May–July
USES: △✄ Borders, Edging

FRAGARIA
(Strawberry) ☀◐

Garden strawberries, grown for their large fruit, are well known across the world. There are also a few unique forms that are grown primarily for their ornamental features. They adapt well to average garden conditions, and most are tolerant of part shade.

× (Frel) 'Pink Panda'   ZONES 2–9
A unique hybrid with large bright pink flowers that appear almost all season long. This hybrid has resulted

from a cross between *Fragaria* and a herbaceous *Potentilla*, selected over many years. Ideal for edging or planting as a groundcover, also excellent in containers and hanging baskets. Tasty bright red fruits are of medium size. Pink Panda is a multi-use plant, performing well in most areas of the country. Plants send out lots of runners, spreading quickly just like any normal garden strawberry. Fairly shade-tolerant. Protected under U.S. Plant Patent Regulations, commercial propagation is prohibited without a licence.

HEIGHT/SPREAD: 15cm (6")/30cm (12")
LOCATION: Average to moist well-drained soil.
BLOOMS: May–September
USES: △◓🏺 Edible fruit. Hanging baskets

vesca   ZONES 2–9
(Alpine Strawberry) Runnerless, small-fruited strawberry. An everbearing type, with an excellent wild-strawberry flavour. Fruit and white flowers are also ornamental. Makes a unique edging.

HEIGHT/SPREAD: 15–25cm (6–10")/30cm (12")
LOCATION: Average to moist soil.
BLOOMS: May–October
USES: △🏺 Edible fruit, Edging

'Improved Rügen' The classic red-fruited European strain.

'Yellow Wonder' Bizarre creamy-white fruit. Unique and tasty!

virginiana 'Variegata'   ZONES 3–9
Unusual and showy deep green foliage, strongly variegated with creamy white. White flowers and small red fruit may be produced, but don't count on making jam. This variety will send out runners, but is not nearly as vigorous as 'Pink Panda'. Best in the rock garden or woodland.

HEIGHT/SPREAD: 10–15cm (4–6")/30cm (12")
LOCATION: Moist, well-drained soil.
BLOOMS: May–June
USES: △◓🏺 Woodland garden

FRANKENIA
(Frankenia) ☀

thymifolia   ZONES 6–9
A heat-loving creeping groundcover, spreading to form a low greyish mat or trailing over rocks. Tiny little pink flowers in summer. Good red winter colour.

HEIGHT/SPREAD: 2cm (1")/15–30cm (6–12")
LOCATION: Needs a well-drained soil.
BLOOMS: June–July
USES: △▲🏺 Walls, Slopes.

FUCHSIA
(Fuchsia) ☀◐●

magellanica   ZONES 7–9
(Hardy Fuchsia) Truly a woody shrub, these associate well with perennials in the border, and benefit from a hard clipping back in early spring. Plants form an upright bush and bear many dangling tubular flowers, crimson with a purple centre. More delicate in appearance than the fancy hanging-basket types, but with a tougher constitution. Often winters in Zone 6 with a mulch.

HEIGHT/SPREAD: 60–120cm (2–4')/60–90cm (2–3')
LOCATION: Prefers a rich, moist soil.
BLOOMS: June–October
USES: △🏺 Borders, Containers

GAILLARDIA
(Blanket Flower) ☀

× grandiflora   ZONES 2–9
Brightly-coloured daisy flowers, often with a contrasting central eye. These are long blooming, excellent for

Filipendula rubra 'Venusta'

Filipendula ulmaria 'Aurea'

Fragaria × 'Pink Panda'

Fragaria virginiana 'Variegata'

Gaillardia × grandiflora 'Monarch Strain'

Galium odoratum

Gaura lindheimeri

Gentiana acaulis

cutting. Good choice for hot, dry areas, very drought-tolerant. Does well in containers. Cut back hard in early September; this forces new leaf growth and prevents plants from blooming to death.

SPREAD: 30cm (12")
LOCATION: Well-drained soil.
BLOOMS: June–September
USES: ✂◄ ☗ ☙ ⚘ Borders, Meadows

'Burgundy' Deep wine-red flowers. HEIGHT: 60–90cm (2–3')

'Dwarf Goblin' Red petals with yellow tips. Compact habit. HEIGHT: 30cm (12")

'Golden Goblin' Solid yellow flowers. HEIGHT: 30cm (12")

'Monarch Strain' Mixed colours, yellow, orange, and red. A superb cutting strain. HEIGHT: 60–90cm (2–3')

GALIUM
(Sweet Woodruff) ☽●

odoratum   ZONES 4–9
(formerly *Asperula odorata*) Attractive, whorled green leaves set off the clusters of starry white flowers. Excellent fast-spreading groundcover, best in shady moist locations but will usually tolerate dryer conditions under trees. Evergreen in mild climates. Useful for planting over spring-blooming bulbs. Spreads quickly, but not terribly invasive. (See also under HERBS.)

> "The pretty little woodruff is in flower;
> what scent is so delicate as that of its
> leaves? They are almost sweeter when
> dried…it is a pleasant surprise to come
> upon these fragrant little stars between
> the leaves of a book." —Gertrude Jekyll,
> *Wood and Garden*

HEIGHT/SPREAD: 10–20cm (4–8")/30–45cm (12–18")
LOCATION: Average to moist soil.
BLOOMS: April–May
USES: ∿▲⚘ Woodland gardens

GAURA
(Gaura) ☀☽

lindheimeri   ZONES 5–9
(Butterfly Gaura) A North American wild-flower, only recently introduced into perennial borders. Plants bloom for many weeks, with loose sprays of white flowers, tinged with very light pink. In the breeze these move constantly, looking like a cloud of small butterflies. Trim plants lightly after their first flush of bloom is over. An interesting new cut flower. Very drought and heat tolerant. Plants may be short-lived in wet winter areas. A winter mulch is recommended in Zones 5–6.

> "Gaura is a fine plant to use as a
> "scrim." The term is borrowed from the
> theater, where it means a gauze curtain
> through which action on stage may be
> seen, but as if through a mist." —Allen
> Lacy, *The Garden in Autumn*

HEIGHT/SPREAD: 90–120cm (3–4')/60–90cm (2–3')
LOCATION: Average well-drained soil.
BLOOMS: June–September
USES: ✂☙⚘ Borders, Meadows

'Whirling Butterflies' A more compact selection, otherwise just like the species. Propagated by cuttings or division. HEIGHT: 60–90cm (2–3')

GENTIANA
(Gentian) ☀☽

Best known are the dwarf, alpine varieties, with their bluer-than-blue trumpet-shaped flowers.

This is a large group of plants; many of the taller species also are useful in the perennial garden, and are generally a lot easier to grow.

acaulis   ZONES 2–9
(Mountain Gentian) A not-so-easy alpine species, always popular for its large sky-blue flowers in spring. This prefers a well-drained but moisture-retentive soil, and therefore is best planted in a rock garden. Forms a low, creeping mat. Dislikes hot afternoon sun.

HEIGHT/SPREAD: 10cm (4")/30cm (12")
LOCATION: Well-drained, humusy soil.
BLOOMS: April–June
USES: △ Scree, Troughs

septemfida   ZONES 2–9
(Every-man's Gentian) One of the easier Gentians, this species is a reasonable substitute if you can't seem to succeed with the alpine types. Plants form a sizeable clump and are nice along the front of a border. Flowers are a good true blue, blooming in summer.

HEIGHT/SPREAD: 15–20cm (6–8")/30–60cm (1–2')
LOCATION: Well-drained, humusy soil.
BLOOMS: July–September
USES: △ Edging, Walls, Slopes

GERANIUM
(Cranesbill) ☀☽

These are hardy relatives of the annual Geraniums (known botanically as *Pelargoniums*) that are so commonly used for summer bedding and window boxes. Cranesbills come in a wide range of heights, forms and colours, to suit most garden purposes, but for the convenience of designers we have indicated each kind as either an alpine (short) or border (medium to tall) variety.

All have similar divided or lobed leaves, forming a mound or mat of foliage. Cup-shaped or star-like flowers generally appear in early summer. Some types take on brilliant red foliage colouring in the fall.

× cantabrigiense   ZONES 4–9
Alpine or Border type. This is a low-growing plant with trailing stems and glossy green, fragrant foliage. Flowers are sterile, and will repeat bloom for most of the summer. Shows much promise as a new groundcover plant. There are two colour forms.

HEIGHT/SPREAD: 20–30cm (8–12")/30cm (12")
LOCATION: Average well-drained soil.
BLOOMS: May–August
USES: △∿⚘ Edging, Borders, Massing

'Biokovo' A natural hybrid selection recently discovered growing wild in Yugoslavia. Large, showy, off-white flowers with a flush of pink in the middle.

'Cambridge' Bred at Cambridge University, bright pink showy flowers.

cinereum   ZONES 5–9
Alpine type. Dense, low mounds of foliage, with large flowers resting on the trailing stems all summer long. Excellent in the rock garden, especially among dwarf conifers. The varieties listed have good vigour, preferring a gravelly soil, especially in areas with winter wet.

HEIGHT/SPREAD: 10–15cm (4–6")/30cm (12")
LOCATION: Very well-drained soil.
BLOOMS: May–September
USES: △∿⚘ Scree, Troughs

'Ballerina' Purplish-pink flowers with exotic dark veins and centre. Greyish leaves. A Bressingham Gardens selection.

'Laurence Flatman' Deep pink flowers with dark crimson veining. Green leaves. Bred by Alan Bloom of Bressingham Gardens.

subcaulescens **'Guiseppii'** Crimson-magenta flowers with a black eye. Greyish foliage. Especially vigorous.

clarkei 'Kashmir White'   ZONES 4–9

(Clarke's Cranesbill) Border type. Deeply-cut green foliage forms a low mound. Large cup-shaped white flowers have darker lilac veins, giving a luminescent effect. An excellent white form for general border use.

HEIGHT/SPREAD:	30–45cm (12–18")/45cm (18")
LOCATION:	Average to moist well-drained soil.
BLOOMS:	June–August
USES:	Borders, Woodland gardens

dalmaticum   ZONES 3–9

(Dalmatian Cranesbill) Alpine type. Forms a low, glossy green cushion covered with clear shell-pink flowers. One of the best varieties. Good red fall colour.

HEIGHT/SPREAD:	10cm (4")/30cm (12")
LOCATION:	Prefers a well-drained soil.
BLOOMS:	May–July
USES:	△▽☼ Troughs, Scree, Walls

endressii   ZONES 3–9

Border type. Vigorous, dense mounds of shiny evergreen leaves, showy bright pink flowers in summer. Excellent groundcover. May need a hard clipping in midsummer.

HEIGHT/SPREAD:	30–45cm (12–18")/30–60cm (12–24")
LOCATION:	Average well-drained soil.
BLOOMS:	June–August
USES:	∿▲☼ Borders, Edging

'Wargrave Pink' Warm salmon-pink flowers, slightly more vigorous.

himalayense   ZONES 2–9

Border type. Mounding clumps of bold leaves and very large, deep violet blue flowers with a reddish-pink caste. Red foliage in fall.

HEIGHT/SPREAD:	30–45cm (12–18")/60cm (24")
LOCATION:	Average well-drained soil.
BLOOMS:	June–July
USES:	Borders, Woodland gardens

'Plenum' (a.k.a. 'Birch Double') Fully double, lavender-violet flowers, tinged with pink. Long blooming and sterile. Not as vigorous.

× 'Johnson's Blue'   ZONES 2–9

Border type. Most popular of all the blue selections. Large, lavender-blue flowers with a tinge of reddish-pink in midsummer. Sterile flowers, good vigorous habit.

HEIGHT/SPREAD:	30–60cm (12–24")/60cm (24")
LOCATION:	Average well-drained soil.
BLOOMS:	June–August
USES:	Borders, Massing

macrorrhizum   ZONES 2–9

Border type. Extremely fragrant leaves form a dense, vigorous groundcover. Magenta pink flowers appear in early summer. Heat tolerant. This is the best species of Geranium for large groundcover plantings in sun or shade, even succeeding in the dry shade under trees. Good fall foliage colour. Several selections exist.

HEIGHT/SPREAD:	30cm (12")/60cm (24")
LOCATION:	Average well-drained soil.
BLOOMS:	June–July
USES:	∿☼ Borders, Massing

'Album' Very pale pink, near-white flowers.

'Ingwersen's Variety' The most widely-grown form. Pale candy-floss pink flowers, light green foliage.

× magnificum   ZONES 2–9

Border type. Abundant display of large violet-blue flowers with darker veins. Attractive divided green leaves with good red fall colour. Sterile.

HEIGHT/SPREAD:	45–60cm (18–24")/60cm (24")
LOCATION:	Average to moist well-drained soil.
BLOOMS:	June–July
USES:	Borders, Massing

× oxonianum 'Claridge Druce'   ZONES 3–9

Border type. Broad mounds of glossy grey-green leaves. Flowers are rose-pink with darker veins. This is a very vigorous selection, excellent for using on a large scale as a weed-proof groundcover.

HEIGHT/SPREAD:	45–60cm (18–24")/60cm (24")
LOCATION:	Average to moist well-drained soil.
BLOOMS:	June–September
USES:	∿▲ Borders, Massing

phaeum   ZONES 5–9

(Mourning Widow) Border type. Unique dark maroon-purple nodding flowers, finely divided leaves. Good choice for moist shady areas, reported to also tolerate deep dry shade.

HEIGHT/SPREAD:	45–60cm (18–24")/60cm (24")
LOCATION:	Average to moist well-drained soil.
BLOOMS:	May–July
USES:	Borders, Massing

psilostemon   ZONES 4–9

(Armenian Cranesbill) (= *G. armenum*) One of the tallest Cranesbills, this plant will be a focal point in the border when its black-centred, magenta flowers appear in early summer. Leaves are very large and deeply cut, with good red fall colour. Plants may require a little extra support and should be placed out of the wind.

> "Grow near *Gladiolus byzantinus* and tall shrub roses with similar flower colors." —Penelope Hobhouse, *Colour in Your Garden*

HEIGHT/SPREAD:	90–120cm (3–4')/90cm (3')
LOCATION:	Prefers a rich, moist soil.
BLOOMS:	June–August
USES:	Borders

renardii   ZONES 4–9

This species has quite unique foliage, sage green in colour with a bumpy puckered texture. Flowers are in clusters, white with bold stripes of violet purple. A little trickier to grow than some Cranesbills, with a need for excellent drainage and lean soil.

HEIGHT/SPREAD:	30cm (12")/30cm (12")
LOCATION:	Needs a very well-drained soil.
BLOOMS:	May–June
USES:	△ Edging

sanguineum   ZONES 3–9

(Bloody Cranesbill) Border type. Low, spreading mat of finely-cut leaves. Flowers are a very showy, bright magenta-pink. Useful little groundcover or edging plant. Moderately drought-tolerant. HEIGHT: 30cm (12"). There are several selections.

SPREAD:	30cm (12")
LOCATION:	Average to moist well-drained soil.
BLOOMS:	June–August
USES:	△∿☼ Borders, Massing

'Album' Clear white flowers, loose habit. HEIGHT: 30–45cm (12–18")

'John Elsley' Low, trailing habit, bright pink flowers. HEIGHT: 10–15cm (4–6")

'Max Frei' Recent German selection. Neat mounds with large deep-magenta flowers. HEIGHT: 20cm (8")

'Shepherd's Warning' Deeper magenta pink than the species. HEIGHT: 20cm (8")

striatum (= 'Lancastriense') Alpine type. Pale blush-pink flowers with dark crimson veins. One of the best! HEIGHT 10–15cm (4–6")

sylvaticum 'Album'   ZONES 4–9

(Wood Cranesbill) Border type. Good in woodland conditions. Forms a broad clump of divided leaves, with upfacing clear white flowers. One of the earliest to bloom. Trim back foliage in late June.

Geranium cinereum 'Laurence Flatman'

Geranium endressii

Geranium × 'Johnson's Blue'

Geranium psilostemon

Gunnera manicata

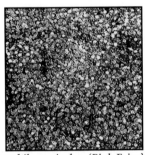

Gypsophila paniculata 'Pink Fairy'

Gypsophila repens 'Pink Beauty'

Hedyotis caerulea

HEIGHT/SPREAD:	45–60cm (18–24")/60cm (24")
LOCATION:	Average to moist well-drained soil.
BLOOMS:	May–June
USES:	Borders, Woodland gardens

wallichianum 'Buxton's Blue'   ZONES 4–9
Alpine or Border type. For the front of the border or growing over a low wall. Makes a sprawling mound of deep green leaves studded for several weeks with flat sky-blue flowers with a large white eye.

HEIGHT/SPREAD:	30cm (12")/60cm (24")
LOCATION:	Average to moist well-drained soil.
BLOOMS:	June–August
USES:	△M Borders, Edging

GEUM
(Avens) ☀◗

These bright and cheerful perennials are always popular in the sunny border, and are valued for their long season of bloom. Branching stems of flowers rise up from a bushy clump of hairy leaves. Good for cutting. Protect from hot afternoon sun.

× 'Borisii'   ZONES 2–9
(Dwarf Orange Geum) (sometimes listed as a form of *G. coccineum*) Bright orange, single flowers in late spring, often reblooming in fall. Compact tidy plants are very hardy and reliable. Clip off flower stems after blooming. This is an excellent low-maintenance plant and is grossly under-used. Evergreen foliage.

HEIGHT/SPREAD:	30cm (12")/30cm (12")
LOCATION:	Prefers a rich, moist soil.
BLOOMS:	May–July
USES:	△⚡<▲ Borders, Edging

quellyon   ZONES 5–9
(= *G. chiloense*) Well-branched stems of flowers are valuable for cutting. Nice filler plant in the summer border. These tend to be short-lived selections and also are not reliably hardy in all winters, but perform very well even if grown as annuals.

HEIGHT/SPREAD:	60–75cm (24–30")/30cm (12")
LOCATION:	Well-drained soil. Dislikes winter wet.
BLOOMS:	May–September
USES:	⚡ Borders, Massing

'Lady Stratheden' Golden-yellow double flowers.

'Mrs. Bradshaw' Orange-red double flowers.

GLECHOMA
(Creeping Charlie, Nepeta) ☀●

hederacea   ZONES 1–9
A rampant groundcover, its trailing stems of rounded leaves rooting wherever they touch the ground. Attractive blue flowers appear in late spring. Often used in baskets and planters, or for hanging down walls. Can easily become an invasive lawn weed!

HEIGHT/SPREAD:	10cm (4")/30–90cm (12–36")
LOCATION:	Prefers a cool, moist location.
BLOOMS:	April–May
USES:	M⚘ Hanging baskets

'Variegata' Leaves are dappled with creamy white. Excellent in hanging baskets. Not as reliably hardy, but less invasive. Zones 4–9.

GONIOLIMON see STATICE

GUNNERA
(Gunnera) ☀◗

manicata   ZONES 7–9
(Giant Gunnera) Enormous rhubarb-like leaves rise from the ground on thick thorny stalks. Often seen in large gardens and parks at the West Coast. Bold feature

plant for the waterside. Flowers appear in midsummer as bizarre bristly cones almost hidden at the base. In colder areas plants can be brought through the winter by covering with a very deep mulch piled inside a four-foot square wooden box in late fall.

HEIGHT/SPREAD:	1.8–3m (6–10')/1.8m (6')
LOCATION:	Rich moist or wet soil.
BLOOMS:	July–August
USES:	Waterside specimen

GYPSOPHILA
(Baby's Breath) ☀

These all have the familiar misty clouds of flowers, but come in a variety of sizes and colours. They flower best in cool-summer areas, but are fairly carefree.

paniculata   ZONES 2–9
Widely grown cut flower, used by florists fresh or dried. Works well to fill gaps left by summer-dormant plants such as Bleeding Hearts or Oriental Poppies. Clumps resent being moved once established. They dislike winter wet.

In Manitoba (and perhaps other adjacent provinces and states?) this species has been placed on the bad list as a nuisance weed; mature plants can act as a tumbleweed and infest pasture land. However, this is highly unlikely to happen in an enclosed garden area. Double-flowered varieties rarely set seed.

> "If you want gypsophila to cover the bare places left by spring bulbs or vanishing Oriental poppies, a few strategically placed twiggy branches will guide the stems where they are needed."
> —Patrick Lima, *The Harrowsmith Perennial Garden*

SPREAD:	60–90cm (2–3')
LOCATION:	Average well-drained soil.
BLOOMS:	June–September
USES:	⚡ Dried Flower, Borders

'Alba' Single white flowers, very hardy. Grown from seed. HEIGHT: 90cm (36")

'Bristol Fairy' Double white flowers, the best type for cutting. HEIGHT: 60–90cm (24–36"). Zones 4–9.

'Pink Fairy' Large, double light-pink flowers. Compact habit. HEIGHT: 30–45cm (12–18"). Zones 2–9.

'Viette's Dwarf' Compact selection with pink flowers. HEIGHT: 45cm (18").

repens   ZONES 2–9
(Creeping Baby's Breath) Low, creeping plants suitable for edging or rock gardens. Mats are smothered with flowers in early summer. Not invasive or weedy in any way. Moderately drought-tolerant.

'Alba' Pure white single flowers.

'Pink Beauty' ('Rosa Schönheit') The deepest pink form available.

'Rosea' Light pink single flowers.

HEIGHT/SPREAD:	10–15cm (4–6")/45–60cm (18–24")
LOCATION:	Well-drained soil. Heat tolerant.
BLOOMS:	May–July
USES:	△M⚘ Walls, Slopes, Edging

HEDYOTIS
(Mountain Bluets) ☀◗

caerulea   ZONES 3–9
(= *Houstonia*) Low, creeping green mat of tiny green leaves, smothered by little blue star flowers in late spring. Easy rock garden perennial that will self-seed nicely. Likes a moist soil while blooming, but doesn't

mind drying out in the summer. Dislikes lime. A native North American wildflower, but most gardeners are not familiar with it.

HEIGHT/SPREAD: 10–15cm (4–6")/30cm (12")
LOCATION: Moist to wet lime-free soil.
BLOOMS: April–June
USES: ⚘ Waterside

HELENIUM
(Sneezeweed, Helen's Flower) ☀

Although relatively unknown perennials in North America, these are valuable for a showy display of bright daisy-type flowers, and are also excellent for cutting. Widely grown in European gardens and commercially as a cut flower. Pinch plants back by half in early June to encourage bushiness. Staking may be required. These garden forms are descendants of native North American wildflowers.

autumnale Hybrids   ZONES 3–9
(Fall Helenium) Reliable performers for the late summer border. Large clusters of flowers are held on tall stems for an impressive background display. These are waterhogs, so give plenty of moisture in the summer. There are many named selections.

HEIGHT/SPREAD: 90–120cm (3–4')/45–60cm (18–24")
LOCATION: Average to moist well-drained soil.
BLOOMS: July–September
USES: ⚘ Borders, Massing

'Bruno' Crimson-mahogany flowers. Late-blooming. Bred by Alan Bloom of Bressingham Gardens. 120cm (4').

'Red and Gold' Seed strain with a mixture of shades, including yellow, orange, red, and gold.

hoopesii   ZONES 2–9
(Orange Helenium) Bright yellow daisies with orange centres. Foliage is grey-green, glossy. Compact and early blooming.

HEIGHT/SPREAD: 60–90cm (2–3')/45cm (18")
LOCATION: Average to moist well-drained soil.
BLOOMS: June–August
USES: ⚘ Borders, Meadows

HELIANTHEMUM
(Rock Rose, Sun Rose) ☀

Hybrids   ZONES 4–9
Versatile evergreen creepers, forming a low spreading mat of green or silvery-grey leaves. Flowers are like small roses, blooming over the summer months. Excellent choice for edging, rock gardens and walls, or in containers. Some varieties may survive to Zone 2 with adequate protection. These all require very good drainage to prevent rotting out in wet winters. Shear plants lightly after the first flush of bloom is over. Moderately drought-tolerant.

HEIGHT/SPREAD: 10–30cm (4–12")/60cm (24")
LOCATION: Well-drained soil. Dislikes winter wet.
BLOOMS: June–September
USES: ⚘ Walls, Slopes

'Annabel' Double, soft-pink flowers. Bushy form, green foliage. Introduced by Bressingham Gardens

'Double Apricot' Butterscotch flowers, an interesting peachy-orange shade, green leaves.

'Fireball' Double red flowers, green leaves.

'Firedragon' Single flame-orange flowers, excellent contrasting grey foliage.

'Henfield Brilliant' Large orange-red single flowers, grey foliage.

'Raspberry Ripple' Single crimson to rose with white streaks, upright grey foliage.

'Single Yellow' Large flowers, green leaves. Very vigorous and hardy.

'Wisley Pink' Large, single soft-pink flowers, grey leaves. Outstanding!

'Wisley Primrose' Pale yellow blooms over silvery-grey foliage.

HELIANTHUS
(Sunflower) ☀

Hardy perennial relatives of the annual birdseed and snack-food varieties. The varieties listed are happiest in a moist sunny location where they will form sizeable non-invasive clumps. All are excellent for cutting.

decapetalus   ZONES 4–9
(= *H. × multiflorus*) This includes selections or hybrids from the wild North American species, with tall, strong stems of deep green, hairy leaves, topped in late summer by bright yellow daisies. Continues blooming well into the fall. Excellent back-of-the-border candidate.

> "…makes a fine background for white phlox and lingers long enough to flower alongside lavender-coloured hardy asters." —Patrick Lima, *The Harrowsmith Perennial Garden*

HEIGHT/SPREAD: 1.5m (5')/60–90cm (2–3')
LOCATION: Prefers a rich moist soil.
BLOOMS: August–September
USES: ⚘ Borders, Meadows

'Loddon Gold' Large double yellow flowers, strong self-supporting stems.

'Plena' Smaller golden-yellow daisies with no centre.

salicifolius   ZONES 4–9
(Willow-leaf Sunflower) A most unique back-of-the-border subject that has been described as a giant asparagus fern. Stems are clothed in drooping, willowy leaves, with an almost tropical appearance. Single yellow daisies appear at the top in late fall and have a charm of their own. An interesting texture plant. Native North American wildflower.

> "This deceives people into thinking it a lily, while its mop-like growing point puts you in mind of a giant papyrus. Whatever it does or does not resemble, this is a most exciting and imposing plant." —Christopher Lloyd, *Foliage Plants*

HEIGHT/SPREAD: 180–240cm (6–8')/60cm (2')
LOCATION: Prefers a rich moist soil.
BLOOMS: September–October
USES: ⚘ Specimen, Borders

HELIOPSIS
(False Sunflower) ☀

helianthoides 'Summer Sun'   ZONES 2–9
The longest flowering of the tall daisy-flowered perennials, with large semi-double golden daisies that bloom in succession over several months. Strong, sturdy stems are excellent for cutting. Terrific background plant for summer and fall colour. Reliable and long-lived. This is a selection from a native North American wildflower.

HEIGHT/SPREAD: 90–120cm (3–4')/45–60cm (18–24")
LOCATION: Average well-drained soil.
BLOOMS: June–October
USES: ⚘ Borders, Massing

Helenium 'Bruno'

Helianthemum 'Wisley Pink'

Helianthemum 'Firedragon'

Helianthus salicifolius

Helleborus niger

Hemerocallis citrina

Hemerocallis fulva

Hemerocallis 'Kwanso'

HELLEBORUS
(Hellebore) ☼•

Much sought-after by perennial enthusiasts every-where, and almost always in short supply. These are invaluable for their mid-winter or early spring display of nodding, cup-shaped flowers. Although they grow best in Zones 6–9, Hellebores are worth a try in colder regions, where the blooming season will be delayed until March or April. A winter mulch of loose leaves or straw is not a bad idea in cold areas.

The different species all require moisture early in the year during their flowering period, but later in the year will tolerate moderate summer drought. Also in common, all species hate being disturbed once they are established; plants will sulk for six months or so just to let you know how unhappy they are. Starting with nursery-grown plants will generally give good results. You may even find that your own plants will self-seed!

argutifolius   ZONES 7–9
(Corsican Hellebore) (= *H. corsicus*) A unique, apple-green flowered species. Forms an outstanding clump of grey-green, leathery foliage, coarsely toothed along the edges. More sun-tolerant than some of the other types. Do not trim until after flowering, if required.

HEIGHT/SPREAD: 45–60cm (18–24″)/60cm (24″)
LOCATION: Well-drained loamy soil.
BLOOMS: March–May
USES: ▲△⌇⌁ Specimen, Borders

foetidus   ZONES 6–9
(Stinking Hellebore) Produces branching stems that hold many nodding cup-shaped flowers, light green with a purple edge. Foliage is evergreen and coarsely divided. One of the better self-seeders! Unique skunk-like fragrance when blooming. Do not trim until after flowering if needed.

HEIGHT/SPREAD: 45–60cm (18–24″)/45cm (18″)
LOCATION: Well-drained loamy soil.
BLOOMS: February–May
USES: ▲△⌇⌁ Borders, Specimen

niger   ZONES 4–9
(Christmas Rose) This species is the one most in demand. Plants form a sturdy clump of leathery, ever-green leaves, not unlike a dwarf peony in appearance. Flowers are large and cup-shaped, pure white or some-times tinged with pinkish green, appearing anytime from Christmas to Easter, depending on the climate. Plants sometimes even bloom under the snow! Slow to establish, but well worth the wait.

> "I always plant Christmas roses…in the near view, close to the house where I can enjoy the flowers from a window when cold weather hardly invites distant inspection." —Helen Van Pelt Wilson,
> *Helen Van Pelt Wilson's Own Garden and Landscape Book*

HEIGHT/SPREAD: 25–30cm (10–12″)/40cm (16″)
LOCATION: Well-drained loamy soil.
BLOOMS: December–March
USES: ▲△⌇⌁ Borders, Specimen

orientalis Hybrids   ZONES 5–9
(Lenten Rose) (now correctly *H. × hybridus*) Forms a tough clump of leathery, evergreen leaves. Flower stalks appear in early spring, holding large nodding flowers in shades of white, cream, pink, rose, red or maroon, often with contrasting spots. Blooms later than the Christmas rose, but considered by many gardeners to be the nicer

of the two. Certainly the easiest species to grow, and very rewarding. Excellent under trees or shrubs. Cut off the old leaves in late winter if they look shabby.

HEIGHT/SPREAD: 40–60cm (16–24″)/45cm (18″)
LOCATION: Well-drained loamy soil.
BLOOMS: February–May
USES: ▲△⌇⌁ Borders, Woodland gardens

HEMEROCALLIS
(Daylily) ☼•☼

Extensive breeding over the last fifty years has brought the Daylily to the top ranks of valuable garden perennials. Over sturdy clumps of grassy leaves stems rise to hold large lily-shaped flowers that open in long succession, each lasting for about a day. By choosing varieties that bloom at different times you can extend the flowering season from May through late August. And there are plenty to choose from; over forty thousand named varieties are registered with the American Hemerocallis Society at last count, with about 1000 more added to the list each year.

Daylilies are suitable for planting in perennial and shrub borders, massing as a groundcover or land-scaping plant, or for planting in large containers. All prefer full sun or part shade, and an average well-drained soil. They are very long-lived, and seldom need to be divided. Once established, Daylilies are also moderately heat and drought tolerant.

In addition to the named hybrids there are some excellent old species forms that are still of value in perennial gardens.

> "They are the most dependable of all perennials with handsome endearing foliage and in my experience they are absolutely pest- and disease-free. I grow them everywhere, even in a dim corner where an astounding red one lights up the darkness." —Helen Van Pelt Wilson,
> *Helen Van Pelt Wilson's Own Garden and Landscape Book*

citrina   ZONES 2–9
(Citron Daylily) A very fragrant evening-blooming species. Large grapefruit-yellow flowers are held on stems above a sizeable clump of dark green leaves. Not invasive. Nice to plant near a patio or deck to enjoy the scent.

HEIGHT/SPREAD: 90–120cm (3–4′)/60cm (2′)
LOCATION: Average to moist soil.
BLOOMS: June–July
USES: ⌇⌁⚘ Borders, Pots

fulva   ZONES 2–9
(Wild Orange Daylily) A familiar sight along the road-sides of eastern North America, this introduced wild-flower is an aggressive colonizer, which makes it an ideal plant for slope stabilizing and covering large areas quickly. A bit too aggressive for most garden situations, but tolerant of difficult areas such as between or under trees and shrubs where little else will grow. Flowers are rusty orange with a brown stripe on each petal.

HEIGHT/SPREAD: 75–120cm (30–48″)/60–90cm (2–3′)
LOCATION: Average to moist soil.
BLOOMS: June–July
USES: ⌁⚘ Massing, Slopes

'Kwanso' This is the not-so-common double-flowered form. Slightly less aggressive.

lilio-asphodelus   ZONES 2–9

(Lemon Daylily) (formerly *H. flava*) An old-fashioned favorite, and always the first daylily to bloom. Flowers are lemon-yellow with a strong citrus fragrance, held on tall arching stems. Plants send out rhizomes and will slowly spread to form a colony.

HEIGHT/SPREAD: 75–90cm (30–36″)/60cm (24″)
LOCATION: Average to moist soil.
BLOOMS: May–June
USES: ✂❦❀ Borders

NAMED HYBRIDS   ZONES 2–9

This is but a short listing from the enormous number of named varieties in existence. In recent years there have been many new colour breakthroughs, particularly with whites, purple and pinks. Some breeders are working on more dwarf varieties with recurrent or continuous blooming, others are selecting for new flower shapes or markings. For those with a serious passion for Daylilies there are specialist nurseries in both the U.S. and Canada that carry the newest and latest (and most expensive!).

SPREAD: 60–90cm (2–3′)
LOCATION: Average well-drained soil.
BLOOMS: Early – late June
           Midseason – mid July
           Late – August
USES: ✂❦❀ Borders, Massing

PINK SHADES

'Annie Welch' Solid soft pink, repeat bloomer. Midseason. 60cm (24″)

'Bama Music' Pale pink, yellow throat. Midseason. 70cm (28″)

'Better Believe It' Medium pink, bright red eye. Midseason. 60cm (24″)

'Bonny Barbara Allen' Rose pink, yellow-green throat. Tetraploid. Midseason-late. 70cm (28″)

'Catherine Woodbury' Fragrant. Pale orchid-pink, lime-green throat. Midseason-late. 75cm (30″)

'Fair Isabell' Apricot-pink, gold throat. Tetraploid. Midseason. 75cm (30″)

'Fashion Model' Pale pink and melon blend, pale green throat. Early-midseason. 90cm (36″)

'Frosty Beauty' Orchid and rose blend, gold throat. Repeat bloomer. Midseason. 80cm (32″)

'Hall's Pink' Light pink flowers, low-growing variety. Late. 50cm (20″)

'Luxury Lace' Lavender-pink, ruffled edges. Repeat bloomer. Midseason. 80cm (32″)

'Melon Balls' Orchid and melon-pink blend, small round flowers. Midseason. 80cm (32″)

'Nob Hill' Two-tone pale pink. Early-midseason. 90cm (36″)

'Patricia Fay' Rose-pink, greenish throat. Midseason. 90cm (36″)

'Vivacious' Silvery rose-pink, ruffled petals. Midseason. 50cm (20″)

ORANGE & GOLD SHADES

'Black-eyed Stella' The much talked-about offspring of 'Stella de Oro'. Bright golden-yellow flowers with a distinct red halo in the centre. Excellent constant flowering habit from June to frost. Early-midseason. 60cm (24″)

'Double Gold' Golden-orange double flowers. Midseason. 60cm (24″)

'Flaming Sword' Burnt orange-red, darker eye. Midseason. 75cm (30″)

'Golden Gate' Large-flowered medium orange-yellow. Midseason. 90cm (36″)

'Golden Prize' Very wide gold flowers. Tetraploid. Excellent foliage! Late. 65cm (26″)

'Manilla Moon' Golden yellow. Tetraploid. Midseason. 70cm (30″)

'Marse Connell' Frilly orange, petals tipped red. Midseason. 95cm (38″)

'Rocket City' Rich bittersweet orange, burnt-orange centre. Tetraploid. Midseason. 90cm (36″)

'Stella de Oro' Very popular repeat-blooming dwarf. Small golden-yellow flowers with a darker throat. Blooms June–September. Excellent for edging or massing. Early-midseason. 30cm (12″)

RED SHADES

'Anzac' Red with a light yellow-green throat. Repeat bloomer. Midseason. 70cm (28″)

'Apple Tart' Rich bright red. Multi award-winning tetraploid. Early-midseason. 70cm (28″)

'Baja' Tetraploid. Red with a green throat. Repeat bloomer. Early-midseason. 65cm (26″)

'Carey Quinn' Deep ruby-red, gold throat. Early/midseason. 75cm (30″)

'Hearts Afire' Solid medium red. Midseason. 90cm (36″)

'Poin Set' Medium-red with a dark eye. Repeat bloomer. Early/midseason. 90cm (36″)

'Red Magic' Medium red, yellow throat. Early/midseason. 90cm (36″)

'Summer Wine' Light wine-red with a green-yellow throat. Midseason. 60cm (24″)

'Velveteen' Solid ruby red flowers. Repeat bloomer. Midseason. 75cm (30″)

YELLOW SHADES

'Beloved Returns' Pale greenish-yellow, ruffled. Repeat bloomer. Midseason. 75cm (30″)

'Channel Islands' Creamy yellow with a green throat. Early. 75cm (30″)

'Daiquiri' Pale yellow blend, green throat. Repeat bloomer. Midseason. 80cm (32″)

'Double Charm' Lemon yellow, double petals. Midseason. 60cm (24″)

'Eenie Weenie' Light yellow with a green throat, lightly ruffled. Dwarf, repeat bloomer. Early-midseason. 25cm (10″)

'Green Flutter' Canary yellow, green throat. Repeat bloomer. Late. 50cm (20″)

'Happy Returns' Prolific canary-yellow flowers, fragrant. Tetraploid. Repeat bloomer. Early. 45cm (18″)

'Holly Herrema' Yellow with a bright green throat, wide petals. Fragrant. Midseason. 70cm (28″)

'Hyperion' Fragrant lemon-yellow flowers. Still one of best. Midseason. 100cm (40″)

'Mary Todd' Buff-yellow, very ruffled. Tetraploid. Award winning. Early. 65cm (26″)

'Pineapple Frost' Cool yellow, green throat. Midseason. 65cm (26″)

'Yellow Stone' Lemon yellow, green throat. Midseason. 60cm (24″)

OTHER SHADES & BICOLOURS

'Bonanza' Light orange-yellow with a maroon-red blotch. Midseason. 85cm (34″)

'Cleo' Butter yellow bicolor, lavender tips. Midseason. 100cm (40″)

'Cocktail Date' Pink and green blend, green throat. Early-midseason. 67cm (27″)

'Helicon' Peach flowers with a darker eye, fragrant. Midseason. 96cm (39″)

'Ice Carnival' Near-white with a green throat. Midseason. 70cm (28″)

Hemerocallis × 'Catherine Woodbury'

Hemerocallis × 'Summer Wine'

Hemerocallis × 'Joan Senior'

Hemerocallis × 'Russian Rhapsody'

Hesperis matronalis

Heuchera americana 'Pewter Veil'

Heuchera americana 'Ruby Veil'

Heuchera micrantha 'Bressingham Bronze'

'Joan Senior', Large near-white flowers. Evergreen. Early-midseason. 60cm (24")

'Magic Dawn' Light lemon yellow, maroon tips on every other petal. Midseason. 90cm (36")

'Raspberry Pixie' Raspberry lavender blend, fragrant. Dwarf. Midseason. 30cm (12")

'Russian Rhapsody' Plum-purple flowers, deep purple eye. Tetraploid. Midseason. 75cm (30")

HERNIARIA
(Rupturewort) ☀◐

glabra   ZONES 4–9
An unusual creeping alpine for sunny areas. Plants form a ground-hugging mat of grey-green leaves. Flowers are inconspicuous. Most effective when tumbling over rocks and walls. Also used in carpet bedding. Turns bronzy-red in winter. Was formerly used in herbal medicine to treat ruptures.

HEIGHT/SPREAD:	1cm (1/2")/30–45cm (12–18")
LOCATION:	Well-drained soil.
USES:	△⋏⋎♠ Walls, Carpet bedding

HESPERIS
(Sweet Rocket) ☀◐

matronalis   ZONES 2–9
Heads of sweetly-scented purple, mauve or white flowers, resembling Summer Phlox. A real old-fashioned garden plant for the early summer border. Often performs as a self-seeding biennial. Naturalized throughout much of eastern North America.

HEIGHT/SPREAD:	60–90cm (2–3')/30cm (12")
LOCATION:	Average to moist soil.
BLOOMS:	June–July
USES:	✂⋎✿ Borders, Meadows, Woodland

HEUCHERA
(Coral Bells) ☀◐

A lot of breeding work is currently going on with the Coral Bells, and each year a dozen or more new selections seem to appear. The older types were grown primarily for their colourful early summer display of flowers, but many of the newer types have been selected more for their outstanding foliage, in previously unimagined shades of purple, brown, red and near-black, often with exotic metallic silver markings to rival the best Rex begonia!

All types are most effective when featured towards the front of a border or in a rockery where their delicate sprays of flowers or attractive leaves can be seen from close range. Flowers are excellent for cutting.

americana   ZONES 4–9
This native North American species has given rise to an overwhelming number of new selections, grown primarily for their beautiful foliage, now in a wide range colours, sizes and shapes. Flowers are greenish-white, held just above the leaves. These all dislike hot afternoon sun, but are tolerant of hot, humid summers. The exotic textures and deep colours seem to associate especially well with ferns and other woodland plants. Foliage stays near-evergreen in mild winter areas.

HEIGHT/SPREAD:	30–45cm (18–24")/30–45cm (12–18")
LOCATION:	Rich average to moist soil.
BLOOMS:	June–July
USES:	△▲✿ Borders, Edging, Specimen

'Eco-magnififolia' Intensely silver leaves with contrasting green veins that turn rich beet-red in the cool of fall and winter.

'Pewter Veil' New leaves are coppery pink, changing to silvery-pewter with darker veins. Large leaves. Outstanding! U.S. Plant Patent applied for.

'Ruby Veil' Huge leaves, metallic ruby-violet with silver-grey veins. Rich effect. U.S. Plant Patent applied for.

'Velvet Night' The darkest variety, near-black leaves overlaid with metallic purple-grey. Dan Heims, the originator, suggests planting this beside a gold-leaved Hosta.

× 'Chocolate Ruffles'   ZONES 4–9
Another newer variety, a complex hybrid bearing enormous ruffled leaves. Foliage is dark chocolate-brown on top, burgundy below. Flowers are creamy, held up on tall purple stems. Nearly evergreen in milder areas. Large than most of the other new forms, perhaps best suited to the border. U.S. Plant Patent applied for.

HEIGHT/SPREAD:	60–75cm (24–30")/45cm (18")
LOCATION:	Rich average to moist soil.
BLOOMS:	June–September
USES:	✂⋏▲ Borders, Specimen

cylindrica 'Green Ivory'   ZONES 4–9
Another North American native wildflower selection. Plants form a low clump of deep green heart-shaped leaves. The tall spikes of greenish-white flowers are a favorite of floral designers. A subtle colour, blending into most border schemes.

HEIGHT/SPREAD:	60–90cm (2–3')/30cm (12")
LOCATION:	Average to moist well-drained soil.
BLOOMS:	June–August
USES:	✂⋏ Borders.

Hybrids   ZONES 3–9
(*H. × brizoides*) This is a catch-all group that includes many of the older flowering garden forms, so popular for edging borders. Foliage is green, forming a low clump that gives rise in late spring to lots of waving stems with sprays of colourful bell-shaped flowers. Superb cut flowers. Divide plants every 2–3 years to maintain vigour.

SPREAD:	30cm (12")
LOCATION:	Average to moist well-drained soil.
BLOOMS:	June–July
USES:	✂➤ Borders, Edging

'Brandon Pink' Prairie-bred hybrid, hardy to Zone 2. Bright coral-pink flowers. HEIGHT: 45–60cm (18–24")

'Bressingham Hybrids' Attractive seed-grown mixture of pink, coral and red flowers, with the occasional white. Flowers vigorously. HEIGHT: 60–75cm (24–30")

'Northern Fire' Another prairie-hardy selection, from the Agriculture Canada Research Station at Morden, Manitoba. Rich scarlet-red flowers. Foliage is deep green, mottled with white. Zones 2–9. Registered with the Canadian Ornamental Plant Foundation. HEIGHT: 45–60cm (18–24")

'Red Spangles' Described by plant breeder Alan Bloom as the ultimate blood-red Coral Bell, blooming over a long season. Raised by him at Bressingham Gardens. HEIGHT: 50cm (20")

micrantha   ZONES 4–9
The species itself is native to the West coast of North America, and from it some excellent purple-leaved selections have been made. Foliage is large and crinkly with an ivy or maple-leaf shape, in shades of deep purple-red. Stems of small whitish-pink flowers appear in early summer but are not very showy. Excellent at the border front, especially when massed. Evergreen in Zones 7–9.

HEIGHT/SPREAD:	30–60cm (12–24")/30–45cm (12–18")
LOCATION:	Average to moist well-drained soil.
BLOOMS:	June–July
USES:	✂⋏▲✿ Borders, Edging

'Bressingham Bronze' An improvement on 'Palace Purple', with outstanding beet-red foliage, maintained more reliably throughout the season. Excellent with blue fescue. A Bressingham Gardens selection.

'Palace Purple' A seed-grown strain, the foliage is deep purple in spring, fading to bronzy-brown for the summer. Plants maintain their colour best with afternoon shade. Rogue out any green-leaved seedlings that might appear. A former *Perennial Plant of the Year*.

sanguinea ZONES 3–9

Among these are many of the excellent old garden forms, mostly of compact size, with a bright display of flowers in late spring. These are the best types for edging purposes, blooming slightly before most other types. Dead-heading faded flowers will encourage continual blooming. Divide every 2–3 years.

HEIGHT/SPREAD:	30–45cm (12–18″)/30cm (12″)
LOCATION:	Average to moist well-drained soil.
BLOOMS:	May–July
USES:	△✂➛ Borders, Edging

'Snow Storm' Extremely bright variegation, the near-white leaves are edged in green. Nicely ruffled. Flowers are cerise pink. Effective in groups.

'Splendens' Bright vermilion-red flowers. Good compact seed strain.

'Splish Splash' Outstanding variegated leaves, deep green heavily mottled with white. The leaf veins turn noticeably raspberry-red in colder months. Light pink flowers.

× HEUCHERELLA
(Foamy Bells) ☼☀☽

Hybrids ZONES 3–9

Interesting hybrids between various *Heuchera* and *Tiarella* species. The result combines the dense foliage texture of Foamflower with the showier flowering habit of Coral Bells. Plants are generally vigorous and hardy. Outstanding in a woodland garden, appreciating part shade. Long flowering.

HEIGHT/SPREAD:	30–45cm (12–18″)/30cm (12″)
LOCATION:	Rich, moist well-drained soil.
BLOOMS:	June–July
USES:	△⋀✂ Edging, Borders

× *alba* **'Bridget Bloom'** Mounding habit, great display of shell-pink flowers for many weeks. An older hybrid raised by Alan Bloom at Bressingham Gardens.

× *tiarelloides* **'Crimson Clouds'** Bizarre double leaves with crimson spots. Pink flowers.

HIBISCUS
(Rose Mallow) ☼

moscheutos 'Southern Belle' ZONES 4–9

(Hardy Hibiscus) Large, shrub-like plants, similar to indoor Hibiscus. Dinner-plate sized flowers are red, rose, pink, or white, usually with a crimson centre. Needs lots of summer heat to bloom really well. Tolerates heat and humidity, but must not be allowed to dry out. A thick mulch for the first winter is advised, and planting before midsummer will increase survival. Selected forms may be propagated by cuttings.

HEIGHT/SPREAD:	90–120cm (3–4′)/60–90cm (2–3′)
LOCATION:	Rich, moist soil.
BLOOMS:	July–September
USES:	Borders, Specimen

HOLLYHOCK see ALCEA

HOSTA
(Hosta, Plantain Lily) ☽●

In ever-increasing demand are these first-class shade plants. Their lush clumps of bold, exotic leaves are the main feature, the stalks of mauve or white lily-like flowers an added bonus. Most varieties are easy reliable plants that adapt well even to densely shaded sites. Both the foliage and flowers are of interest to floral designers.

With extensive breeding work still being undertaken there seems to be no end in sight to the number of Hosta varieties; close to *one thousand* are circulating among the specialists and collectors, from five-foot giants to 4-inch miniatures. Gardeners with a passion for these shade-lovers are advised to join the American Hosta Society. Many gardeners are still quite unaware of the fascinating selection that this diverse group of plants has to offer. As one specialist grower, who lists over 150 varieties puts it:

> "Our specialty is hostas…you know, 'I've got both— the green and the variegated one.'"— Tony & Michelle Avent, Plant Delights Nursery.

Hosta are easily divided in spring or early fall but most varieties can be left for years before they become crowded and start to decline. Slugs and snails are often troublesome, particularly the monster slugs at the West coast. Aside from hand-picking, trapping or baiting slugs, an alternative approach is to select those Hosta varieties marked "slug-resistant"; these have especially thick and waxy leaves that slugs find difficult to eat.

LOCATION: Rich, moist but well-drained soil. Golden-leaved and variegated varieties are generally more sun tolerant than green or blue-leaved types.

USES: Each variety has been placed in one of the categories listed below. This should help you to choose the best Hosta for your landscape situation. As a general rule most varieties grow as wide as the height of the foliage, or perhaps half again. See below regarding heights.

HEIGHTS given are for the *foliage*, the flower stems usually rising 30–45cm (12–18″) above that. Each variety is placed into one or more of the following groups, largely based on height.

DWARF: 20cm (8″) or less. Suitable for rock gardens or containers. Usually slow growing.

EDGING: 30cm (12″) or less, vigorous growth.

GROUNDCOVER: 45cm (18″) or less, very vigorous growth. Excellent for massed, low-maintenance plantings.

BACKGROUND: 60cm (24″) or taller.

SPECIMEN: Good choice for a closely-viewed focal point. Interesting leaf texture, colour, shape, or flowers. Does not always indicate monstrous types.

STANDARD VARIETIES ZONES 2–9

Older varieties and species, these are tried and true landscape performers, usually readily available and at quite reasonable prices. If you have a garden with well-established clumps of Hosta they will most likely to turn out to be one of these.

'August Moon' GROUNDCOVER. Large and deeply crinkled gold leaves. Near-white flowers in July. Excellent, Award-winning. 50cm (20″)

fortunei **'Albo-picta'** GROUNDCOVER. Spring foliage is bright yellow with a dark green margin. Slowly changes to all green by summer. Pale lilac flowers in late July. 35cm (14″).

fortunei **'Hyacinthina'** GROUNDCOVER. Powdery-green pointed leaves, white on the underside. Upright mounds. Pale purple flowers in July. 45cm (18″)

Heuchera micrantha 'Palace Purple'

Hosta 'August Moon'

Hosta fortunei 'Albo-picta'

Hosta 'Royal Standard'

Hosta 'Blue Umbrellas'

Hosta 'Ginko Craig'

Hosta 'Krossa Regal'

Hosta 'Kabitan'

'Honeybells' GROUNDCOVER. Fragrant pale-mauve flowers in August. Large light green leaves. 30cm (12″)

lancifolia EDGING. Glossy green spear-shaped leaves, forming a tidy mound. Deep lilac flowers in August. Tolerates drier, sunnier sites better than most other varieties. 25cm (10″)

'Royal Standard' GROUNDCOVER. Rich green, deeply-veined large leaves. Fragrant white flowers in August. Fairly sun-tolerant. 60cm (24″)

undulata **'Albo-marginata'** GROUNDCOVER. Slightly wavy leaves, two-tone green with a broad creamy-white margin. Lilac flowers in July. This is the old standard "variegated" hosta. 30cm (12″).

undulata **'Variegata'** (sometimes listed as 'Medio-variegata') EDGING. Wavy, twisted leaves are green with feathery creamy-white streaks in the centre. Lilac flowers in July. Compact. 25cm (10″).

NOVELTY HOSTA   ZONES 2–9

This section includes a sampling from the many newer varieties as well as some unusual species types. Many are slow to increase, therefore they are generally more costly than the older standard varieties. Some of the newest forms are increased by micro-propagation (also known as tissue-culture) which makes them widely available in a relatively short period of time.

> "I've never seen a hosta I didn't like, but I do have some favorites. I'm especially partial to those with golden leaves, which pump color into dull and shady corners." —Allen Lacy, *The Garden in Autumn*

'Antioch' BACKGROUND. Large light green leaves with a wide cream edge, forming large clumps. Pale lavender flowers in July. Outstanding. 60cm (24″)

'Aphrodite' see *plantaginea* 'Aphrodite'

'Big Daddy' BACKGROUND. Huge, heavily quilted, deep blue leaves. Light lavender flowers in July. Slug-resistance is excellent! 75cm (30″)

'Big Mama' BACKGROUND. Thick blue-green leaves, heavily quilted. Near-white flowers in July. 70cm (28″)

'Birchwood Parky's Gold' EDGING. Compact golden mounds, bright gold in the fall. Showy mauve flowers in July. Sun-tolerant and fast-growing. 30cm (12″)

'Blue Boy' GROUNDCOVER. Rounded mound of small frosted blue leaves, rich texture. Nice for edging. 45cm (18″)

'Blue Dimples' EDGING. Thick-substanced, waxy leaves with an intense powdery-blue colour. Pale lavender flowers in July. 38cm (15″)

'Blue Umbrellas' BACKGROUND. Huge puckered leaves, forming a giant mound, blue in spring later fading to green. Pale lavender flowers in June. One of the best blue-leaved monster Hostas. 75cm (30″)

'Blue Wedgewood' EDGING or GROUNDCOVER. Good slug-resistance! Vigorous, grey-blue leaves with thick substance. Soft lavender flowers in July. 38cm (15″)

'Bold Ruffles' BACKGROUND. Large blue-grey leaves with ruffled edges. White flowers June–July. Excellent slug-resistance. 60cm (24″)

'Bressingham Blue' see *sieboldiana* 'Bressingham Blue'

'Bright Glow' EDGING. Waxy golden leaves, very thick substance. White clusters of flowers in July. 30cm (12″)

'Candy Hearts' GROUNDCOVER. Perfect rounded clump of green heart-shaped leaves. Lavender flowers in July. 45cm (18″)

'Christmas Tree' SPECIMEN. Medium-sized clump of corrugated deep-green leaves with a creamy-white edge. Leaves continue up the flower stems. Lavender flowers in July. A variegated *sieboldiana* type. 40cm (16″)

'Colossal' BACKGROUND. Massive clump of huge corrugated dark-green leaves. Lavender flowers in July. One of the biggest. 75cm (30″)

'Dorset Blue' EDGING. An outstanding dwarf blue type. Round, cupped powdery-blue leaves, lavender flowers in August. 25cm (10″)

fluctuans **'Variegated'** SPECIMEN. Very highly-rated among collectors, considered to be the finest variegated Hosta ever! Large grey-green leaves with wide, bright yellow margins. Forms a stunning upright mound. Lavender flowers in July. Find a prime spot for this baby. 70cm (28″)

fortunei **'Aureo-marginata'** GROUNDCOVER. Attractive dark-green leaves with a strong yellow-gold edging. Pale violet flowers in July. 40cm (16″)

'Francee' GROUNDCOVER. Elegant mound of dark green leaves with a perfect white edge; refined and elegant. Lilac flowers in July. Award winning. 60cm (24″)

'Frances Williams' see *sieboldiana* 'Frances Williams'

'Ginko Craig' EDGING. Narrow lance-shaped leaves, green with a white edge. This fast-growing variety is excellent for edging. Medium purple flowers in August. 25cm (10″)

'Gold Edger' EDGING. One of the best for edging, the heart-shaped leaves are reliably golden-green all season. Fast grower. Mauve flowers in July. 30cm (12″)

'Gold Standard' GROUNDCOVER. All-green in spring, the leaves soon changing to bright yellow with a green margin, the centres near white by fall. Lavender flowers in July. Should receive a few hours of direct sun each day for best colouring to develop. 60cm (24″)

'Golden Scepter' EDGING. An all-gold version of 'Golden Tiara', colours up early. Lavender-purple flowers in July. Vigorous grower. 30cm (12″)

'Golden Sunburst' see *sieboldiana* 'Golden Sunburst'

'Golden Tiara' EDGING. Perhaps the most popular edging variety. Light green heart-shaped leaves with a distinctive yellow edge. Fast grower. Purple flowers in July. 30cm (12″)

'Great Expectations' SPECIMEN. Widely thought to be one of the best Hosta of all time! A mutation of *sieboldiana* 'Elegans', the deep blue leaves have an unusual bold centre variegation of golden-yellow, later changing to creamy-white. Truly exotic in appearance, a must for the collector. Near-white flowers in June. 45cm (18″)

'Green Piecrust' SPECIMEN or GROUNDCOVER. Large dark green leaves with unique heavily ruffled edges. Most effective when viewed up close. Lavender flowers in June. 73cm (29″)

'Ground Sulphur' DWARF. Low, dense mound of bright sulphur-yellow leaves. Appreciates some direct sun to bring out the colour. Lavender flowers in July. 20cm (8″)

'Halcyon' GROUNDCOVER. Deep blue-green leaves forming a dense mound. Thick substance means good slug-resistance. Tall stems of pale lavender flowers in August. 40cm (16″)

'Invincible' GROUNDCOVER. Pointy green foliage with a shiny, highly-polished finish. Sun-tolerant and slug-resistant. An excellent choice for landscaping, with a showy display of fragrant lavender flowers in August. Highly rated. 40cm (16″)

'Janet' GROUNDCOVER. Bright gold-centred leaves with a green margin. Pale lavender flowers in July. Highly rated. 43cm (17″)

'Kabitan' EDGING. Long, narrow yellow leaves are edged in green and slightly ruffled. Dark lavender flowers are a lovely contrast in July. A form of *H. sieboldii*. Very bright and cheery. 25cm (10″)

'Krossa Regal' SPECIMEN. Upright vase-shaped habit. Outstanding powdery blue-green leaves. Stems of lavender flowers in August reaching up to five feet! Good slug-resistance. Very highly rated. 75–90cm (30–36″)

'Lemon Lime' EDGING or GROUNDCOVER. Small clumps of chartreuse-green leaves, vigorous habit. Good display of lavender-purple flowers in July, held well above the leaves. 28cm (11″)

'Love Pat' SPECIMEN. Outstanding frosty-blue leaves, heavily quilted and cup-shaped. Very highly rated variety. Near-white flowers in July. Heat-tolerant. 48cm (19″)

'Marilyn' GROUNDCOVER. Excellent golden foliage with wavy edges. Lavender flower in July. 43cm (17″)

montana **'Aureo-marginata'** SPECIMEN. Large, glossy leaves, deep green with irregular yellow margins, forming an upright vase-shaped mound. Outstanding all season long. White flowers in late July on very tall stems. Very early to emerge in the spring, may need some frost protection. 75cm (30″)

nigrescens BACKGROUND. Strongly upright clump of shiny grey-green leaves. Near-white flowers appear in July on five-foot tall stems. 60cm (24″)

'Northern Halo' see *sieboldiana* 'Northern Halo'

'Pearl Lake' GROUNDCOVER. Profuse bloomer. Lavender flowers in July, over heart-shaped green leaves. Vigorous grower. Award-winning. 35cm (14″)

'Piedmont Gold' BACKGROUND or GROUNDCOVER. Large golden-yellow leaves, holding well in shade or sun. White flowers in July. Fast grower. Still one of the most impressive yellow varieties for lighting up a shady corner! 45cm (18″)

plantaginea BACKGROUND or SPECIMEN. Very fragrant, huge white flowers in August are held just above the leaves, exceptionally showy. Shiny light-green foliage with good heat-tolerance. Also known as the old "August Lily", this is one of the original Hosta species first planted in North American gardens. 60cm (24″)

plantaginea **'Aphrodite'** SPECIMEN. A rare and unusual form with large double trumpet flowers. Recently introduced from China where it has been grown for years. Foliage and habit are identical to the species, listed above. Plant this where it can be appreciated! 60cm (24″)

'Sea Lotus Leaf' GROUNDCOVER. Thick blue-green foliage, upwardly cupped like a lotus leaf. Very pale lavender flowers in June. 47cm (19″)

'Sea Octopus' DWARF or EDGING. Narrow dark-green leaves, heavily ruffled. Mauve flowers. Most unusual! Grow on a ledge or in a trough so it can be easily seen. 15cm (6″)

'Shade Fanfare' GROUNDCOVER. Soft golden-green leaves with a wide creamy-white margin. Popular variety, vigorous grower. Lavender flowers in July. 45cm (18″)

sieboldiana **'Bressingham Blue'** SPECIMEN or BACKGROUND. Deeply ribbed, powdery blue-green leaves, puckering upward. Tall stems of white flowers in June. Introduced by Bressingham Gardens. 60cm (24″)

sieboldiana **'Elegans'** SPECIMEN or BACKGROUND. The original, and still one of the best large-leaved true blue Hostas. Frosted powdery-blue leaves are heavily corrugated. Short stems of almost-white flowers in July. Slow to establish, but eventually becomes an enormous clump. 70cm (28″)

sieboldiana **'Frances Williams'** BACKGROUND or SPECIMEN. Long considered to be one of the best Hosta of all time. Round, puckered leaves are blue-green with a wide yellow margin. Near-white flowers in July. Sometimes scorches in direct sun. Spectacular! 62cm (25″)

sieboldiana **'Golden Sunburst'** BACKGROUND. An all-yellow version of 'Frances Williams', best planted in the shade for bold effect. Good heavy texture. 60cm (24″)

sieboldiana **'Northern Halo'** BACKGROUND or SPECIMEN. Heavily corrugated blue-grey leaves, thick creamy-white margins. This is a white-margined

sieboldiana 'Elegans'. Slow to establish, but outstanding! White flowers in July. 70cm (28″)

sieboldii **'Alba'** GROUNDCOVER. An older form that is still excellent for general groundcover use, as it spreads quickly to form a patch of lance-shaped green leaves. White flowers appear in August. 45cm (18″)

'Sugar and Cream' GROUNDCOVER or SPECIMEN. Large wavy green leaves with white margins. Quickly makes a dense wide mound. Fragrant white flowers in August. 55cm (22″)

'Sum and Substance' SPECIMEN or BACKGROUND. Enormous golden-chartreuse leaves, the largest of any Hosta, forming a huge mound up to six feet wide. Very highly rated! Pale lavender flowers in August. Slug-resistant. 75cm (30″)

'Summer Fragrance' SPECIMEN or BACKGROUND. Quickly forms a large, upright mound of white-edged green leaves. Very fragrant pale lavender flowers in August. 65cm (26″)

'Sun Power' BACKGROUND. Brilliant golden-yellow leaves, lightly ruffled and twisted. Rapid grower. A highly regarded gold form with an upright vase-shaped habit. Lavender flowers in July. 75cm (30″)

tardiflora EDGING. Leathery, dark green leaves. Valued for its showy display of lavender-purple flowers in late September, long after other varieties have finished. 20cm (8″)

tokudama **'Aureo-nebulosa'** SPECIMEN. Unusual centre variegation. Blue-green margins with a chartreuse and gold centre. Very choice, slow-growing variety for the enthusiast. Clusters of white flowers in July. Excellent slug-resistance. 38cm (15″)

ventricosa GROUNDCOVER. Sturdy, indestructible mounds of pointed green leaves, shiny on the underside. Good dense habit, tolerates very heavy shade. Flowers are very showy deep-purple bells with light lavender stripes, appearing in July. Has a tendency to self-seed. 60cm (24″)

ventricosa **'Aureo-marginata'** SPECIMEN or GROUNDCOVER. Another old garden form, but still very highly regarded. Leaves are deep green with irregular wide yellow to creamy-white margins. Showy bell-shaped purple flower in July. A must for collectors. 55cm (22″)

'Wide Brim' GROUNDCOVER or SPECIMEN. Rounded green leaves with wide cream to gold margins, lightly quilted. Lots of lavender flowers in July. Vigorous and classy. 45cm (18″)

'Wrinkles and Crinkles' GROUNDCOVER or SPECIMEN. Heavily corrugated green leaves with extremely wavy edges. White flowers in July. 45cm (18″)

'Zounds' GROUNDCOVER. Outstanding bright golden-yellow corrugated foliage, standing out like a beacon. Clean white flowers in late June. Good slug-resistance. 50cm (20″)

HOUSTONIA *see* **HEDYOTIS**

HOUTTUYNIA
(Chameleon Plant) ☀◐☼

cordata 'Chameleon'   ZONES 5–9
(often listed as 'Variegata') Forms a thick patch of brightly-coloured leaves splashed with a bold combination of green, red, yellow and cream, and with an intense fragrance of tangerines that is not appealing to everyone. Plants spread quickly by underground rhizomes, especially in moist locations, and should be kept out of most borders. Flowers are insignificant. A useful groundcover although very late to come up in spring. Nice in containers or at the waterside. Plants will spread more slowly in dry locations.

Hosta 'Sea Octopus'

Hosta sieboldiana 'Elegans'

Hosta 'Sum and Substance'

Hosta 'Summer Fragrance'

Hypericum polyphyllum 'Grandiflora'

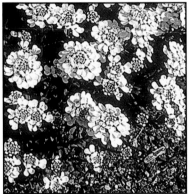

Iberis sempervirens 'Findel'

Incarvillea delavayi

Iris ensata Violet

HEIGHT/SPREAD:	15–45cm (6–18")/45cm (18")
LOCATION:	Prefers a damp to wet soil.
BLOOMS:	August
USES:	⋀⋎ Waterside

HUMULUS
(Hops) ☀ ◑

lupulus   ZONES 2–9
Vigorous climbing vine, useful as a fast cover for a screen or fence. This can be trained up pergolas or trellises, or allowed to clamber up a tree. Cone-shaped dried fruits are used in beer making. Plants are herbaceous, growing back from the ground each year. Can become invasive, spreading quickly underground. Handsome lobed foliage. There is a gold-leaved form ('Aureus') that is difficult to find; it is an outstanding garden plant and much less vigorous.

HEIGHT/SPREAD:	3–6m (10–20')/60cm (2')
LOCATION:	Prefers a rich, moist soil.
BLOOMS:	July–August
USES:	⋎ Climbing vine

HYPERICUM
(St. John's-Wort) ☀ ◑

polyphyllum 'Grandiflora'   ZONES 5–9
Small, finely-textured leaves form a spreading clump set with large golden-yellow flowers in summer. Useful in the rockery, or over walls. Not evergreen like *H. calycinum*, which is listed under GROUNDCOVERS.

HEIGHT/SPREAD:	15–30cm (6–12")/30cm (12")
LOCATION:	Average well-drained soil.
BLOOMS:	June–August
USES:	◭ Walls, Edging

HYSSOPUS
(Hyssop) ☀

officinalis 'Pink Delight'   ZONES 4–9
A selection of the normally blue-flowered herb (see under HERBS), this variety has spikes of shell-pink flowers in early summer for several weeks. Foliage is fragrant, and the plant can be used for flavoring, the same as any other hyssop. Plants are fairly woody and benefit from a hard pruning to 10cm (4") in early spring to keep them dense and bushy. Very drought-tolerant.

HEIGHT/SPREAD:	60–75cm (24–30")/60cm (24")
LOCATION:	Well-drained soil.
BLOOMS:	July–August
USES:	✄⋖🍴 Borders, Herb gardens

IBERIS
(Candytuft) ☀ ◑

sempervirens   ZONES 3–9
A spring-blooming favorite, usually seen cascading over rocks and walls or used as a groundcover. Evergreen foliage forms a compact mat or bush, smothered with white flowers for many weeks. Slightly drought-tolerant.

SPREAD:	30–90cm (1–3')
LOCATION:	Well-drained soil.
BLOOMS:	April–June
USES:	◭⋀⋎▲🍴 Walls, Slopes, Edging

'Findel' Very big heads of snow-white flowers. A rare form, difficult for nurseries to produce, and worth seeking out! HEIGHT: 20–25cm (8–10")

'Little Gem' Especially compact selection, very tidy. Masses of small white flowers. HEIGHT: 15cm (6")

'Snowflake' Larger form, good for edging borders. Clean white flowers in medium-size clusters. HEIGHT: 25cm (10")

INCARVILLEA
(Hardy Gloxinia) ☀ ◑

delavayi   ZONES 5–9
Large rose-purple, trumpet-shaped flowers above low clumps of bold dark green leaves. Winter protection is recommended in Zones 5–6. Worth growing as a container plant in Zones 1–4, bringing indoors for the winter, or treating as an annual. The fleshy roots are inclined to rot out where soils are heavy or stay wet in the winter. Excellent for cutting.

HEIGHT/SPREAD:	45–60cm (18–24")/30cm (12")
LOCATION:	Well-drained soil. Dislikes winter wet.
BLOOMS:	May–July
USES:	✄⋖⋎ Borders

INULA
(Inula) ☀

orientalis   ZONES 4–9
(Golden Inula) Woolly buds open into large, shaggy yellow daisies. Interesting cut flower. Coarse, rough light-green foliage. Nice in the border.

HEIGHT/SPREAD:	45–75cm (18–30")/45cm (18")
LOCATION:	Well-drained soil.
BLOOMS:	July–August
USES:	✄⋖ Borders

IRIS
(Iris) ☀ ◑

A wonderful and diverse group of plants, with flowers in virtually every colour of the rainbow. Few gardens would be complete without at least one representative from the Iris ranks. All have grassy, sword-shaped leaves forming a clump. Most prefer a rich, well-drained soil with plenty of water during flowering.

Certain types, most notably the modern hybrid Bearded Irises, are susceptible to the Iris Borer. This nasty pest lays its eggs inside the leaves, which hatch and develop quickly into green worms that tunnel their way down to the fleshy rhizomes. See the section on PESTS & DISEASES at the end of this guide for more information.

cristata   ZONES 3–9
(Crested Iris) A dwarf species, native to Eastern North America. Quickly spreads to form a colony of grassy green leaves with stems of pale blue-and-yellow flowers in late spring. Tolerates part to heavy shade, and is best suited to woodland gardens or massing as a groundcover under shrubs.

HEIGHT/SPREAD:	15–20cm (6–9")/30cm (12")
LOCATION:	Prefers a moist slightly acid soil.
BLOOMS:	April–May
USES:	◭⋀⋎ Edging, Woodland gardens

ensata (= *I. kaempferi*)   ZONES 4–9
(Japanese Iris) Large, flat crepe-textured flowers appear over tall grassy clumps that somewhat resemble cattails. These have been selected and bred in Japan for hundreds of years. Plants must have plenty of moisture until they bloom, followed by a dryer period for the rest of the growing season. Also they are not tolerant of lime soils or hot, dry conditions. Japanese Iris are set in their ways, and without the specific conditions just mentioned they will seldom thrive. There are now hundreds of named selections but growers often sell them by colour only, so try to buy plants in flower whenever possible to be sure of what you are getting. Flowers come in shades of blue, pink, purple and white, in both single and double forms.

HEIGHT/SPREAD: 60–120cm (2–4')/45cm (18")
LOCATION: Evenly moist rich soil, see above.
BLOOMS: June–July
USES: ✄ ⚘ Waterside, Borders

florentina   ZONES 4–9
(Orris Root) Grown in gardens for centuries, the root of this Iris is dried and ground to produce Orris powder used in potpourri and perfume making. Looks very much like a Bearded Iris, the flowers are pale blue-grey with a yellow beard.
HEIGHT/SPREAD: 45–60cm (18–24")/30cm (12")
LOCATION: Rich well-drained loamy soil.
BLOOMS: May–June
USES   ✄ Border, Herb garden

foetidissima   ZONES 6–9
(Gladwyn Iris) An evergreen species, grown for its clusters of colourful scarlet fruit which look attractive in fall and winter, and are sometimes used in dried arrangements. Flowers are insignificant. Tolerates part shade.
HEIGHT/SPREAD: 45–60cm (18–24")/45cm (18")
LOCATION: Prefers a rich moist soil.
BLOOMS: May–July
USES: ✄ Borders, Winter interest

× germanica Hybrids   ZONES 3–9
(Tall Bearded Iris) Familiar to everyone, these are the most popular and widely grown type. Their large satiny flowers put on a short but spectacular display in spring. Modern Bearded Iris flowers come in nearly every colour and combination imaginable, including blue, bronzy-brown, maroon-black, orange, peach, pink, purple, white, and yellow. There are over twenty thousand named varieties that have been selected over the last fifty years or so. Since most growers handle just a small selection of cultivars, gardeners wishing to build up a collection should consider joining one of the Iris societies or contact a specialist Iris grower that does mail-order.

> "I've also heard of a gardener who, every three years, rips out his iris beds and replaces his poor passé sorts with the latest developments, It is foolishness, I say, and not even gardening as I know it." —Patrick Lima, *The Harrowsmith Perennial Garden*

Bearded Iris are grouped into several categories from Tall (28" plus), down through Border, Intermediate, Standard Dwarf and Miniature Dwarf (the last two listed separately under *Iris pumila*). By far the Tall Bearded group is the most popular, although they have a tendency to look tired after flowering and remain rather shabby for the rest of the season. They are heavy feeders, requiring additional fertilizer in early spring, again before blooming and once more in mid-August.

Divide plants every 3–4 years in July/August, making sure each division has at least one fan of leaves. Plant into rich well-prepared soil with excellent drainage and in a sunny location. It is very important that the top of the horizontal rhizome should be just showing at the surface of the soil, not too deep nor too shallow. Modern Bearded Iris are terribly overbred and seem to be susceptible to various insects and diseases, most notably Iris borers, aphids, various kinds of leaf spots and rots. See the PESTS & DISEASES section for some ideas on controlling these.
HEIGHT/SPREAD: 70cm (28")/30–45cm (12–18")
LOCATION: Rich well-drained loamy soil, better on the dry side.
BLOOMS: May–June
USES: ✄ Borders

pallida   ZONES 3–9
(Sweet Iris) The species itself is seldom grown, but the striped forms listed below are very popular both for their handsome foliage, and showy lavender-blue flowers. Both forms are good for edging, or anywhere a splash of bright foliage would be effective in a border. These are reliable and disease-resistant. Evergreen in mild areas.
HEIGHT/SPREAD: 60cm (24")/30cm (12")
LOCATION: Average well-drained loamy soil.
BLOOMS: June–July
USES: ✄ ⚘ Borders, Edging

'Aureo-variegata' Attractive stripes of gold and bright green.
'Variegata' The more commonly seen form. Leaves are striped lengthwise with cream and grey-green.

pseudacorus   ZONES 2–9
(Yellow Flag Iris) Large cattail-sized clumps, attractive at the waterside but also happy in the border. Canary-yellow flowers put on a nice display. Naturalized in many parts of North America along lakes and rivers.
HEIGHT/SPREAD: 90–120cm (3–4')/60cm (24")
LOCATION: Rich average to wet soil.
BLOOMS: May–June
USES: ✄ Border, Waterside

× pumila Hybrids   ZONES 2–9
(Dwarf Bearded Iris) Included here are the Standard Dwarf and Miniature Dwarf Bearded Iris. These have a similar appearance, but both these groups bloom well before the main flush of Tall Beardeds. Their flowers bloom in a wide range of colours although there are not nearly as many named selections in existence; one advantage however is that as a group these are not nearly so overbred, and they naturally have a tougher constitution. Their preference is for a warm site and well-drained soil. Good choice for the rock garden, or grouped at the border front. These are much easier to grow than the Tall Bearded group, and are generally long-lived and pest free.
HEIGHT/SPREAD: 15–30cm (8–12")/20–30cm (8–12")
LOCATION: Average to dry well-drained soil.
BLOOMS: April–May
USES: ✄◢ Borders, Edging

setosa   ZONES 2–9
(Arctic Iris) Compact, grassy foliage makes a nice edging. Good-sized lavender-blue flowers are similar in appearance to the Siberian Iris but plants are more compact. A very hardy species native to Siberia and Alaska. Could be massed effectively as a groundcover in Zones 2–6, much the way *Liriope* is used in the southern States.
HEIGHT/SPREAD: 15–30cm (6–12")/30cm (12")
LOCATION: Average to moist well-drained soil.
BLOOMS: May–June
USES: ◢✄⚘ Wildflower, Borders, Edging

sibirica   ZONES 2–9
(Siberian Iris) These have strong clumps of grassy leaves that remain attractive all season. Delicate-looking flowers rise above on slender stems in late spring. Tolerates shade better than most Iris as well as wet soils. Siberian Iris are very long-lived and need to be divided only when the flowers start to become small or few in number. Blooms are generally in shades of blue to rose, purple and white, with many named cultivars in existence. Flowers are nice for cutting, the seed-pods for dried arrangements.
HEIGHT/SPREAD: 60–100cm (24–40")/60cm (24")
LOCATION: Rich, average to wet soil.
BLOOMS: May–June
USES: ✄ Borders, Waterside

'Caesar's Brother' Deep violet-blue flowers. Excellent older selection. HEIGHT: 100cm (40")
'Eric the Red' Dark wine-purple flowers, close to red. HEIGHT: 90cm (3')
'Flight of Butterflies' Violet-blue flowers with intricate white veins, like a butterfly wing. HEIGHT: 90cm (3')
'Papillon' Soft, light blue. HEIGHT: 90cm (3')
'Persimmon' Rich mid-blue flowers. HEIGHT: 90cm (3')

Iris × germanica Pink

Iris pallida 'Aureo-variegata'

Iris setosa

Iris sibirica 'Caesar's Brother'

Iris versicolor

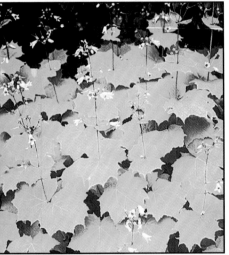

Kirengeshoma palmata

Kniphofia × 'Cobra'

Kniphofia × 'Primrose Beauty'

'Ruffled Velvet' Velvet-purple flowers with black and gold markings. HEIGHT: 60–75cm (24–30")

stylosa   ZONES 8–9
(Winter Iris) (= *I. unguicularis*) Totally unlike any of the other Iris, this species opens its blossoms one by one from late fall to early spring. Plants make an evergreen grassy clump, the lavender flowers hiding among them for some extra protection. Prefers a hot, dry site, especially against a wall or house. Performs especially well at the West coast. Plants resent disturbance; divide or move only if absolutely necessary.

HEIGHT/SPREAD: 30–45cm (12–18")/45cm (18")
LOCATION: Average well-drained soil.
BLOOMS: December–March
USES: Borders

tectorum   ZONES 4–9
(Japanese Roof Iris) An unusual species, with foliage similar to Bearded Iris, but nearly evergreen. Flowers are up to 15cm (6") wide, lilac purple with dark purple blotches and streaks with an exotic, slightly wavy appearance. Prefers a moist site but tolerant of extended summer drought. Was once grown on top of thatched roofs in Japan. Good heat-tolerance.

HEIGHT/SPREAD: 30–40cm (12–16")/30cm (12")
LOCATION: Average to moist well-drained soil.
BLOOMS: June–July
USES: Borders, Waterside

versicolor   ZONES 2–9
(Blueflag Iris) Native to eastern North America, this species is like a blue-flowered version of *I. pseudacorus*. The bold, upright clumps of green foliage are attractive beside a pond or stream. Plants also adapt nicely to average border conditions.

HEIGHT/SPREAD: 90–120cm (3–4')/60cm (24")
LOCATION: Average to wet soil.
BLOOMS: May–June
USES: Wildflower, Borders, Waterside

ISOTOMA see LAURENTIA

JASIONE
(Shepherd's Bit)

laevis   ZONES 4–9
(= *J. perennis*) Violet-blue balls of flowers appear all summer. Nice frontal or edging plant. Related to the *Campanulas*, these are especially nice combined with summer-blooming heathers, enjoying similar conditions. Flowers are good for cutting.

HEIGHT/SPREAD: 25–45cm (10–18")/30cm (12")
LOCATION: Well-drained light soil, preferably acidic.
BLOOMS: July–September
USES: Borders, Heather beds

KALIMERIS
(Double Japanese Aster)

mongolica 'Hortensis'   ZONES 4–9
(= *Asteromoea mongolica*) A recently rediscovered plant, once again becoming available to gardeners. Plants form an upright loosely-growing green bush, covered with small semi-double white daisies with a light yellow centre. Flowers appear for many weeks, the plants combining well with practically anything in the border, acting as a general filler wherever needed.

"It grows about two feet tall, with a very dainty and delicate form, quite open and airy. The multitude of little pompom flowers from midsummer until the first killing freeze look like a doll's powderpuff—or like tiny double Shasta daisies, white, with a buttery yellow centre." —Allen Lacy, *The Garden in Autumn*

HEIGHT/SPREAD: 60–90cm (24–36")/45cm (18")
LOCATION: Average to moist well-drained soil.
BLOOMS: June–September
USES: Massing, Borders

KIRENGESHOMA
(Yellow Waxbells)
HEIGHT/SPREAD: 90–120cm (3–4')/60–90cm (2–3')
LOCATION: Rich, moist woodland soil, preferably acidic.
BLOOMS: August–October
USES: Shady borders, Woodland gardens

koreana   ZONES 5–9
Similar in effect to the species below, but more upright. Flowers are pale yellow bells held in upright spikes. Said to be slightly hardier. Both species require similar woodland conditions.

palmata   ZONES 5–9
A first-rate foliage plant, with exotic-looking upright clumps of toothed green maple-like leaves. Flowers are pendulous yellow bells rising above on purple-black stems. Good candidate for a cool woodland garden. Somewhat slow to establish.

"It is, *par excellence*, a subject for the foliage border, where its flowers will not be metaphorically killed by showy neighbours." —Christopher Lloyd, *Foliage Plants*

KNAUTIA
(Crimson Scabious)

macedonica   ZONES 5–9
(= *Scabiosa rumelica*) A bushy-growing border perennial, valued for its long succession of crimson red, double pincushion flowers. Excellent for cutting. This is a good "filler" plant for summer schemes, and one of the few perennials available in this rich shade of deep red. Sometimes performs as a biennial.

HEIGHT/SPREAD: 60–75cm (24–30")/60cm (24")
LOCATION: Average well-drained soil.
BLOOMS: June–September
USES: Borders

KNIPHOFIA
(Red-Hot Poker, Torchlily)
(formerly *Tritoma*) Tufts of sword-shaped leaves, forming a broad clump that remains evergreen in milder regions. Flowers are arranged in a bottle-brush shaped head, held on strong upright stems. Recent hybrids have extended the range of colours beyond the old red and yellow combination. In Zones 5–6 the leaves should be tied up and the plants mulched for the winter to protect the sensitive crown. Trim back any damaged leaf-tips in early spring. These demand excellent drainage, yet appreciate a good supply of moisture when blooming. Planting before midsummer is recommended.

Hybrids   ZONES 5–9

Much breeding work and selection has happened over the last twenty years, aiming to produce a wider range of colours on sturdy cold-hardy plants. A great deal of variation in plant heights, blooming times, and hardiness has resulted. Moderately drought-tolerant.

SPREAD:	45cm (18″)
LOCATION:	Rich well-drained soil. Dislikes winter wet.
BLOOMS:	June–September
USES:	✂◀🌾 Borders

'Bressingham Comet' Compact selection. Grassy foliage, flowers are a yellow and flame orange bicolor. August–October. HEIGHT: 60cm (24″)

'Cobra' A new tall variety from Blooms of Bressingham. Flower buds open dark bronze changing to copper and pale yellow. August–September. HEIGHT: 90cm (36″)

'Ice Queen' Another Bressingham selection. Ivory flowers with a green caste. September–October. HEIGHT: 120cm (48″)

'Little Maid' Ivory and light yellow flowers, very compact. June–October. HEIGHT: 50–60cm (20–24″)

'Primrose Beauty' Flowers are soft primrose yellow, June–September. This stoloniferous variety seems to be hardy over a wide area. HEIGHT: 75–90cm (30–36″)

'Royal Castle Hybrids' Flowers are in various combinations of red, yellow and orange, heads often bicoloured. A seed-grown strain. June–August. HEIGHT: 90cm (3′)

'Shining Sceptre' Glowing golden-orange flowers. July–September. Another of the famous hybrids by Alan Bloom of Bressingham Gardens. HEIGHT: 100cm (40″)

LAMIASTRUM
(False Lamium, Yellow Archangel) ☼●

galeobdolon   ZONES 2–9

Attractive groundcover plants for shady areas, the foliage remaining evergreen in mild winter regions. Small but showy yellow flowers appear briefly in the spring. Great in containers.

HEIGHT/SPREAD:	20–30cm (8–12″)/30cm (12″)
LOCATION:	Average to moist soil.
BLOOMS:	May–June
USES:	〰◀🌾 Shady borders, Woodland

'Herman's Pride' Pointed leaves, heavily veined with metallic silver. Forms a neat, non-spreading mound, well-behaved and excellent for edging.

'Variegatum' (= 'Florentinum') Very fast-spreading mat of handsome green and silver striped foliage, the stems running and rooting where they touch the ground. Easily controlled by removing runners or clipping. An especially good groundcover for difficult shady areas, like under trees. Keep this out of the border.

> "Their foliage, though course, is very beautiful, and though we often say "silver" when we mean white or cream, these leaves seem licked with metallic paint, a lovely foil for their pastel yellow flowers." —Ann Lovejoy, *The American Mixed Border*

LAMIUM
(Lamium, False Salvia) ☼●

maculatum   ZONES 2–9

Handsome tidy groundcover plants, with small silver and green leaves. Clusters of flowers appear in spring and sporadically until late fall. Perfect for edging, walls, and in containers, but a bit too vigorous for the rock garden. Evergreen in mild regions. The various selections have become extremely popular in recent years, particularly for landscaping.

> "'Beacon Silver' makes a nice combination swirling around the extremely hardy and hearty chrysanthemum 'Mei-Kyo'" —Allen Lacy, *The Garden in Autumn*

HEIGHT/SPREAD:	15–30cm (6–12″)/30–60cm (12–24″)
LOCATION:	Average to moist well-drained soil.
BLOOMS:	May–September
USES:	〰◀🌾 Edging, Borders

'Aureum' Golden-yellow leaves, pink flowers. Will not tolerate direct sun, much less vigorous.

'Beacon Silver' Metallic silver leaves, edged in green. Turns bronzy in cold weather, and always has a slight red caste in the leaf. Pink flowers are a bright contrast. This variety has mysteriously lost much of its former vigour in recent years. For large plantings we suggest any of the other selections as alternatives.

'Chequers' Very vigorous variety. Leaves are dark green with central silver stripes. Pink flowers throughout the summer. Will sometimes self-seed.

'Pink Pewter' Similar to 'Beacon Silver', but with no hint of red in the leaves. Clear pink flowers. Good vigour.

'White Nancy' Leaves are almost completely silver, the clear white flowers appear to almost float on top. Excellent choice for covering large or small areas.

LATHYRUS
(Sweet Pea) ☼

latifolius   ZONES 3–9

(Everlasting Pea) Trailing perennial vine, will climb on fences and trellises, or clamber over slopes. Flowers are in shades of rose, pink, and white. Good cut-flower, fresh or dried, but unfortunately lacking the fragrance of the annual Sweet Pea. This has naturalized throughout much of North America, but is not at all invasive in the garden.

HEIGHT/SPREAD:	30cm–2.4m (1–8′)/30cm (12″)
LOCATION:	Average well-drained soil.
BLOOMS:	June–September
USES:	✂ Slopes, Climbing vine

LAURENTIA
(Blue Star Creeper) ☼☼

fluviatilis   ZONES 6–9

(= *Isotoma fluviatilis*) Flat carpet of tiny, green leaves, smothered in light blue starry flowers all summer long. Ideal for planting between paving stones, will stand light traffic. Worth growing even as an annual in colder regions for its showy display. Proving to be hardier than first thought. May winter in Zone 5 with snowcover.

HEIGHT/SPREAD:	4cm (2″)/30cm (12″)
LOCATION:	Average to moist well-drained soil.
BLOOMS:	May–September
USES:	◢〰◀🌾 Patios, walkways

LAVANDULA
(Lavender) ☼

A group of low woody shrubs from the Mediterranean, often grown with perennials in borders and mixed plantings. Lavenders are native to areas with hot dry summers and mild winters, so they are extremely happy at the West coast, but there are some varieties of English Lavender that adapt well right across the country. All types have that same unmistakable sweet fragrance and

Kniphofia × 'Bressingham Comet'

Lamiastrum 'Herman's Pride'

Lamium 'Pink Pewter'

Laurentia fluviatilis

Lavandula angustifolia 'Hidcote Blue'

Lavandula angustifolia 'Jean Davies'

Liatris spicata

Liatris spicata 'Floristan White'

spikes of showy flowers in summer. Shearing the bushes back lightly after flowering or in early spring will keep them dense and compact. Most types are moderately drought-tolerant.

angustifolia   ZONES 4–9
(English Lavender) (formerly *L. vera*) Old-fashioned plant with a long history as a scented herb, but always appreciated for its showy spikes of flowers and attractive grey leaves. Lavender is especially effective when planted around shrub roses. Acts as an evergreen shrub in milder regions and can be used to make a low hedge. Mulch for the winter in cold areas. Several forms of this species exist.

SPREAD:	30–45cm (12–18″)
LOCATION:	Average well-drained soil.
BLOOMS:	June–August
USES:	✂◄▲♥ ⚘ Dried, Borders, Edging

'Hidcote Blue' Rich purple flower spikes, long blooming. Compact habit. A seed-grown strain. HEIGHT: 30–40cm (12–16″)

'Jean Davies' Pale pink flowers, very unusual. Vegetatively grown. HEIGHT: 35cm (14″)

'Munstead' Bright lavender-blue flowers. The most compact form and generally quite reliable. A seed-grown strain. HEIGHT: 30–40cm (12–16″)

stoechas   ZONES 7–9
(Spanish Lavender) Plant habit is similar to English Lavender, but more tender. Spikes of mauve flowers are crowned by dark purple petals that wave like little flags. Unique and showy. Could be wintered indoors in colder areas.

HEIGHT/SPREAD:	45cm (18″)/18cm (45″)
LOCATION:	Well-drained soil.
BLOOMS:	June–August
USES:	✂◄▲♥ ⚘ Borders

LAVATERA
(Mallow) ☀
These are now all the rage in Europe but only starting to be widely seen in North American gardens. Their funnel-shaped flowers bring to mind a Rose-of-Sharon or a small single hollyhock, and all of these plants are close relatives. Lavatera will be in constant bloom summer through fall, and combine effectively with so many other flowers. These are not long-lived plants but generally last three to five years before dying out.

olbia Hybrids   ZONES 7–9
(Tree Mallow) Plants form a large mound of lobed grey-green leaves, covered in bright hollyhock-type flowers from midsummer to frost. These are actually woody shrubs that should be back hard each spring to 15cm (6″), forcing new bushy growth from the base. The various colour selections look equally at home with both perennials and shrubs. Planting before midsummer is recommended. Use a deep winter mulch in colder areas.

> "Plant in a gray and pink color scheme; there are few pink-flowering shrubs so late in the season." —Penelope Hobhouse, *Colour in Your Garden*

HEIGHT/SPREAD:	1.2–3m (4–10′)/1.5m (5′)
LOCATION:	Average well-drained soil.
BLOOMS:	July–October
USES:	✂◄ Borders, Mixed plantings.

'Candy Floss' Pale pink flowers.

'Barnsley' White flowers with a red eye, fading to pink. Remove any stems that revert to pink. Reported to be hardy to Zone 5 with protection.

'Rosea' Clear pink flowers, free-flowering.

thuringiaca   ZONES 5–9
Similar in effect to the selections listed above, but a little hardier and more compact in habit. Plants have downy, sage-green foliage, with branching stems of soft-pink flowers from midsummer on. This is woody at the base and should be cut back to 15cm (6″) in early spring.

HEIGHT/SPREAD:	1.2–1.5m (4–5′)/90cm (3′)
LOCATION:	Average well-drained soil.
BLOOMS:	July–October
USES:	✂ Borders, Mixed plantings

LEONTOPODIUM
(Edelweiss) ☀

alpinum   ZONES 2–9
Well-known rockery plant from the Swiss Alps. Foliage is silver-grey, bearing woolly white flowers, sometimes used for dried arrangements. Best in a well-drained rock garden. Interesting and unique, particularly if you like the song. Extremely drought-tolerant.

HEIGHT/SPREAD:	15cm (6″)/25cm (10″)
LOCATION:	Very well-drained soil.
BLOOMS:	June–July
USES:	▲⚘ Gravel gardens

LEUCANTHEMUM see CHRYSANTHEMUM

LEWISIA
(Lewisia) ☀◐

cotyledon   ZONES 3–9
A challenging but rewarding plant for the rock garden, forming a flat rosette of evergreen foliage. Sprays of brightly-coloured flowers are held above in early summer. Modern hybrid strains produce both solid-coloured and striped flowers, from pink through salmon, orange, yellow and white shades. Lewisia demands perfect drainage, best achieved by placing plants almost vertically between rocks in a wall or planting in a scree garden. A mulch of gravel around the crown is required to keep plants high and dry. Very showy!

HEIGHT/SPREAD:	15–20cm (6–8″)/15cm (6″)
LOCATION:	Perfectly drained soil.
BLOOMS:	May–July
USES:	▲▲♥ Troughs, Screes

LIATRIS
(Blazing Star, Gayfeather) ☀
These are popular as commercial cut flowers for their tall, long-lasting spikes. Also excellent border perennials, and easy to naturalize in a meadow planting. Blazing Stars are tough, drought-tolerant North American native wildflowers.

spicata   ZONES 2–9
Plants form a low grassy clump of leaves, with tall spikes of rosy-purple flowers appearing in midsummer. An easy, reliable border perennial. HEIGHT: 90cm (3′)

SPREAD:	45cm (18″)
LOCATION:	Well-drained soil. Dislikes winter wet.
BLOOMS:	July–September
USES:	✂⚘ Borders, Meadows

'Floristan White' Spikes of fluffy white flowers, especially nice together with the purple. HEIGHT: 90cm (3′)

'Kobold' Good compact habit, mauve flowers. Good height for the front or mid-border. HEIGHT: 45–60cm (18–24″)

LIGULARIA
(Ligularia) ☀◐
Bold background or specimen plants, these produce tall clumps of large rounded leaves with upright spikes or clusters of yellow daisy flowers in summer.

At their best in a cool, moist location, especially beside water. Avoid planting Ligularia under trees where they will have to compete for water. During periods of heat or drought the plants may look sad and wilted towards the end of the day, only to bounce back fresh and perky by morning. These are long-lived plants that seldom need dividing.

dentata   ZONES 3–9
(= *L. clivorum*) The most commonly seen species with its large green, rhubarb-like rounded leaves that form a large clump. Tall spikes of golden-yellow flowers put on a great show at the back of a summer border. Excellent waterside specimen. Heat tolerant.

HEIGHT/SPREAD:	90–120cm (3–4′)/60–90cm (2–3′)
LOCATION:	Rich, moist to wet soil.
BLOOMS:	July–September
USES:	✄ Borders, Waterside, Specimen

'Desdemona' Large handsome purplish leaves, contrasting branching heads of bright-orange daisies. An unforgettable combination!

'Othello' Very similar, slightly earlier to bloom.

stenocephala 'The Rocket'   ZONES 4–9
Purple-black stems ending in long bottle-brush spikes of yellow flowers. Leaves are deeply toothed or divided, lighter in form and reportedly slug-resistant. Excellent as a background plant. An Alan Bloom selection first introduced by Bressingham Gardens.

HEIGHT/SPREAD:	120–180cm (4–6′)/60–90cm (2–3′)
LOCATION:	Rich, moist soil.
BLOOMS:	June–July
USES:	✄ Borders, Waterside, Specimen

LILIUM
(Lily) ☀◐◑

Lilies can provide bold effect in the summer border with their large flowers. The various types offer a wide range of colours, shapes, and blooming times from which to choose. As cut-flowers they are strong stemmed and long-lasting. Divide the clumps every few years in late fall, separating the bulbs and replanting in a different site. Gardeners interested in building up a collection of lilies might consider joining one of the many Lily societies.

Asiatic Hybrids   ZONES 2–9
Easy to grow, early blooming and very hardy. Flowers open wide, either upfacing, outfacing, or nodding, in an incredibly wide range of colours and blends. Some of the newer selections are free of spots or have bold splotches (brushmarks) of a contrasting colour on each petal. The general range includes orange, pink, red, white, and yellow, with many pastels, bicolours and in-between shades available.

> "The garden that grows a crop of lilies cannot help making the transition from June's abundance to midsummer in the most beautiful way." —Patrick Lima, *The Harrowsmith Perennial Garden*

HEIGHT/SPREAD:	60–120cm (2–4′)/30cm (12″)
LOCATION:	Average well-drained soil.
BLOOMS:	June–July
USES:	✄☘ Borders, Massing

Aurelian Hybrids   ZONES 4–8
(Trumpet Lily) Immense flaring trumpet flowers, excellent as a background planting in the border or massed among shrubs. Strongly fragrant. These will require staking but otherwise are easy and trouble-free. The range of named cultivars is not nearly as extensive as the Asiatics

but includes a good range of colours, including shades of pink, apricot, orange, white, and yellow.

HEIGHT/SPREAD:	120–180cm (4–6′)/45cm (18″)
LOCATION:	Average well-drained soil.
BLOOMS:	July–August
USES:	✄ Borders

lancifolium   ZONES 2–9
(Tiger Lily) (formerly *L. tigrinum*) Out-facing or nodding orange flowers with black spots, held on strong stems in a long branching raceme. Petals curl back attractively behind the flowers. A classic old-fashioned flower, superb for cutting. The tiny little black bulbils held along the stems can be planted like seeds; these will form blooming-size bulbs in about three years.

HEIGHT/SPREAD:	120–150cm (4–5′)/45cm (18″)
LOCATION:	Average well-drained soil.
BLOOMS:	August–September
USES:	✄ Borders, Woodland gardens

Oriental Hybrids   ZONES 4–9
Late-blooming and very fragrant, their large star-shaped flowers are superb for cutting. These deserve a place in every border. Oriental lilies have a reputation for being fussy and short-lived. They are often planted near Rhododendrons as the requirements for growing each are similar; light sandy-loam soils that are rich in compost or peat, preferably on the acid side. Gardeners in mild coastal climates most often succeed with these, but they are well worth trying in other areas. Winter mulching is recommended in Zones 4–5. There are many named selections of these but in a fairly small range of colour: mostly in shades of white, pink or red, sometimes attractively banded or spotted.

HEIGHT/SPREAD:	90–180cm (3–6′)/45cm (18″)
LOCATION:	Well-drained lime-free soil. Dislikes winter wet.
BLOOMS:	August–September
USES	✄ Borders, Woodlands

speciosum 'Rubrum'   ZONES 4–9
(Red Japanese Lily) A late-blooming species with branching stems of fragrant ruby-red flowers with a white margin. An old-fashioned favorite for lime-free soils. Very popular flower in wedding bouquets. Prefers a cool exposure.

HEIGHT/SPREAD:	120–150cm (4–5′)/45cm (18″)
LOCATION:	Well-drained lime-free soil.
BLOOMS:	August–September
USES:	✄ Borders, Woodland gardens

LIMONIUM see STATICE

LINUM
(Flax) ☀

Although we usually think of flax as blue, other varieties are available with white or yellow flowers. All will bloom for several weeks, the flowers followed by attractive round seed pods. Drought-tolerant.

flavum 'Compactum'   ZONES 5–9
Low, compact bushes, covered by large golden-yellow flowers throughout the summer. Especially nice for edging or rock gardens. This little gem deserves to be used more often! Not a short-lived species, but sometimes slow to establish. Moderately drought-tolerant.

HEIGHT/SPREAD:	15–30cm (6–12″)/30–45cm (12–18″)
LOCATION:	Well-drained soil. Dislikes winter wet.
BLOOMS:	June–August
USES:	⛰❋ Borders, Edging

perenne   ZONES 2–9
Heavenly-blue flowers in early summer on an upright arching clump. Nice display when planted in groups. Prune hard after flowering to encourage a second flush.

Ligularia stenocephala 'The Rocket'

Lilium Asiatic Orange

Lilium × 'Casa Blanca' Oriental

Linum flavum 'Compactum'

Liriope 'Variegata'

Lithodora diffusa 'Grace Ward'

Lobelia splendens 'Queen Victoria'

Lobelia syphilitica

Needs excellent winter drainage. Short-lived, but readily self seeds. The species itself grows up to 60cm (24") tall. Very drought-tolerant. The compact selections below are especially good.

SPREAD:	30cm (12")
LOCATION:	Well-drained soil. Dislikes winter wet.
BLOOMS:	May–August
USES:	⬧🜂 Borders, Meadows

'Sapphire' Dwarf, compact form. Excellent for edging or rock gardens. HEIGHT: 25–30cm (10–12")

'White Diamond' White-flowered, compact form. Good companion to 'Sapphire'.

LIRIOPE
(Lily-turf) ☀ ◐

Widely grown as a groundcover in the southern U.S., this is a sturdy group of plants valued for their heat-tolerance and resistance to pests and diseases. The grassy evergreen leaves form a dense clump or mat, with short spikes of showy flowers in late summer. Liriope prefer a shady exposure, particularly in hot summer areas. Although tolerant of a wide range of sites their preference is for a moist but well-drained soil with plenty of humus, preferably on the acid side. A light trim in early spring will tidy up any brown tips caused by winter winds. These perform surprisingly well in many parts of Canada and the northern U.S.

muscari   ZONES 6–9
(Blue Lily-turf) Plants quickly develop into dense evergreen clumps. Showy spikes of flowers are followed by black berries that remain through the winter. This is the species most used as a groundcover or edging, with close to one hundred named varieties in existence.

HEIGHT/SPREAD:	20–40cm (8–16")/30cm (12")
LOCATION:	Average to moist well-drained soil, preferably acidic.
BLOOMS:	July–September
USES:	⬧🌢🜂 Massing, Edging

'Big Blue' Large spikes of blue flowers, held well above the leaves.

'Majestic' Large, mauve-blue flowers, vigorous habit.

'Silvery Sunproof' Green and white leaves.

'Variegata' Leaves brightly striped with green and cream. Lavender flowers.

spicata   ZONES 5–9
(Creeping Lily-turf) The hardiest species, rapidly forming a dense mat of grassy green foliage. Spikes of pale lavender are held among the leaves. Inclined to look quite tired by late winter; mow or trim back in early spring to encourage fresh growth.

HEIGHT/SPREAD:	30cm (12")/30–60cm (1–2')
LOCATION:	Average to moist well-drained soil, preferably acidic.
BLOOMS:	July–August
USES:	🌢🜂 Massing, Edging

LITHODORA
(Lithospermum) ☀ ◐

diffusa 'Grace Ward'   ZONES 5–9
An excellent groundcover or rockery plant with brilliant sky-blue flowers all summer long. Foliage is evergreen, an attractive grey-green colour, forming a low creeping mat. Very popular at the West coast where it seems to grow especially well. Inclined to be fussy and short-lived in cold-winter areas; use a winter mulch in Zones 5–6. Must have acidic conditions and perfect drainage to thrive. 'Heavenly Blue' is a very similar selection.

HEIGHT/SPREAD:	15cm (6")/30–45cm (12–18")
LOCATION:	Well-drained acid soil. Dislikes lime.
BLOOMS:	May–August
USES:	⬧🌢🜂 Slopes, Walls

LOBELIA
(Lobelia) ☀ ◐

Showy late-summer blooming perennials with large upright spikes of flowers, not at all like the more familiar trailing annual types grown in hanging baskets. These short-lived perennials appreciate a moist site and look perfect growing beside a stream or pond where they will often naturalize by self-seeding. Flowers are excellent for cutting. Use a winter mulch in cold regions, or treat as annuals.

× speciosa   ZONES 6–9
(Hybrid Cardinal Flower) A hybrid group that includes a number of older selections that have traditionally been grown from cuttings and are seldom available in North America. Recent breeding work in Europe has resulted in some excellent new seed strains that offer a good range of colours with superior vigour. The clumps of bright green or bronze leaves have good strong stems. Hardiness is not yet widely tested but plants are expected to need a winter mulch in Zones 5–7. The long blooming season makes these useful even as bedding annuals.

SPREAD:	30cm (12")
LOCATION:	Rich moist, well-drained soil.
BLOOMS:	July–October
USES:	✂🌢🜂➤ Borders, Massing

'Compliment Series' Taller, large-flowered plants developed for the floral industry. Foliage is bright green with spikes of blue, deep red or scarlet. HEIGHT: 75cm (30")

'Fan Series' A compact bushy habit with spikes in shades of deep red, scarlet, deep cinnabar rose and soft orchid rose. Excellent for bedding. HEIGHT: 50–60cm (20–24")

splendens 'Queen Victoria'   ZONES 7–9
(Red-leaved Cardinal Flower) Rich maroon-red foliage, contrasting with spikes of scarlet-red flowers. Superb for mass planting, or using in containers, this is widely considered to be one of the best perennials for foliage colour. Not reliably hardy in all areas, but worth growing even as an annual.

HEIGHT/SPREAD:	90cm (3')/30cm (12")
LOCATION:	Moist but well-drained soil.
BLOOMS:	July–September
USES:	✂🌢➤ Specimen, Borders, Waterside

syphilitica   ZONES 4–9
(Giant Blue Lobelia) Stately upright spikes of flowers, from dark blue to white over leafy clumps of green foliage. Great for cutting. This is a native North American wildflower, easy to naturalize in any moist sunny area where it will happily self-seed.

HEIGHT/SPREAD:	60–90cm (2–3')/30cm (12")
LOCATION:	Average to moist or wet soil.
BLOOMS:	August–October
USES:	✂ Borders, Waterside

LOTUS
(Golden Bird's-Foot) ☀

corniculatus 'Flore-Pleno'   ZONES 2–9
A creeping green mat, smothered with double golden pea-flowers in early summer. Good groundcover for difficult sunny areas. Not overly invasive, tolerant of very poor soils.

HEIGHT/SPREAD:	10cm (4")/30cm (12")
LOCATION:	Average well-drained soil.
BLOOMS:	June–July
USES:	⬧🌢🜂 Walls, Slopes

LUNARIA
(Money Plant, Honesty) ☀◐

annua ZONES 2–9
(formerly *L. biennis*) Sprays of pretty purple or white flowers are followed by interesting coin-shaped seedheads. The branches of papery dried pods are popular for indoor decoration. A self-seeding biennial, useful in the shade garden and not weedy.

HEIGHT/SPREAD:	60–90cm (2–3')/30cm (12")
LOCATION:	Rich average to moist soil.
BLOOMS:	May–June
USES:	✄❦ Woodland gardens, Meadows

LUPINUS
(Lupine) ☀◐

The tall spires of Lupines are an unforgettable sight in the late spring garden. Excellent for cutting, the flowers are available in a rainbow of colours. Plants grow best in a deep, rich soil on the neutral to acidic side. Good drainage is essential. Use a winter mulch in cold regions. Since Lupines are short-lived, renew plantings every other year. Cutting plants back to the base after blooming may encourage them to live an extra year. Lupines often look scruffy after blooming; plant something in front that will get big later in the summer to hide them. Aphids have a special liking for them.

Hybrids ZONES 3–9
Extensive breeding has created a choice of colours as well as plant heights. Spikes can now be had in shades of blue, pink, rose, red, white, or yellow, sometimes attractively bi-coloured. Plants will self-seed if allowed but seedlings will usually revert to mixed colours.

SPREAD:	30cm (12")
LOCATION:	Average to moist soil, preferable acidic.
BLOOMS:	June–July
USES:	✄❦ Borders

'Dwarf Minarette' Dwarf, compact plants in an attractive range of colours. HEIGHT: 45–60cm (18–24")

'Russell Hybrids' Classic tall spikes, often available as separate or mixed colours. HEIGHT: 75–100cm (30–40")

LYCHNIS
(Campion) ☀

Related to *Dianthus*, the Campions have flowers in bright pink, magenta, red or orange shades, mostly vibrant, hot shades that don't easily fit into soft pastel colour schemes. However, they are hardy, easy-to-grow plants, mostly for the summer border. Gardeners who develop a more daring sense of colour design will find these interesting and useful.

alpina ZONES 1–9
(Arctic Campion) From short tufts of grassy leaves, clusters of bright pink flowers appear in late spring. Short-lived but readily self-seeds. An easy little rock garden plant, especially useful in brand-new rock gardens or walls.

HEIGHT/SPREAD:	10–15cm (4–6")/15cm (6")
LOCATION:	Average well-drained soil, preferably acidic.
BLOOMS:	May–June
USES:	⛰ Walls

arkwrightii 'Vesuvius' ZONES 3–9
Clusters of large scarlet-orange flowers, over a compact clump of burgundy leaves. Very showy for the border front. Not long-lived where drainage is poor. Nice for cutting.

HEIGHT/SPREAD:	30–45cm (12–18")/30cm (12")
LOCATION:	Average well-drained soil.
BLOOMS:	June–July
USES:	✄ Borders, Edging

chalcedonica ZONES 2–9
(Maltese Cross) Very old-fashioned, long-lived cottage garden plants. Domed clusters of flaming scarlet-orange flowers are held aloft on strong stems. Excellent for cutting. Shear back hard (to 12 inches) after flowering to encourage a repeat bloom in fall. A unique salmon-rose shade ('Rosea') is seldom available but worth seeking.

> "…invaluable for its pure bright colour, and can be used in daring color schemes. Grow next to deeper reds, or experiment with neighbouring bronze and purple leaves which absorb some of the 'hot' color." —Penelope Hobhouse, *Colour in Your Garden*

HEIGHT/SPREAD:	90–120cm (3–4')/30cm (12")
LOCATION:	Average well-drained soil.
BLOOMS:	June–August
USES:	✄ Borders

coronaria ZONES 3–9
(Rose Campion) Attractive rosettes of felty grey leaves. Branching stems of bright magenta-rose flowers bloom through the summer. Not a long-lived species, but readily self-seeds. Can be used for cutting. See below for other colour forms.

HEIGHT/SPREAD:	45–75cm (18–30")/30cm (12")
LOCATION:	Average well-drained soil.
BLOOMS:	June–August
USES:	✄ Borders, Meadows

'Alba' White-flowered form, excellent in pastel or white border schemes.

'Angel Blush' Flowers are a delicate soft-pink and white combination. Subtle.

LYSIMACHIA
(Loosestrife) ☀●

NOT the same as Purple Loosestrife (see LYTHRUM). These true Loosestrife are all moisture-loving perennials, typically with short spikes of white or yellow flowers. They vary from low creeping types to taller border varieties. Most share the trait of spreading fairly quickly, so some extra consideration should be given to their placement.

ciliata 'Atropurpurea' ZONES 3–9
(Fringed Loosestrife) (= *Steironema ciliata*) A species native to the eastern U.S., this select form has rich bronze-purple leaves, forming a loose upright clump. The nodding yellow flowers contrast beautifully. Although this spreads to form a patch it is not too invasive for the border.

HEIGHT/SPREAD:	75–90cm (30–36")/60cm (24")
LOCATION:	Prefers a rich moist soil.
BLOOMS:	June–August
USES:	✄ Borders, Woodland gardens

clethroides ZONES 2–9
(Gooseneck Loosestrife) Unusual spikes of white flowers, bent just like a goose's neck, and highly valued by floral arrangers. Foliage can develop good red fall colour. Quickly spreads to form a patch and may swamp slower-growing neighbours. Best at the waterside or a similar moist location. Tolerates semi-shade. Great for massing.

HEIGHT/SPREAD:	60–90cm (2–3')/90cm (3')
LOCATION:	Rich, average to moist soil.
BLOOMS:	July–September
USES:	✄ Borders, Waterside, Woodland

Lupinus Dwarf Mixture

Lychnis arkwrightii 'Vesuvius'

Lychnis coronaria

Lysimachia clethroides

Lysimachia nummularia

Macleaya cordata

Mazus reptans

Monarda × 'Marshall's Delight'

nummularia   ZONES 2–9

(Creeping Jenny) Low trailing stems quickly form a bright green carpet. Golden-yellow flowers appear among the leaves from spring to fall. Also excellent in hanging baskets. Remains evergreen in mild climates. Can become invasive but runners are easily removed or weeded out. Quite tolerant of heavy shade.

HEIGHT/SPREAD:	5–10cm (2–4″)/45cm (18″)
LOCATION:	Prefers a rich moist soil.
BLOOMS:	May–August
USES:	∿▲✿ Lawn substitute, Waterside

'Aurea' Bright golden leaves make a glowing display. Must be planted in the shade to avoid scorching. Outstanding carpeter below blue *Pulmonaria*.

> "The plant creeps about at ground level and is ideally suited, it seems to me, for linking the units in a group of ferns." — Christopher Lloyd, *Foliage Plants*

punctata   ZONES 2–9

(Yellow Loosestrife) Upright, bushy clumps spreading to form a large patch. Star-shaped yellow flowers appear in leafy spikes in summer. Good waterside plant, but adapts well to the border and will even grow in shade under trees. Excellent for cutting.

HEIGHT/SPREAD:	45–90cm (18–36″)/60cm (24″)
LOCATION:	Prefers a rich moist soil.
BLOOMS:	June–August
USES:	✄ Borders, Woodland gardens

LYTHRUM
(Purple Loosestrife)

The spread of *Lythrum salicaria* in wetland areas throughout North America has recently become an issue of major environmental concern. For awhile some of the hybrid varieties (for example 'Morden Pink', 'Dropmore Purple' and many others) were considered to be largely sterile. The most recent studies have shown, however, that virtually all hybrid cultivars may set seed if they cross with local populations of *Lythrum salicaria* thereby possibly contributing to the wetland problem.

Lythrum salicaria has been declared a noxious weed in many states and provinces already, including Alberta, Manitoba, Ontario, Prince Edward Island, Arkansas, Colorado, Illinois, Minnesota, Missouri, Montana, North Carolina, North Dakota, Ohio, Oregon, South Dakota, Washington and Wisconsin. It is strongly recommended that growers and nurseries in these areas discontinue selling *Lythrum*. Gardeners within ten miles of a local wetland population of *Lythrum* are advised to watch any hybrids already in their gardens very closely to insure that no seed is formed, perhaps dead-heading faded flowers as a precaution or even removing and destroying plants entirely.

There are many other perennials available as substitutes to take the place of Lythrum in our gardens. Consider any of these: Aster, Astilbe, Buddleia, Echinacea, Lavatera, Liatris, Malva, Monarda, Perovskia, Physostegia, Sidalcea.

MACLEAYA
(Plume Poppy) ☀◐

cordata   ZONES 2–9

A giant background plant with handsome, deeply lobed blue-green leaves, topped in summer by cream-coloured plumes. Plants will spread fairly quickly to make a large patch and can become a tad invasive unless restrained each spring. Otherwise, this is a good bold specimen plant.

HEIGHT/SPREAD:	1.8–2.4m (6–8′)/60–90cm (2–3′)
LOCATION:	Prefers a deep, rich soil.
BLOOMS:	July–August
USES:	✄ Borders, Specimen

MALVA
(Mallow) ☀

moschata 'Rosea'   ZONES 3–9

(Pink Musk Mallow) Satiny pink flowers, like a miniature Hibiscus. The deeply cut leaves give off a pleasant musky smell when crushed. Upright clumps, blooming for many weeks. Cut these back in late summer before they bloom themselves to death. Short-lived.

HEIGHT/SPREAD:	60–90cm (2–3′)/45cm (18″)
LOCATION:	Average well-drained soil.
BLOOMS:	July–September
USES:	✄✿ Borders, Meadows

sylvestris mauritiana   ZONES 3–9

(Striped Mallow) Large bright rose-purple flowers, exotically striped with deep maroon veins. Often behaves as a self-seeding biennial or annual, sometimes lasting longer. An old European cottage garden plant. Blooms over a very long season, well into late fall.

HEIGHT/SPREAD:	60–120cm (2–4′)/45cm (18″)
LOCATION:	Average well-drained soil.
BLOOMS:	July–October
USES:	✄ Borders, Meadows

MATRICARIA see CHRYSANTHEMUM

MAZUS
(Mazus) ☀◐

reptans   ZONES 5–9

(Creeping Mazus) Ground-hugging green mats are studded with yellow-spotted lavender flowers. Nice between paving stones or in the rock garden. Prefers a good moist location. Evergreen in Zones 8–9.

HEIGHT/SPREAD:	5–10cm (2–4″)/30cm (12″)
LOCATION:	Moist well-drained soil.
BLOOMS:	April–June
USES:	△∿▲ Between patio stones, Waterside

MENTHA
(Mint) ◐●

requienii   ZONES 7–9

(Corsican Mint) Tiny green leaves create a flat carpet with the fragrance of creme-de-menthe. Minute mauve flowers appear in July. Very nice growing in rock gardens and patio cracks, even as a self-seeding annual. Looks a bit like Baby-tears.

> "If you are a *laissez-faire* gardener with a shady piece of lawn that you don't treat with weed-killers, this is an ideal spot to introduce the creeping peppermint. As you tread and mow, a pungent waft from the plant will vie with the smell of oil and petrol fumes." —Christopher Lloyd, *Foliage Plants*

HEIGHT/SPREAD:	2.5cm (1″)/15–30cm (6–12″)
LOCATION:	Likes a rich moist soil.
BLOOMS:	July–August
USES:	△∿✿ Between patio stones

MONARDA
(Bee-Balm, Bergamot) ☀◐

Tall, bushy plants with aromatic mint-like foliage. Their bright shaggy flower heads attract bees and butterflies. Plants are suited to the border or wildflower garden, having been developed from native North American species. A good range of colours is available and there are some exciting new dwarf selections being developed that should become available in the near future.

Plants spread to form a vigorous patch that thins out in the middle; divide every other year and replant only the younger outside pieces. Powdery mildew on the foliage is often a problem. See the section on PESTS & DISEASES for some ideas on controlling this, or choose some of the resistant varieties

didyma Hybrids   ZONES 3–9

The varieties listed below are all fairly tall growing, long-flowering and excellent for cutting. They grow best with a moist, rich soil and full sun. Mildew is often a sign of stress due to lack of water. Very attractive to hummingbirds and butterflies.

HEIGHT/SPREAD: 75–120cm (30–48")/45cm (18")
LOCATION: Rich, moist well-drained soil.
BLOOMS: June–September
USES: ✂ ➤ ❦ Borders, Woodland edge

'Gardenview Scarlet' An older variety but with good mildew resistance. Brilliant red flowers. Usually does much better than 'Cambridge Scarlet'.

'Marshall's Delight' A newer hybrid from Agriculture Canada, registered with the Canadian Ornamental Plant Foundation. Hot-pink flowers on good strong stems. Highly resistant to powdery mildew. Outstanding!

'Panorama Mix' Seed-strain with a nice range of scarlet, bright red, pink, salmon, and crimson shades.

'Prairie Night' ('Prärienacht') Very tall German selection, dark purple-lilac flowers.

'Snow White' ('Schneewittchen') Small creamy-white flower heads.

'Violet Queen' Deep purple-blue flowers.

MYOSOTIS
(Forget-Me-Not) ☀●

Few other flowers can match the true sky-blue of Forget-me-nots. Their long display combines perfectly with all sorts of spring-blooming bulbs and perennials. These are ideal "tuck-in" plants for the spring garden, self-seeding anywhere that pleases them.

scorpioides 'Spring Carpet'   ZONES 3–9

(True Forget-Me-Not) (= *M. palustris*) A true perennial species that prefers a constantly moist or wet soil and a sunny site. Low, creeping stems form a low spreading patch. Flowers are bright blue with a yellow eye. Good waterside plant. Trim back lightly after blooming.

HEIGHT/SPREAD: 15–20cm (6–8")/20cm (8")
LOCATION: Moist to wet soil.
BLOOMS: April–June
USES: ❦ Waterside, Wet sites

sylvatica   ZONES 3–9

(Woodland Forget-Me-Not) The more commonly grown species, these always make a bright spring display. Widely used to underplant spring bulbs, especially tulips. This is a true biennial that will almost always perenniate by self-seeding. Fairly shade tolerant, especially below deciduous trees. There are strains available in various shades of blue as well as pink and white.

HEIGHT/SPREAD: 15–25cm (6–9")/15cm (6")
LOCATION: Average to moist well-drained soil.
BLOOMS: April–June
USES: △❦ Borders, Woodland gardens, Bedding

NEPETA
(Catmint) ☀

Showy, fragrant relatives of the mints. These give us a good range of blues to use in the summer border, combining so nicely with the flashier border plants. Taller varieties are useful for cutting.

× 'Dropmore Blue'   ZONES 2–9

A Canadian hybrid of high merit bred by Dr. Frank Skinner and introduced by him in 1932. Excellent choice for edging or mass planting, with masses of sterile bright blue flowers that appear throughout the summer. The dense fragrant grey-green foliage stands up well to heat, although plants often benefit from clipping back in early July. Great in containers. An effective companion to roses. Moderately drought-tolerant.

HEIGHT/SPREAD: 30cm (12")/30cm (12")
LOCATION: Average well-drained soil.
BLOOMS: June–September
USES: ❦ Edging, Borders, Massing

sibirica 'Blue Beauty'   ZONES 2–9

(Siberian Catmint) This variety is known in Europe as 'Souvenir d'André Chaudron'. Whatever you call it, this is a robust and long-blooming plant for the border. Spikes of fragrant tubular flowers are deep lavender blue, held above an upright clump of foliage. Inclined to spread a bit, but easily restrained with a spade. A little-known perennial, superb for cutting!

HEIGHT/SPREAD: 60–90cm (2–3')/45cm (18")
LOCATION: Average well-drained soil.
BLOOMS: June–August
USES: ✂ Borders

NIPPONICANTHEMUM see CHRYSANTHEMUM

OENANTHE
(Oenanthe) ◐

javanica 'Flamingo'   ZONES 4–9

Recently brought over from Korea, this interesting foliage plant is related to parsley. The leaves are large and lacy, blue-green dappled with cream and lavender pink. Umbels of white flowers are held above. This forms a fast-spreading mat that roots wherever it touches the ground but can be easily controlled by clipping back the runners. Could be interesting in a hanging basket or window box.

HEIGHT/SPREAD: 10cm (4")/45cm (18")
LOCATION: Prefers a rich, moist soil.
BLOOMS: July–August
USES: ∧❦ Baskets

OENOTHERA
(Evening Primrose, Sundrop) ☀

Sun-loving plants, very tolerant of hot sites and lean dry soils. Flowers are poppy-shaped, with a soft satiny texture. Sundrops are daytime blooming, while Evening Primroses open late in the day and close before the next morning. All types are originally native North American wildflowers.

berlandieri 'Siskiyou'   ZONES 5–9

(Mexican Evening Primrose) A vigorous and extremely floriferous selection, with upfacing cup-shaped flowers in a beautiful light rose shade. This shows good potential as a landscaping plant with a long season of bloom. Foliage is olive green. Plants form a low mat. Because of its wandering habit, this should probably be restrained or edged regularly. Very drought-tolerant.

Monarda × 'Prairie Night'

Myosotis scorpioides 'Spring Carpet'

Nepeta × 'Dropmore Blue'

Oenothera berlandieri 'Siskiyou'

Oenethera tetragona

Ophiopogon planiscapus 'Nigrescens'

Origanum × 'Herrenhausen'

Paeonia × 'Bowl of Beauty'

HEIGHT/SPREAD: 20–30cm (8–12")/60–75cm (24–30")
LOCATION: Needs a well-drained soil.
BLOOMS: June–September
USES: ⋔⌄♥⫚ Edging, Massing

missouriensis   ZONES 3–9
(Ozark Sundrops) Large yellow blossoms with a crepe-like texture. With low, sprawling stems this is best suited to the rock garden or for edging. Very drought-tolerant.

HEIGHT/SPREAD: 15–30cm (6–12")/30cm (12")
LOCATION: Deep, well-drained soil.
BLOOMS: June–August
USES: △♥⫚ Edging

pallida   ZONES 4–9
(White Evening Primrose) Large white crepe flowers, aging to shell pink. A short-lived perennial, but will self-seed if happy. Needs excellent drainage. Very drought-tolerant.

HEIGHT/SPREAD: 30cm (12")/30cm (12")
LOCATION: Average to poor well-drained soil.
BLOOMS: June–August
USES: △⫚ Walls, Slopes

tetragona   ZONES 3–9
(Yellow Sundrops) (formerly *O. fruticosa youngii*) Flowers begin as red buds, opening into lemon-yellow blossoms over several weeks. Plants eventually spread to form a wide patch. Divide every other year. These are reliable, long-lived garden perennials. Several named varieties exist. Very drought-tolerant.

HEIGHT/SPREAD: 45–60cm (18–24")/30–60cm (12–24")
LOCATION: Average well-drained soil.
BLOOMS: June–August
USES: ⫚ Borders, Massing

'Sonnewende' Excellent German selection. Bronzy-red tinged foliage forms a sturdy upright clump. Large, bright yellow flowers over a long season. A great improvement.

OPHIOPOGON
(Lilyturf) ☀◐

Many varieties of Lilyturf (or Mondo Grass) are used in the Southern U.S. as groundcovers. Generally not as hardy as the closely related *Liriope*, a winter mulch of evergreen boughs is recommended in Zones 5–6. These form evergreen grassy tufts, the small flowers almost hidden among the leaves.

planiscapus 'Nigrescens'   ZONES 6–9
(Black Lilyturf) With its nearly jet-black leaves this makes a most unique specimen for edging or mass planting. Short spikes of pale pink flowers are followed by black berries in the fall. At its best when contrasted with yellow or silver foliage, such as *Lysimachia nummularia* 'Aurea' or *Lamium* 'White Nancy'. This is not a fast grower. Prefers a sheltered, partly shaded location.

> "The color is difficult to place in a garden, exotic and unusual but drawing the eye as firmly as a patch of red. Make a feature of it by emphasizing its dramatic potential with yet more deep purple foliage." —Penelope Hobhouse, *Colour in Your Garden*

HEIGHT/SPREAD: 15–30cm (6–12")/20–30cm (8–12")
LOCATION: Rich, moist well-drained soil.
BLOOMS: July–August
USES: △⋔⌄♥ Massing, Edging

ORIGANUM
(Oregano) ☀

In addition to the more herbal, pizza-flavoring varieties, there are a few types of Oregano that are showy border perennials worthy of a bright sunny spot.

× 'Herrenhausen'   ZONES 5–9
Fragrant, bushy clumps bear many clusters of mauve-pink flowers through the summer. A recent German hybrid gaining much attention here. This is most effective when allowed to romp and trail through and over other border plants. Good for cutting. May prove to be much hardier.

HEIGHT/SPREAD: 45–60cm (18–24")/45cm (18")
LOCATION: Average well-drained soil.
BLOOMS: July–September
USES: ✂◄♥ Borders, Walls

vulgare 'Aureum'   ZONES 4–9
Excellent bright yellow foliage forming a low, spreading mat. A terrific edging plant in the border. Seems to colour up well in either sun or shade. Fragrant pale mauve flowers appear in early summer. Some gardeners prefer to keep this low throughout the season by clipping lightly every six weeks or so. This also serves to maintain the leaf colour into late fall. Nice on walls or slopes.

HEIGHT/SPREAD: 15–30cm (6–12")/45cm (18")
LOCATION: Average well-drained soil.
BLOOMS: July–August
USES: ♥ Borders, Edging, Walls

PAEONIA
(Garden Peony) ☀

Old favorites for the late spring border, prized for their large satiny flowers, which are so superb for cutting. The handsome foliage remains attractive all season, particularly when hoops or rings are used to hold clumps together. Breeding has created thousands of named cultivars, many of which are available only through specialist growers. A small number of excellent varieties are listed below, offering a good starting point for newer gardeners.

Peonies prefer a deep, rich well-drained loamy soil and full sun exposure. New plants take several years to become established, and resent being disturbed at any time. Many years can go by before Peonies actually require dividing; as many as ten or fifteen. When necessary, divide plants in the early fall only; be sure that each division has several growth points or eyes, and that they are planted no deeper than they were originally growing. Established plants should be fertilized in the early spring and again immediately after blooming. Peonies can easily be damaged by rain, especially the double-flowered forms, unless adequately staked or grown in special peony hoops.

> "As landscaping tools, peonies are more versatile than most perennials. In addition to spectacular blooms, the symmetrical yard-high growth of elegant, long-lasting leaves makes the plants naturals for focal points or massed display." —Patrick Lima, *The Harrowsmith Perennial Garden*

Peonies are fairly free of pests. Ants are often seen feeding on the sugar that coats the sticky flower buds, but they are in no way harmful or helpful. A fungal infection known as Botrytis can sometimes damage the flowers, turning them black. Thrips are occasionally a problem. See the PESTS & DISEASES section for information on controlling these.

lactiflora Hybrids ZONES 2–9

(Common Garden Peony) The very large number of named cultivars have been categorized into Single, Japanese, Semi-double, and Double forms, each category basically having more petals than the one previous. Flowers vary tremendously in size, blooming time, and fragrance, with the range of colours including every shade of pink, magenta, red, white and cream imaginable. As some nurseries sell by colour only, it is wise to buy plants in flower whenever possible, or else look for named varieties.

HEIGHT/SPREAD:	75–100cm (30–40")/90cm (3')
LOCATION:	Rich, well-drained loamy soil.
BLOOMS:	late May–June, divided into early, middle and late.
USES:	✂ Borders, Massing

'Bowl of Beauty' Japanese; fuchsia-pink with creamy-white stamens; early.

'Claire de Lune' Single; creamy-yellow petals, fragrant; very early.

'Constance' Japanese; pink with yellow stamens; middle.

'Dia Jo Kuhan' Japanese; small-flowered, magenta with a pink edge, yellow stamens; middle.

'Duchess de Nemours' Double; white; early.

'Karl Rosenfield' Double; deep purple-red; middle.

'Lady Alexandra Duff' Double; soft-pink, compact; middle.

'Laura Dessert' Double; creamy-white with a yellow flush; middle-early.

'Okinawa' Japanese; carmine red, yellow stamens; middle.

'Romance' Japanese; large pink flowers; middle.

tenuifolia ZONES 2–9

(Fernleaf Peony) Rare and much in demand. The finely-cut leaves make this quite unlike any other Peony. The delicate, crimson-red single flowers seem to rest on the leaves, appearing well before the main flush of Garden Peonies begins. Even more rare and expensive is the double red flowered 'Plena', a collector's gem!

HEIGHT/SPREAD:	30–45cm (12–18")/30–45cm (12–18")
LOCATION:	Rich, well-drained loamy soil.
BLOOMS:	May–June
USES:	⌂⚲✂ Borders, Edging

PAPAVER
(Poppy) ☀

Satiny poppy flowers are a traditional favorite. They are useful for cutting if picked in bud, the cut ends then seared over a flame. Good drainage is crucial, particularly where winters are wet. Most species are short-lived perennials that happily self-seed in any sunny border, the exception to this is the longer-lived Oriental Poppy. All species prefer lighter soils and a warm, sunny location.

alpinum Hybrids ZONES 3–9

(Alpine Poppy) Short and graceful little poppies, in shades of yellow, orange, pink, and white, the petals sometimes intricately fringed. The ferny leaves form a low tuft. Short lived, but freely self-seeding into rock garden cracks and crevices. Moderately drought-tolerant. This species name is invalid, *P. burseri* currently is considered acceptable.

HEIGHT/SPREAD:	15–20cm (6–8")/15cm (6")
LOCATION:	Well-drained soil.
BLOOMS:	May–August
USES:	⌂⚲✶ Screes, Troughs, Walls

alboroseum ⬇ ZONES 2–9

(Arctic Poppy) This species is like a more refined, dwarf version of *P. atlanticum*. Plants form a low rosette of sil-very green, hairy leaves, bearing upright stems of satiny flowers in shades of salmon to white. A little gem for the rock garden.

HEIGHT/SPREAD:	10–15cm (4–6")/10cm (4")
LOCATION:	Well-drained, gritty soil.
BLOOMS:	May–June
USES:	⌂⚲ Troughs, Scree

atlanticum ZONES 5–9

(Atlas Poppy) Low silvery-green tufts of hairy leaves are a pretty contrast to the soft sherbet-orange flowers. Short lived, but freely self-seeding. Nice scattered in a sunny border.

HEIGHT/SPREAD:	30cm (12")/20cm (8")
LOCATION:	Well-drained soil.
BLOOMS:	May–August
USES:	⌂⚲✂ Borders, Meadows

nudicaule ZONES 2–9

(Iceland Poppy) Tufts of light-green leaves, with cheerful flowers in shades of yellow, orange, red, pink, or white, sometimes strikingly bicoloured. Long blooming season. Usually biennial but freely self-seeding. Many strains exist, each with a slightly different range of colours. Good for cutting if picked in bud. Moderately drought-tolerant.

HEIGHT/SPREAD:	30–45cm (12–18")/30cm (12")
LOCATION:	Average well-drained soil.
BLOOMS:	May–October
USES:	⌂⚲✂✶ Borders, Walls

orientale ZONES 2–9

(Oriental Poppy) Large clumps of coarse, hairy foliage, producing enormous satiny flowers in late spring. Nice in the border, but because they usually go completely dormant after flowering, plant something nearby that gets bushy in the summer to fill in the gap. There are several good seed strains available in shades of orange, salmon and red, typically with a dark zone or eye in the middle. Many named hybrids also exist; these are propagated from root-cuttings and include both single and double-flowered forms in shades of orange, true pink, white, and deep red, sometimes bicoloured or with exotically fringed petals.

> "The two perennials that speak to me most strongly of early summer are lupins and oriental poppies. 'What about bearded irises?' you may well ask. Sad to say, I have grown out of them."
> —Christopher Lloyd, *Christopher Lloyd's Flower Garden*

HEIGHT/SPREAD:	75–100cm (30–40")/60cm (24")
LOCATION:	Well-drained soil, preferably sandy loam.
BLOOMS:	May–June
USES:	✂ Borders

'Allegro' Orange-scarlet blooms, compact. Seed strain. HEIGHT: 45–60cm (18–24")

'Beauty of Livermere' Deep ox-blood red. Seed strain.

'Brilliant' Vivid, fiery scarlet. Seed strain.

'Carneum' Shades of salmon to flesh pink. Seed strain.

'Doubloon' Early blooming double orange.

'Perry's White' Large white flowers, black base spots.

'Picotee' Wide salmon-pink edges with a white base.

PELTIPHYLLUM
(Umbrella Plant) ☀◐

peltatum ZONES 5–9

(now correctly *Darmera peltata*) An interesting water-side plant, with large round rhubarb-like leaves that form a wide clump. Bizarre clusters of pink flowers appear before the leaves in early spring. In effect like a small *Gunnera* but far hardier. This is a wildflower native to southern Oregon.

Paeonia lactiflora × 'Okinawa'

Paeonia tenuifolia

Papaver nudicaule

Papaver orientale 'Carneum'

Penstemon digitalis 'Husker Red'

Penstemon fruticosus 'Purple Haze'

Penstemon × 'King George'

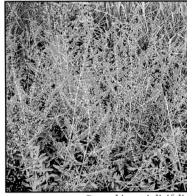

Perovskia atriplicifolia

HEIGHT/SPREAD:	90–120cm (3–4')/90cm (3')
LOCATION:	Rich, constantly moist soil.
BLOOMS:	April–May
USES:	Waterside, Specimen

PENSTEMON
(Beard-Tongue) ☀

A large and diverse group of plants, mostly wild-flowers native to areas of North America with warm arid summers. Their showy, tubular flowers are usually held above the foliage in upright spikes. Taller types make excellent cut-flowers. Penstemon cannot tolerate wet feet, so very good drainage is a basic requirement for all types, especially so for the lower alpine species.

barbatus Hybrids   ZONES 3–9
These are among the hardiest *Penstemon* available. Plants typically form a low mound of green foliage, with spikes of trumpet flowers rising above in early summer. Taller varieties are quite good for cutting. Divide plants every other year to keep them vigorous. Moderately drought and heat tolerant.

SPREAD:	30cm (12")
LOCATION:	Average well-drained soil.
BLOOMS:	June–August
USES:	✂ ➤ 🌸 Borders, Wildflower gardens

'**Coccineus**' Deep scarlet-red flowers. HEIGHT: 30–45cm (12–18")

'**Elfin Pink**' Compact spikes of clear pink flowers. Good companion to 'Prairie Dusk', and equally as reliable. HEIGHT: 30–45cm (12–18")

'**Hyacinth Mix**' The hardiest type, this seed strain produces compact clumps of flowers in a mixture of blue, lilac, pink, and scarlet. HEIGHT: 30cm (12")

'**Prairie Dusk**' Strong stems of vivid purple flowers over a long season. Very effective in combination with *Achillea* 'Moonshine'. HEIGHT: 60cm (24")

digitalis 'Husker Red'   ZONES 4–9
A recent selection from the University of Nebraska. Attractive upright clumps of maroon-red foliage are a wonderful contrast in the border, retaining their colour all season long. Flowers are very pale pink, held on stems well above the leaves. Especially effective when mass planted. This is sure to become a popular variety in the near future. Selected as the 1996 PERENNIAL PLANT OF THE YEAR by the Perennial Plant Association.

HEIGHT/SPREAD:	75–90cm (30–36")/30cm (12")
LOCATION:	Average well-drained soil.
BLOOMS:	July–August
USES:	✂ Wildflower, Borders, Massing

fruticosus 'Purple Haze'   ZONES 4–9
Introduced by the Native Plant Program at the U.B.C. Botanical Garden in 1992, this sub-shrub is native to the hot interior of British Columbia. Plants are smothered with showy lilac-purple flowers for several weeks in late spring. Foliage is evergreen, the plant forming a low bushy mound that will cascade nicely over banks and walls. Suitable for rock gardens or edging. This plant will not be happy in heavy wet soils or with regular overhead irrigation. Very drought-tolerant. Registered with the Canadian Ornamental Plant Foundation.

HEIGHT/SPREAD:	20cm (8")/60cm (24")
LOCATION:	Very well-drained soil.
BLOOMS:	May–June
USES:	▲△⋀⋁▲➤🌸 Wildflower, Walls, Slopes

Hybrids   ZONES 8–9
(Hybrid Beard-tongue) The showiest varieties by far, these put on a terrific display of colour in the summer and fall border. Plants form a bushy upright clump, bearing several spikes of large trumpet flowers. Used in England for massed bedding. Unfortunately they are not reliably hardy and should be mulched even in mild winter areas, or treated as bedding annuals. Excellent in pots and tubs. Many named forms have been selected.

SPREAD:	45cm (18")
LOCATION:	Average well-drained soil.
BLOOMS:	June–October
USES:	✂◀🌱 Borders, Massing

'**Garnet**' Wine red flowers. HEIGHT: 50cm (20")

'**King George**' Salmon-red with a white throat. HEIGHT: 60cm (24")

'**Sour Grapes**' Large, pale purple flowers. HEIGHT: 70cm (28")

PEROVSKIA
(Russian Sage) ☀

atriplicifolia   ZONES 5–9
Chosen as the 1995 PERENNIAL PLANT OF THE YEAR by the Perennial Plant Association. Not really a sage at all, *Perovskia* forms an upright bush of fine-textured grey-green leaves that are pleasantly fragrant when rubbed. The plant becomes a haze of lavender blue by mid-summer when spikes of tiny flowers appear. These continue to bloom well into the fall, contrasting beautifully with the various late-blooming Rudbeckias and other daisies in bloom then. Russian Sage is an excellent filler plant for the border, but can also make an effective display when mass planted on its own, or featured with waving ornamental grasses. Some of the woody stem must be left each year for new shoots to develop in the spring; prune plants back to 15cm (6") in late fall or early spring. Moderately drought-tolerant.

HEIGHT/SPREAD:	90–150cm (3–5')/60cm (2')
LOCATION:	Well-drained soil. Dislikes winter wet.
BLOOMS:	July–September
USES:	✂🌸 Borders, Massing

PERSICARIA see POLYGONUM

PETASITES
(Butterbur) ☀◐

japonicus 'Giganteus'   ZONES 4–9
(Giant Japanese Butterbur) A monster plant for the waterside, bearing enormous rounded leaves, not unlike rhubarb. Greenish flowers appear on naked stems in very early spring. This is a bold textural plant that looks great beside a pond or stream. Place carefully, as this is an aggressive spreader and difficult to eradicate. The leaf-stems are edible, if you are adventurous!

HEIGHT/SPREAD:	120–180cm (4–6')/120cm (4')
LOCATION:	Moist to wet soil, even in shallow water.
BLOOMS:	March–April
USES:	Waterside specimen

PETRORHAGIA see TUNICA

PHLOX
(Phlox) ☀◐

Among the most popular of garden perennials, these range in form from low creeping alpines to tall border plants. The flowers of most types have a heavy, sweet perfume, so the taller varieties are especially valued for cutting. All are selections or hybrids of native North American wildflowers.

borealis   ZONES 1–9
(Arctic Phlox) Very similar to a pink-flowered *P. subulata*, but sturdier and more reliable. Could be used as a groundcover for small areas or in the rock garden. Forms a low mat of evergreen leaves, studded with small pink flowers in spring. Fairly drought-tolerant. Prefers full sun.

HEIGHT/SPREAD:	5–10cm (2–4″)/30cm (12″)
LOCATION:	Well-drained soil.
BLOOMS:	April–May
USES:	△〜▲▼ᕷ Walls, Edging

× chattahoochee   ZONES 4–9

(Chattahoochee Phlox) A chance hybrid found growing wild in northern Florida. This is an excellent newer variety suited to a lightly shaded woodland setting, but does equally well in full sun. Low, bushy plants are covered in brilliant blue flowers with a maroon-purple eye. Trim plants back lightly after flowering. May prove to be hardier.

HEIGHT/SPREAD:	15–25cm (6–10″)/30cm (12″)
LOCATION:	Prefers a rich, moist soil.
BLOOMS:	April–June
USES:	△▼ Edging, Woodland gardens

divaricata   ZONES 3–9

(Woodland Phlox) These medium-sized clumps are ideal for edging along a shady border. Loose clusters of flowers appear in spring. Nice groundcover under shrubs or trees, preferring partial shade. Shear plants lightly after blooming. There are a few named colour selections.

> "One of the prettiest flowers of April is the wild blue phlox. Along with the Virginia bluebell, it is one of the handsomest and showiest of American wildflowers." —Henry Mitchell, *One Man's Garden*

HEIGHT/SPREAD:	30cm (12″)/30cm (12″)
LOCATION:	Moist, rich woodland soil.
BLOOMS:	April–June
USES:	△〜✂ Woodland gardens

'Fuller's White' Strong stems of clear white flowers. Freely flowering.

laphamii Dark blue flowers.

'Louisiana' Purple-blue flowers with a dark eye. Early.

douglasii   ZONES 2–9

These are dwarf creepers, similar to *P. subulata* but even more compact, forming a dense, low carpet of evergreen leaves smothered with flowers in spring. Good choice for rock gardens or edging. More resistant to downy mildew and other disease problems that so often bother the *subulata* varieties. Best in full sun. Fairly drought-tolerant.

HEIGHT/SPREAD:	5–10cm (2–4″)/30cm (12″)
LOCATION:	Well-drained soil.
BLOOMS:	April–May
USES:	△〜▲▼ᕷ Edging, Scree

'Crackerjack' Large flowers, intense carmine-red. Good grower!

'Red Admiral' Bright rose red flowers.

'Rose Cushion' Delicate soft baby pink. Very unusual.

maculata Hybrids   ZONES 3–9

(Meadow Phlox) This group of hybrid Phlox is often recommended as a substitute for Summer Phlox in areas where powdery mildew is a problem. Plants have a similar upright habit, but the foliage is darker green and the cone-shaped flower heads appear a little bit earlier. Flowers are fragrant, excellent for cutting. Though mildew-resistance is excellent, the choice of colours is more limited.

HEIGHT/SPREAD:	90cm (3′)/60cm (2′)
LOCATION:	Average to moist well-drained soil.
BLOOMS:	June–August
USES:	✂ Borders, Meadow gardens

'Alpha' Rose-pink flowers with a darker eye.

'Miss Lingard' Large heads of pure white flowers; early-blooming, extremely fragrant. Often classified as *P. carolina*.

'Rosalinde' Carmine-pink flowers.

paniculata   ZONES 3–9

(Summer Phlox, Garden Phlox) These luxurious panicles of bright flowers can be spectacular in the summer border.

The many named selections offer a wide choice of colours to match any border scheme. Shorter plants should be placed in front of Summer Phlox, to hide the withering lower leaves at blooming time. Superb cut flowers.

Powdery mildew is often a problem, see the section on PESTS & DISEASES for some ideas on how to control it. Simply growing Summer Phlox on a moist site or keeping it well watered will help to prevent mildew. Fertilize in early spring and again just before flowering as these are heavy feeders. Plants should be divided about every three years.

A great number of named cultivars have been developed over the years. These range in colour from pink through salmon, orange and red, to blue, mauve-purple and white. Some selections have a contrasting eye in the centre of each flower. As many growers sell Summer Phlox only by colour, it might be wise to select those plants in flower to be sure of the exact shade. A sampling of modern named varieties follows.

HEIGHT/SPREAD:	60–120cm (2–4′)/60–75cm (24–30″)
LOCATION:	Rich, moist well-drained soil.
BLOOMS:	July–September
USES:	✂〜▼ Wildflower, Borders

'Blue Boy' Bluish-mauve flowers, the closest to true blue. HEIGHT: 100cm (40″)

'David' A new white variety with very fragrant flowers, highly mildew resistant. HEIGHT: 90–100cm (36–40″)

'Dodo Hanbury Forbes' Large trusses, pure pink with a red eye. HEIGHT: 90cm (36″)

'Eva Cullum' Large heads, clear pink flowers with a dark red eye. Compact habit. Selected by Alan Bloom of Bressingham Gardens. HEIGHT: 60–75cm (24–30″)

'Franz Schubert' Lilac-blue flowers with a darker eye. Another long-blooming Alan Bloom selection. HEIGHT: 90cm (36″)

'Fuchsia' Deep purple-blue. HEIGHT: 90cm (36″)

'Juliet' Pale-pink flowers, compact. HEIGHT: 60cm (24″)

'Orange Perfection' The closest to a true orange. HEIGHT: 90cm (36″)

'Mt. Fujiyama' Excellent late-blooming white. HEIGHT: 90cm (36″)

'Norah Leigh' Extremely difficult-to-obtain variety, the leaves are strongly variegated with cream and green. Flowers are pale lilac purple. Not particularly vigorous. HEIGHT: 75cm (30″)

'Prime Minister' Pure white with a red eye. HEIGHT: 90cm (36″)

'Starfire' Cherry-red flowers, bronzy green foliage. HEIGHT: 90cm (36″)

'The King' Very deep wine purple, large trusses. HEIGHT: 60–75cm (24–30″)

× procumbens 'Variegata'   ZONES 3–9

An outstanding variety, the foliage is strongly variegated with creamy-yellow and green. Mauve-pink flowers are held in upright clusters. A little gem for the woodland or rock garden, preferring part shade.

HEIGHT/SPREAD:	20cm (8″)/30cm (12″)
LOCATION:	Well-drained soil.
BLOOMS:	April–May
USES:	△▲▼ Woodland garden

× 'Spring Delight'   ZONES 3–9

A late-spring blooming hybrid of medium height, with many clusters of rose-pink flowers. Vigorous habit, best in partial shade. Good for cutting.

HEIGHT/SPREAD:	30–50cm (12–16″)/30cm (12″)
LOCATION:	Average well-drained soil.
BLOOMS:	May–June
USES:	✂ Borders, Edging

Phlox divaricata laphamii

Phlox douglasii 'Red Admiral'

Phlox paniculata (Mixed Bed)

Phlox × procumbens 'Variegata'

Phlox subulata 'Emerald Blue'

Phygelius capensis

Physalis alkekengi

Physostegia virginiana 'Variegata'

stolonifera **ZONES 2-9**

(Creeping Phlox) A dense evergreen groundcover, tolerant of heavy shade. Small but showy clusters of flowers appear in late spring. Excellent under shrubs. Very different from the other spring-blooming varieties. Keep out of full sun. A former *Perennial Plant of the Year.*

HEIGHT/SPREAD: 15–30cm (6–12″)/30cm (12″)
LOCATION: Rich, moist well-drained soil.
BLOOMS: April–May
USES: Edging, Woodland gardens

'Blue Ridge' Lilac-blue flowers.

'Bruce's White' White flowers with a yellow eye.

'Pink Ridge' Dark mauve-pink flowers.

'Sherwood Purple' Good strong purple-blue.

subulata **ZONES 2-9**

(Moss Phlox, Creeping Phlox) Low mats of evergreen leaves are smothered with flowers in spring. Very popular rock garden and edging plants. Not recommended as a groundcover for large areas as the plants thin out too quickly. Divide clumps every other year to maintain vigour. Shear plants lightly after blooming. Downy mildew is a common problem and is difficult to prevent; choosing a sunny well-drained site to begin with will help in avoiding it. Fairly drought-tolerant. Several colour selections are commonly available.

HEIGHT/SPREAD: 5–15cm (2–6″)/30–45cm (12–18″)
LOCATION: Well-drained soil.
BLOOMS: April–May
USES: Edging, Walls

'Atropurpurea' Rosy-red flowers.

'Benita' Lilac blue with a darker eye.

'Candy Stripes' A new variety with very attractive flowers; white and rose-pink stripes, with a crimson eye.

'Emerald Blue' Pale lilac-blue flowers. Excellent foliage.

'Laura' Pale pink with a darker eye.

'Marjorie' Dark pink with a red eye.

'Rosette' Very compact and distinctly mound-forming. Rose-pink flowers.

'Snow Queen' The best of the whites. Clear white flowers and a vigorous habit.

PHYGELIUS
(Cape Fuchsia)

Upright, bushy plants from South Africa, with tubular flowers similar to *Fuchsia.* They are perennial shrubs at the West coast, but also worth trying outdoors in the milder parts of Zone 6. Plants should be cut back hard to 15cm (6″) in early spring, and pinching occasionally through the season will maintain a more compact and bushy habit. Cuttings taken in fall will root easily in a greenhouse or under lights, providing a backup to plants wintering outside. These make excellent container plants for the patio or deck. Good for cutting.

aequalis 'Yellow Trumpet' **ZONES 7-9**

(Yellow Cape Fuchsia) Clusters of soft yellow hanging bells appear throughout the summer and fall.

HEIGHT/SPREAD: 90cm (3′)/45–60cm (18–24″)
LOCATION: Average to moist well-drained soil.
BLOOMS: July–September
USES: Borders, Tubs

capensis **ZONES 7-9**

(Orange Cape Fuchsia) Large orange-red flowers with a yellow throat. Reported to be slightly hardier. If left to get shrubby this may grow as tall as six or eight feet.

HEIGHT/SPREAD: 90cm (3′)/45–60cm (18–24″)
LOCATION: Average to moist well-drained soil.
BLOOMS: July–September
USES: Borders, Tubs

PHYSALIS
(Chinese Lantern)

alkekengi **ZONES 2-9**

Showy scarlet-orange inflated pods appear in September, and are useful for dried arrangements. Flowers are insignificant. An aggressive spreader, best kept in the cutting garden or back lane, or allowed to naturalize at the edge of a woodland. Fertilize yearly for good-quality lanterns. For a little fun try tucking a vase full of the cut lantern stems next to a large gold-leaved hosta!

HEIGHT/SPREAD: 60–90cm (2–3′)/60cm (2′)
LOCATION: Moist but well-drained soil.
USES: Cutting gardens, *Not* in borders

PHYSOSTEGIA
(Obedient Plant)

virginiana **ZONES 2-9**

Another native North American wildflower. Tall wand-like spikes of flowers appear in midsummer, the common name comes from the fact that the individual flowers in the spikes will stay wherever you move them. Very useful as a background plant in the border or wild garden. Excellent cut flowers. These form a large clump that may be inclined to spread, but can be easily controlled with an edging spade. Several colour selections exist.

"If you have nothing else to do, you can reposition the individual flowers, which are attached to their stems by the botanical equivalent of a ball-and-socket joint…" —Patrick Lima, *The Harrowsmith Perennial Garden*

SPREAD: 60cm (24″)
LOCATION: Prefers a rich moist soil.
BLOOMS: July–September
USES: Borders, Woodland gardens

'Pink Bouquet' Bright pink flowers. HEIGHT: 90–120cm (3–4′)

'Summer Snow' Pure white flowers. Slower spreading. HEIGHT: 60–75cm (24–30″)

'Variegata' Green leaves are heavily blotched with cream. Lilac flowers. Much less aggressive, very choice! HEIGHT: 60–90cm (2–3′)

PLATYCODON
(Balloon Flower)

grandiflorus

These are a real novelty in the garden when their inflated buds actually "pop" open into star-shaped flowers. The long-lived plants form an upright clump in the border that seldom needs dividing, with flowers available in shades of blue, pink or white. Because Balloon Flowers are very slow to make an appearance in spring they can be easily damaged by early weeding or digging; you can easily mark the spot by planting crocuses or other small bulbs underneath them.

HEIGHT/SPREAD: 60–75cm (24–30″)/60cm (24″)
LOCATION: Average well-drained soil.
BLOOMS: June–August
USES: Borders

POLEMONIUM
(Jacob's Ladder) ☼●

caeruleum   ZONES 2–9

These form lush clumps of fresh green leaves that can easily be mistaken for some kind of fern. Later in the spring the upright stems appear, topped with clusters of small bright blue or white bell-shaped flowers. Showy in the shade garden. Can be a prolific self-seeder unless the fading flower stems are removed.

HEIGHT/SPREAD:	45–90cm (18–36")/30cm (12")
LOCATION:	Average to moist soil.
BLOOMS:	May–July
USES:	✄◁▲ Borders, Woodland gardens

POLYGONATUM
(Solomon's Seal) ☽●

Their graceful, arching stems add an exotic touch to the shade garden and are often described as being architectural. Delicate creamy bell flowers hang from the stems in late spring to be followed later by black berries. Solomon's Seal are the perfect woodland companions to Hostas, Astilbes, and ferns. These are highly regarded for cutting by flower arrangers. New plantings may take a year or two to become established.

odoratum 'Variegatum'   ZONES 2–9

(Fragrant Solomon's Seal) Green leaves are edged with broad creamy-white stripes. Fragrant waxy bells appear in spring, followed by black berries. Brightens up a shady site. Slow to establish.

HEIGHT/SPREAD:	60cm (24")/30cm (12")
LOCATION:	Moist woodland soil.
BLOOMS:	May–June
USES:	△ Borders, Woodland gardens

commutatum   ZONES 3–9

(Giant Solomon's Seal) (= *P. giganteum*) These bold, arching stems of green leaves can form a wide clump. This species is a North American wildflower that eventually needs lots of space or regular division.

HEIGHT/SPREAD:	90–120cm (3–4')/60–90cm (2–3')
LOCATION:	Moist woodland soil.
BLOOMS:	May–June
USES:	✄ Borders, Woodland gardens

POLYGONUM
(Fleece-Flower) ☼ ☽

Many of these varieties are relatively new to North American gardens but can be depended on to create attention with their showy late summer and fall display. They all feature short spikes of pink or red poker flowers, usually held over top of the foliage. Botanists have recently split these into several genera, but we are listing them together for convenience sake, with the currently accepted name in brackets.

affine 'Dimity'   ZONES 3–9

(Dwarf Fleeceflower) (now *Persicaria affinis*) Forms a low carpet of leathery green leaves, turning bronzy-red in fall. Short poker spikes of red flowers fade to pink as they age. A nice groundcover or rock garden plant, appreciating part shade. This form is more reliably perennial than some of the older ones. Raised and introduced by Alan Bloom of Bressingham Gardens. Extremely drought-tolerant.

HEIGHT/SPREAD:	15–20cm (6–8")/30–60cm (12–24")
LOCATION:	Moist to average well-drained soil.
BLOOMS:	June–August
USES:	△⋏ Borders, Edging

amplexicaule   ZONES 5–9

(Mountain Fleece) (now *Persicaria amplexicaulis*) Quite new to North American gardens, these bushy plants are upright, ideal for massed landscape planting but yet not too invasive for the border. They are covered with showy poker flowers from midsummer on. Good choice for difficult wet sites.

> "An amazing plant, in beauty from the end of June until the frost of autumn."
> —Graham Stuart Thomas,
> *Perennial Garden Plants*

HEIGHT/SPREAD:	90–120cm (3–4')/60cm (24")
LOCATION:	Rich moist well-drained soil.
BLOOMS:	June–September
USES:	✄⋏ Massing, Borders, Waterside

'Atrosanguinea' An older selection with good deep red flowers.

'Firetail' Bright salmon-red flowers, larger spikes. Selected by Alan Bloom of Bressingham Gardens.

'Taurus' Rich scarlet-red pokers on a fairly compact bush, excellent for cutting. A new hybrid from Alan Bloom. HEIGHT: 90cm (3').

bistorta 'Superbum'   ZONES 3–9

(Bistort) (now *Persicaria bistorta*) Large bright-pink spikes are held well above the dense green foliage. Another good perennial for mass planting, or in the border. Spreading but not invasive. Especially good for cutting.

HEIGHT/SPREAD:	75cm (30")/60cm (24")
LOCATION:	Average to moist well-drained soil.
BLOOMS:	June–August
USES:	✄ Borders, Massing

cuspidatum 'Compactum'   ZONES 3–9

(Japanese Fleeceflower) (now *Fallopia japonica* 'Compacta') A spreading groundcover with fairly invasive tendencies, best used for extensive massed plantings around shrubs or trees, or in tubs where it can be contained. Plants form an upright bushy green clump, with attractive beet-red stems and short spikes of rose-red flowers that are half hidden among the leathery leaves, followed by crimson seedheads. Foliage often has excellent red fall colour. Keep this out of the border.

HEIGHT/SPREAD:	60cm (24")/60cm (24")
LOCATION:	Average to moist well-drained soil.
BLOOMS:	August–September
USES:	⋏☙ Shrub borders, Median plantings

POTENTILLA
(Cinquefoil) ☼

Although the Shrubby Cinquefoils are familiar landscape plants, these herbaceous types are not nearly so well known. Their wild-rose shaped flowers appear in shades of red, orange, yellow, or white. Most are happy in average sunny border conditions.

fragiformis   ZONES 2–9

(Woolly Cinquefoil) (= *P. megalantha*) Clumps of beautiful felty green strawberry-shaped leaves. Golden-yellow flowers are in clusters, blooming in early summer. Good rockery or edging plant. Excellent showy foliage.

HEIGHT/SPREAD:	30cm (12")/30cm (12")
LOCATION:	Average well-drained soil.
BLOOMS:	May–June
USES:	△☙ Borders, Edging

nepalensis 'Miss Willmott'   ZONES 2–9

Scarlet-red single flowers, with a lighter pink centre. Good front-of-the-border or edging plant. Shear plants back after their first flush of bloom to keep them tidy and to encourage a second flush in the fall.

HEIGHT/SPREAD:	30cm (12")/30cm (12")
LOCATION:	Average well-drained soil.
BLOOMS:	June–September
USES:	△ Borders, Edging

Polygonatum odoratum 'Variegatum'

Polygonum amplexicaule 'Atrosanguinea'

Polygonum cuspidatum 'Compactum'

Potentilla nepalensis 'Miss Willmott'

Potentilla verna 'Nana'

Primula auricula

Primula × pruhoniciana 'Wanda'

Primula vialii

verna 'Nana'   ZONES 3–9

(Alpine Cinquefoil) A very low, non-spreading rockery plant. Single yellow buttercup flowers nestle on a compact evergreen mound. Very showy. Fairly drought-tolerant. This name is in dispute, the botanists favouring either *P. tabernaemontani* or *P. neumanniana*.

HEIGHT/SPREAD: 10cm (4")/15–30cm (6–12")
LOCATION: Average well-drained soil.
BLOOMS: April–June
USES: △▲▼ᵀ Troughs, Walls

PRATIA
(Creeping Pratia) ☀☼

angulata   ZONES 7–9

Low creeping carpet of evergreen leaves. Starry white flowers appear in spring and summer, followed by dark purple berries. Excellent between paving stones, in the rockery, or as a lawn substitute over a small area. Reliably hardy only in milder areas. From New Zealand.

HEIGHT/SPREAD: 5–15cm (2–6")/30cm (12")
LOCATION: Rich moist soil.
BLOOMS: May–September
USES: △⋀▲

PRIMULA
(Primrose) ☼

Primrose flowers are a true sign of spring, associating well with all sorts of flowering bulbs. They are moisture-lovers, and seem to do best in cooler climates, particularly in coastal areas. Where winters are severe apply a thick mulch in late fall. Certain species are even hardy on the prairies.

> "No spring perennials bloom as long—
> a full five weeks on average—and no
> perennials at all, with the exception of
> bearded irises, display as wide and
> lovely a colour range as primroses." —
> Patrick Lima, *The Harrowsmith
> Perennial Garden*

auricula Hybrids   ZONES 2–9

(Auricula Primrose) Rosettes of waxy, evergreen leaves bear clusters of flowers in muted shades of yellow, mauve, pink, red and wine, usually with a contrasting eye. These were extremely popular in Victorian England where hundreds of named varieties were selected and collected.

HEIGHT/SPREAD: 15–20cm (6–8")/20–30cm (8–12")
LOCATION: Well-drained moist soil.
BLOOMS: March–May
USES: △▲⋇▼ Edging, Borders

× bullesiana   ZONES 4–9

(Hybrid Candelabra Primrose) A delightful hybrid group, generally grown from seed, that gives a mixture of yellow, violet and red shades. Flowers are held in whorls on upright stems. These are definitely vigorous moisture lovers.

HEIGHT/SPREAD: 50cm (20")/25cm (10")
LOCATION: Rich moist soil.
BLOOMS: June–August
USES: ⋇⋖△ Borders, Waterside

denticulata   ZONES 2–9

(Drumstick Primrose) Flowers are in a ball-shaped cluster, in shades of blue, lilac, pink, and white. These are vigorous, durable and tough garden plants; hardy almost anywhere with reliable snow cover or a light mulch.

HEIGHT/SPREAD: 30cm (12")/25cm (10")
LOCATION: Rich moist soil.
BLOOMS: March–May
USES   ⋇⋖△ Borders, Woodland gardens

florindae   ZONES 3–9

(Himalayan Cowslip) A late-blooming Primrose, sending up large umbels of fragrant, dangling yellow or orange flowers in the summer. Excellent for cutting. Long-lived if planted in a good moist site.

HEIGHT/SPREAD: 60–90cm (2–3')/30–60cm (1–2')
LOCATION: Rich moist to wet soil.
BLOOMS: June–August
USES: ⋇ Borders, Waterside

japonica   ZONES 5–9

(Japanese Primrose) A Candelabra-flowered type, with several whorls of red, pink or white blossoms on each upright stem. Leaves form a low, cabbage-like clump of fresh green. This species prefers a constantly moist soil, perhaps beside a stream or pond, but will adapt to a semi-shaded border.

HEIGHT/SPREAD: 30–60cm (12–24")/30cm (12")
LOCATION: Rich moist soil.
BLOOMS: May–July
USES: ⋇⋖△ Borders, Woodland gardens

× pruhoniciana 'Wanda'   ZONES 2–9

An extremely popular, very old variety. Magenta-purple flowers smother the bright green leaves in early spring. Perhaps the toughest Primrose of all, the plants quickly form a dense patch. Divide plants every two to three years after blooming.

HEIGHT/SPREAD: 15cm (6")/30cm (12")
LOCATION: Average to moist well-drained soil.
BLOOMS: March–May
USES: △⋀ Edging, Woodland gardens

'Lilac Wanda' A sport with lighter lilac-pink flowers. Not quite so shocking a colour.

'Wanda Hybrid Mix' A special seed-strain offering the same habit and vigour as the original 'Wanda' but in a wider range of colours, including yellow, red, pink and white.

sieboldii   ZONES 4–9

(Japanese Star Primrose) Large clusters of flowers are held above a low rosette of downy leaves in spring. Very showy species. Plants will become dormant and disappear by midsummer. Combines well in a border with taller-growing perennials. Prefers an acidic soil. There are several selections.

HEIGHT/SPREAD: 15–25 (6–9")/15cm (6")
LOCATION: Moist, well-drained soil, preferable acidic.
BLOOMS: April–May
USES: ⋇⋖△ Borders, Woodland gardens.

'Geisha Girl' Clear light pink.

'Mikado' Deep rose-pink.

'Snowflake' Pure white flowers.

vialii   ZONES 3–9

(Chinese Pagoda Primrose) Bizarre-looking rocket-shaped spikes of flowers in a dazzling mauve and scarlet combination. A short-lived summer bloomer, often self seeding when grown in a bright, cool woodland setting.

HEIGHT/SPREAD: 30–60cm (1–2')/20–30cm (8–12")
LOCATION: Moist well-drained soil.
BLOOMS: May–July
USES: ⋇⋖△ Woodland gardens, Borders

WOODLAND JEWELS

Primula vulgaris   ZONES 4–9

RARE DOUBLE ENGLISH PRIMROSES. These charming clusters of fully-double primrose flowers put on a tremendous display over the spring season. Double Primroses have been cherished in English Cottage gardens for centuries. Thanks to modern tissue culture techniques these have been cleaned up of nasty viruses and are once again vigorous, healthy and available to today's gardeners.

As easy to grow as any other hardy *Primula*, these plants need a rich, moist soil with plenty of peat and well rotted manure. Choose a site that is protected from hot afternoon sun and can easily be watered during dry spells. Divide double primroses every two to three years to keep plants young and floriferous.

Gardeners all across the country will rejoice at the opportunity to try these rare and delightful plants that had all but disappeared for so many years.

HEIGHT/SPREAD: 10–15cm (4–6")/20cm (8")
LOCATION: Rich average to moist soil, preferably on the heavy side.
BLOOMS: March–May
USES: ⚎ Borders, Edging

'Alan Robb' Pale apricot.

'April Rose' Deep ruby red.

'Dawn Ansell' Clear white.

'Lilian Harvey' Magenta-pink, flowers like little roses.

'Marianne Davey' Creamy yellow.

'Miss Indigo' Deep purple with a white edge.

'Quaker's Bonnet' Lavender mauve, early. Very dainty.

'Sunshine Susie' Golden-yellow.

PRUNELLA
(Self-heal) ☀☽

grandiflora   ZONES 5–9
(sometimes listed as *P. × webbiana*) Little-known in North American gardens, these add a bright splash to the early summer garden. Short spikes of flowers rise above a low mat of bright green leaves. Best used for edging or in the rock garden. There are a few named selections, the species itself is seldom grown.

HEIGHT/SPREAD: 15–20cm (6–8")/30cm (12")
LOCATION: Average to moist, well-drained soil.
BLOOMS: May–July
USES: ⚎ Edging, Walls, Borders

'Blue Loveliness' or simply 'Loveliness'. Pale lavender-blue flowers.

'Little Red Riding Hood' ('Rotkäppchen') Rosy-red flowers.

'Pink Loveliness' Bright pink flowers.

PULMONARIA
(Lungwort) ☽●

Despite being stuck with such an unfortunate common name, these spring-blooming perennials are anything but unappealing. They create low mounds of handsome leaves, often heavily splotched or dotted with silvery-grey. Clusters of flowers are held above the leaves in various shades, from sky blue through to pink, red, and white. These look at home in a woodland setting, growing very well beneath trees and shrubs. Trim off any tired-looking leaves in very early spring. Any of these combine beautifully with spring-flowering primroses.

angustifolia 'Azurea'   ZONES 3–9
(Blue Lungwort) This form has long been grown in gardens. The unspotted green leaves emerge along with a bright display of pink buds, changing to rich gentian-blue bell flowers. A good choice for massing under shrubs and deciduous trees. Leaves may look a bit tired by the end of summer.

HEIGHT/SPREAD: 30cm (12")/30cm (12")
LOCATION: Rich, moist woodland soil.
BLOOMS: March–May
USES: ⚎ Edging, Massing, Borders

Hybrids   ZONES 3–9
Several newer American hybrids are now becoming available. These have been selected for superior form, leaf colour, mildew resistance and, of course, better flowers. Many more varieties are sure to come out of current breeding programs.

HEIGHT/SPREAD: 30–45cm (12–18")/30cm (12")
LOCATION: Rich, moist woodland soil.
BLOOMS: March–May
USES: ⚎ Edging, Massing, Borders

'Excalibur' Leaves are all silver, with just an edging of dark green. Good mildew resistance. Rosy-purple flowers. U.S. Plant Patent applied for.

'Spilled Milk' Wide leaves, very silvered with a few blotches of green. Compact habit. Flowers begin pink fading to rose.

longifolia   ZONES 3–9
(Joseph and Mary) Leaves are long, narrow and pointed in this species, with showy silver spots. Blooms appear a week or two later than other types, and are held in tight clusters. These usually remain attractive all season long.

HEIGHT/SPREAD: 25cm (10")/30cm (12")
LOCATION: Rich, moist woodland soil.
BLOOMS: March–May
USES: ⚎ Edging, Massing, Borders

'Bertram Anderson' Deep violet-blue flowers.

'Roy Davidson' Lighter blue flowers.

rubra 'Redstart'   ZONES 3–9
(Red Lungwort) This blooms in an unusual deep red shade with flowers appearing earlier than the other species. Foliage is bright green, remaining evergreen in milder areas but not nearly as appealing as the spotted forms. Compact habit.

HEIGHT/SPREAD: 30–45cm (12–18")/30cm (12")
LOCATION: Rich, moist woodland soil.
BLOOMS: March–May
USES: ⚎ Edging, Massing, Borders

saccharata   ZONES 2–9
(Bethlehem Sage) Low green foliage is usually heavily spotted with silver. Clusters of flowers open pink and soon turn to bright blue. Evergreen in milder areas. Still the most popular species.

HEIGHT/SPREAD: 25cm (10")/30cm (12")
LOCATION: Rich, moist woodland soil.
BLOOMS: March–May
USES: ⚎ Edging, Massing, Borders

'Argentea' Leaves are almost totally silver.

'Mrs. Moon' An older variety, heavily spotted with silver.

'Pierre's Pure Pink' Pale salmon-pink, does not change to blue.

'Sissinghurst White' Large white flowers, nice contrast to the blue forms.

PULSATILLA see ANEMONE pulsatilla

PYRETHRUM see CHRYSANTHEMUM coccineum

RAOULIA
(Raoulia) ☀

australis   ZONES 5–9
A little-known alpine from New Zealand. This forms an absolutely flat carpet of grey foliage that will crawl in between and over rocks. An interesting choice for trough gardens and alpine screes. Flowers are tiny and insignificant. Must have perfect drainage.

HEIGHT/SPREAD: 1cm (1/2")/30cm (12")
LOCATION: Very well-drained, gravelly soil.
USES: ⚎ Troughs, Walls, Screes

Primula × 'Sunshine Susie'

Prunella grandiflora 'Little Red Riding Hood'

Primula × 'Miss Indigo'

Pulmonaria saccharata 'Mrs. Moon'

Rodgersia pinnata 'Superba'

Roscoea purpurea procera

Rudbeckia fulgida 'Goldsturm'

Rudbeckia hirta × 'Rustic Mixture'

RHEUM
(Rhubarb) ☀ ☼

There are several ornamental species, all of them related to the common edible back-yard rhubarb, but with more exotic-looking leaves. Impressive specimen plants for moist sites.

× 'Ace of Hearts'   ZONES 4–9

Reasonably compact selection suited even to smaller gardens. Heart-shaped leaves are dark green tinged with crimson. Tall spikes of pale-pink flowers appear in late spring.

HEIGHT/SPREAD: 120cm (4')/90cm (3')
LOCATION: Rich, moist soil.
BLOOMS: May–June
USES: ✄ ❦ Specimen, Borders, Waterside

RODGERSIA
(Rodgersia) ☀ ☼

These make exotic bold-leaved clumps for the waterside or moist woodland areas. Fluffy plumes of flowers rise above in the summer. Unique specimen plants, but slow to establish, preferring the dappled shade of high trees.

aesculifolia   ZONES 3–9

(Fingerleaf Rodgersia) Leaves are large and shaped like those of the horse chestnut, dark green with some bronzy overtones. The creamy-white flowers are held above in a wide airy panicle, blooming later than the other species.

HEIGHT/SPREAD: 90cm (3')/60–90cm (2–3')
LOCATION: Rich, moist soil.
BLOOMS: July–August
USES: ✄ Dried Flower, Borders, Waterside

pinnata   ZONES 4–9

(Featherleaf Rodgersia) Large upright clumps of compound leaves. Large heads of flowers are held well above the foliage. Both the flowers and showy red seed heads are interesting for cutting.

HEIGHT/SPREAD: 90–120cm (3–4')/60–90cm (2–3')
LOCATION: Rich, moist soil.
BLOOMS: June–July
USES: ✄ Dried Flower, Borders, Waterside

'Elegans' Showy display of creamy white flowers.

'Superba' Foliage is tinged with purple, rose-pink flower heads. Considered by some to be the separate species *R. henrici*.

tabularis   ZONES 3–9

(Shieldleaf Rodgersia) (= *Astilboides tabularis*) Very large round umbrella-like leaves, not compound like the other varieties. Big plumes of creamy flowers resembling an Astilbe.

HEIGHT/SPREAD: 90–120cm (3–4')/60–90cm (2–3')
LOCATION: Rich, moist soil.
BLOOMS: June–July
USES: ✄ Dried Flower, Borders, Waterside

ROSCOEA
(Roscoea) ☀ ☼

Exotic plants in the Ginger family, from the Himalayas. They bear short spikes of orchid-like flowers. The roots are easily stored for the winter like a Dahlia, or plants can be overwintered outdoors in milder regions, although a thick mulch is recommended. Best in bright woodland conditions.

cautleoides 'Kew Beauty'   ZONES 6–9

(Yellow Roscoea) Blue-green sword-shaped leaves. Large primrose-yellow flowers make an attractive display.

HEIGHT/SPREAD: 30–45cm (12–18")/30cm (12")
LOCATION: Rich, moist woodland soil.
BLOOMS: June–August
USES: ✄◣❦ Borders, Woodland gardens.

purpurea procera   ZONES 6–9

(Purple Roscoea) Arching green leaves and large purplish-violet flowers. A vigorous form.

HEIGHT/SPREAD: 30–45cm (12–18")/30cm (12")
LOCATION: Rich, moist woodland soil.
BLOOMS: June–August
USES: ✄◣❦ Borders, Woodland gardens

RUDBECKIA
(Cone-flower, Gloriosa Daisy) ☀

For a long display of bright colour in the late summer border it is hard to beat this tough group of plants, all of them descending from native North American wildflower species. The name "Black-eyed Susan" describes these coneflowers well, their large golden daisies centred with a deep brown or black eye. All varieties prefer a warm sunny location with rich moist soil. Superb cutting flowers, some also have attractive seed-heads for drying.

hirta Hybrids   ZONES 5–9

(Gloriosa Daisy) More or less biennial, these hybrids are best treated as self-seeding annuals in most regions. Their large flowers put on a constant display from midsummer to very late fall, and they will grow in hot locations with only the occasional deep soaking. Excellent as filler plants in the summer border, also a good choice for containers. Some unusual deep bronze colours are to be found among the modern tetraploid seed strains. Very drought-tolerant.

> "If I were starting a garden from scratch in a sunny spot, wanted bright color quickly, needed a steady source of excellent cut flowers, and had no budget to speak of, there's no question about what I would plant—the hybrid rudbeckias called gloriosa daisies." — Allen Lacy, *The Garden in Autumn*

HEIGHT/SPREAD: 45–90cm (18–36")/30cm (12")
LOCATION: Average to moist well-drained soil.
BLOOMS: July–October
USES: ✄❦✤❦ Borders, Massing

'Double Gold' Extra-full golden-yellow flowers. The original Gloriosa Daisy. HEIGHT: 75–90cm (30–36")

'Irish Eyes' Single yellow flowers with green eyes. Charming selection. HEIGHT: 75cm (30")

'Rustic Mixture' Compact mixture of singles, in yellow, orange, bronze and deep, rich mahogany.

fulgida 'Goldsturm'   ZONES 3–9

The best of the Coneflowers and still ranking among the best top ten perennials of all time! Compact plants are covered with deep orange-yellow brown-centred flowers for many weeks. Especially popular for mass planting with ornamental grasses and *Sedum* 'Autumn Joy'. Reliable and long-lived.

HEIGHT/SPREAD: 45–60cm (18–24")/45cm (18")
LOCATION: Average to moist well-drained soil.
BLOOMS: July–October
USES: ✄❦ Borders, Massing

laciniata 'Goldquelle'   ZONES 2–9

(Golden Fountain Coneflower) This is a compact, slower spreading version of the old-fashioned 'Golden Glow' with double chrome-yellow daisies held on strong, self-supporting stems. An outstanding cut flower, and reliable border perennial. Deadheading will encourage plants to continue flowering.

HEIGHT/SPREAD: 90–100cm (36–40")/60cm (24")
LOCATION: Average to moist well-drained soil.
BLOOMS: July–September
USES: ✄ Borders

maxima   ZONES 6–9

(Giant Coneflower) This native of the southern states is quite new to gardens. Plants first make a beautiful clump of powdery-blue basal leaves; then tall stems of drooping black-eyed Susan flowers appear in midsummer, making this a double-use plant. May prove to be hardy in colder regions. Good for cutting. Worth growing for the blue leaves alone!

> "There are many rudbeckias with yellow flowers and black centres, but there is nothing like this one." —Graham Stuart Thomas, *Perennial Garden Plants*

HEIGHT/SPREAD:	1.8–2.1m (6–7′)/60cm (2′)
LOCATION:	Prefers a deep, rich moist soil.
BLOOMS:	July–September
USES:	✂ Specimen, Borders

nitida 'Herbstsonne'   ZONES 2–9

(Autumn Sun Coneflower) This has been aptly described as "the Godzilla of Coneflowers," forming an enormous upright clump best suited to the back of a large border. The flowers are huge lemon-yellow daisies with drooping petals. Excellent for cutting. Appreciates a moist site. Long-lived.

HEIGHT/SPREAD:	1.5–2.4m (5–8′)/90cm (3′)
LOCATION:	Moist to average well-drained soil.
BLOOMS:	July–October
USES:	✂🦋 Borders, Specimen, Waterside

RUTA
(Rue) ☀

graveolens 'Curly Girl'   ZONES 4–9

Used as a herb since medieval times, Rue has always been appreciated for its ferny blue-green foliage. This especially dense and compact variety is a nice foliage accent for the front of a border, and can also be grown as a low hedge. A definite improvement over the species. Shy to flower. Clip plants back to 15cm (6″) in early spring if they get leggy. Evergreen in Zones 7–9. Fairly drought-tolerant.

HEIGHT/SPREAD:	30–40cm (12–16″)/30cm (12″)
LOCATION:	Well-drained soil.
BLOOMS:	July–August
USES:	▲▼🌿 Herb gardens, Borders

SAGINA
(Pearl Wort) ☀◐

subulata   ZONES 4–9

(Irish Moss) Creeping moss-like groundcover for small areas, sometimes used as a lawn substitute. Also nice between paving stones or in the rock garden. The bright green foliage is studded with tiny white flowers in summer. Evergreen in mild climates. Keep this out of hot afternoon sun. 'Aurea' (Scotch Moss) has neon bright golden-yellow leaves.

HEIGHT/SPREAD:	2cm (1″)/30cm (12″)
LOCATION:	Prefers a moist well-drained soil.
BLOOMS:	June–August
USES:	△〰▲▼ Walls, Between flagstones

SALVIA
(Perennial Salvia, Sage) ☀

Some of these are valued for their long summer display of flowers, others more for their handsome foliage. Salvia is a large and diverse group of hardy and tender perennials that includes the familiar Common Sage and its many colour varieties (see HERBS). Almost all of these appreciate a warm sunny site and are fairly drought-tolerant. Salvias are currently gaining wide interest.

argentea   ZONES 5–9

(Silver Sage) An unusual foliage plant, valued for its intensely silver, fuzzy leaves that are arranged in a low rosette. Spikes of yellowish flowers will rise above to about 120cm (4′) but these are often removed. Plants are biennial or short-lived perennials. Place this towards the front of the border where the impressive leaves can be easily viewed.

HEIGHT/SPREAD:	30–45cm (12–18″)/40cm (16″)
LOCATION:	Needs a well-drained soil.
BLOOMS:	June–July
USES:	▼▲ Specimen, Borders

azurea 'Grandiflora'   ZONES 5–9

(Azure Sage) (= *S. pitcheri*) Tall branching spikes of bright clear blue in late summer and fall. A native of the southeastern U.S., tolerant of heat and humidity. These are fairly tall and may require staking. Some say this is the best hardy Salvia of all.

HEIGHT/SPREAD:	90–120cm (3–4′)/45cm (18″)
LOCATION:	Average well-drained soil.
BLOOMS:	August–October
USES:	✂ Wildflower, Borders, Meadows

haematodes 'Lye End'   ZONES 5–9

(Meadow Clary) Branching stems with spikes of deep lavender-blue flowers continue to appear through the summer, held well above the low foliage. Especially good for cutting. These are short-lived and should be encouraged to self seed.

HEIGHT/SPREAD:	90cm (36″)/45cm (18″)
LOCATION:	Average well-drained soil.
BLOOMS:	June–August
USES:	✂ Borders, Meadows

officinalis 'Berggarten'   ZONES 4–9

(Common Sage) A newer selection from Germany, featuring unusually large, rounded leaves in the classic sage-green tone. Serves double duty as both a border perennial and an herb. Spikes of violet flowers appear in summer. Makes good foliage for floral design. Fragrant.

HEIGHT/SPREAD:	30–60cm (12–20″)/30cm (12″)
LOCATION:	Well-drained soil.
BLOOMS:	July–August
USES:	✂▲▼ Herb gardens, Edging

× superba Hybrids   ZONES 3–9

(Perennial Salvia) Dense spikes of flowers are held above low clumps of grey-green leaves. Very showy plants for the summer border often reblooming in the fall if deadheaded. Excellent for cutting. Fairly drought-tolerant. There are a good number of selections in existence.

HEIGHT/SPREAD:	45–60cm (18–24″)/45–60cm (18–24″)
LOCATION:	Average well-drained soil.
BLOOMS:	June–July
USES:	✂➤ Borders, Massing

'Blue Queen' Rich violet-blue flowers.

'East Friesland' Dark violet-purple, compact habit.

'Lubeca' A taller hybrid with long lasting spikes of violet-blue flowers in summer. HEIGHT: 75cm (30″)

'Miss Indigo' Showy deep purple-blue spikes. A long-lived Alan Bloom hybrid. HEIGHT: 75cm (30″)

'Rose Queen' Distinctive rosy-violet. Inclined to be a bit floppy.

verticillata 'Purple Rain'   ZONES 5–9

A unique new selection from Europe that holds a lot of promise for North American gardens. Plants form a bushy mound of fuzzy green leaves. Arching stems rise above, holding rich violet-purple flowers that are held in clusters spaced evenly apart to the tip. Dead-head for continual bloom.

HEIGHT/SPREAD:	45cm (18″)/45cm (18″)
LOCATION:	Average well-drained soil.
BLOOMS:	July–September
USES:	✂ Massing, Borders

Rudbeckia nitida 'Herbstsonne'

Ruta graveolens 'Curly Girl'

Salvia argentea

Salvia superba × 'East Friesland'

Santolina chamaecyparissus

Saponaria × 'Bressingham'

Saxifraga cotyledon

Saxifraga × *arendsii*

SANTOLINA
(Cotton Lavender) ☀

chamaecyparissus   ZONES 6–9
Low bushes of soft feathery silver-grey leaves, sometimes used as a miniature clipped hedge or edging. Yellow button-flowers appear in summer but are sometimes clipped off. The entire plant has a pleasant camphor-like fragrance. Evergreen in mild regions. Often treated as a bedding annual or used for carpet bedding. Give plants a good hard clipping to 10cm (4″) in early spring to keep them bushy. Very drought-tolerant.

HEIGHT/SPREAD: 30–45cm (12–18″)/30cm (12″)
LOCATION: Well-drained soil. Dislikes wet feet.
BLOOMS: June–July
USES: ♥⚘ Dried Flower, Edging, Herb gardens

SAPONARIA
(Soapwort) ☀

The vigorous border species are best known, but there are also several cushion-forming types for the alpine enthusiast.

× 'Bressingham'   ZONES 4–9
Slowly spreads to form a dome of green foliage, studded with stemless bright pink flowers in late spring. A choice alpine variety for the rock garden or trough. Selected by Alan Bloom.

HEIGHT/SPREAD: 5cm (2″)/15cm (6″)
LOCATION: Gritty, humus-rich soil.
BLOOMS: May–June
USES   △▲ Troughs, Screes

× lempergii 'Max Frei'   ZONES 4–9
A German selection, forms a low bushy mound with clusters of deep pink flowers for many weeks. Blooms when most rock garden plants are long finished flowering. Excellent for massing or edging. Not invasive.

HEIGHT/SPREAD: 20–40cm (8–16″)/45cm (18″)
LOCATION: Average well-drained soil.
BLOOMS: June–September
USES: △⋎⚘ Massing, Edging

ocymoides   ZONES 2–9
(Rock Soapwort) Vigorous, trailing rockery or edging plant. The bright green foliage is smothered with pink flowers in late spring. Fine for tumbling over walls or slopes. Shear plants back hard after blooming. Fairly drought-tolerant.

HEIGHT/SPREAD: 15–20cm (6–8″)/30–45cm (12–18″)
LOCATION: Lean, well-drained soil.
BLOOMS: May–June
USES: △⋎▲♥⚘ Walls, Slopes

officinalis 'Rosea Plena'   ZONES 2–9
(Double Pink Bouncing Bet) An old-fashioned perennial with a very long history in gardens. Its clusters of pale rose-pink double flowers are sweetly scented, similar to phlox. Plants form an upright clump, benefiting from a light pinching in May to encourage bushiness. Spreading but not invasive.

HEIGHT/SPREAD: 60–90cm (2–3′)/60cm (2′)
LOCATION: Average to moist well-drained soil.
BLOOMS: June–August
USES: ✂ Borders, Woodland gardens

SAXIFRAGA
(Saxifrage, Rockfoil) ◐

This huge group of plants includes many easy rock garden specimens, although many types are best left to the experienced alpine connoisseur. Their starry flowers are usually held in airy sprays during late spring. Rosettes of evergreen foliage develop into a neat clump. Most require excellent drainage and prefer a cool location, a rockery or scree providing the ideal conditions.

× arendsii   ZONES 4–9
(Mossy Saxifrage) Low cushions of bright green foliage with short stems of upfacing cup-shaped blossoms in shades of red through pink and white. Showy display in late spring. These require a cool, moist location and will not tolerate drought. Best in a shady rock garden or wall.

HEIGHT/SPREAD: 10–20cm (4–8″)/30cm (12″)
LOCATION: Moist, well-drained soil.
BLOOMS: April–June
USES: △▲⚘ Walls, Troughs

cotyledon   ZONES 3–9
(Pyramidal Saxifrage) Very wide, flat rosettes of grey-green leaves. Tall, branching panicles of white flowers in early summer, most attractive when arching out from a wall.

HEIGHT/SPREAD: 45–60cm (18–24″)/20cm (8″)
LOCATION: Moist, well-drained lime-free soil.
BLOOMS: June
USES   △✂▲⚘ Walls, Troughs

paniculata   ZONES 3–9
(Encrusted Saxifrage) Clusters of grey-green rosettes form a neat tight mound, the leaf edges are trimmed with a curious silver deposit of lime. Short sprays of white starry flowers. One of the easiest types to grow in sun or part shade.

HEIGHT/SPREAD: 25cm (10″)/30cm (12″)
LOCATION: Average to moist well-drained soil.
BLOOMS: May–June
USES: △✂▲⚘ Walls, Edging

× urbium   ZONES 4–9
(London Pride) Vigorous habit, spreading into low evergreen mats. Short stems of airy pale pink flowers in late spring. Excellent groundcover or edging plant for shady areas, even in dense shade under trees. There are a few selections available.

SPREAD: 15–30cm (6–12″)
LOCATION: Average to moist soil.
BLOOMS: May–June
USES: △⋎▲⚘ Edging, Walls

'Aureopunctata' (Golden London Pride) Leaves are heavily spotted with gold. Unique edging plant. HEIGHT: 20–30cm (8–12″)

primuloides Miniature variety, with small rosettes of green leaves, for shaded rockeries. HEIGHT: 10cm (4″)

SCABIOSA
(Pincushion Flower) ☀

Popular old-fashioned favourites, especially valued for cutting. The round, flat quilled flowers appear over a long season. Dead-heading will encourage continued blooming well into the fall. Foliage is dark green and lacy. All are attractive to butterflies.

alpina   ZONES 4–9
(Dwarf Pincushion Flower) A cute little summer bloomer for the rock garden. Makes a mound of grey-green foliage, topped with mauve-blue pincushions.

HEIGHT/SPREAD: 15–20cm (6–8″)/30cm (12″)
LOCATION: Well-drained soil.
BLOOMS: May–August
USES: △⚘ Edging

caucasica 'Hybrid Mix'   ZONES 2–9
Large globe-shaped flowers, in shades of rich blue and lavender through white. Good strong stems. Flowers best in cool-summer regions.

HEIGHT/SPREAD: 45–75cm (18–30″)/30–45cm (12–18″)
LOCATION: Average well-drained soil. Dislikes
                winter wet.
BLOOMS: June–October
USES: ✂⚘ Borders

columbaria
ZONES 3–9

Two new selections of this species have recently become available here in North America. These are creating quite a lot of excitement with their constant display of small pincushion flowers from late spring through fall. The effect is especially good when mass planted around shrubs or at the front of a border. Also worth a try in containers.

HEIGHT/SPREAD: 30–45cm (12–18″)/30cm (12″)
LOCATION: Average well-drained soil.
BLOOMS: June–September
USES: ✂❦✿ Massing, Edging, Borders

'Butterfly Blue' Small lavender-blue flowers in profusion all season long.

'Pink Mist' Pale soft pink flowers, beautiful companion to the blue. (Note: U.S. Plant Patent applied for, can be commercially propagated under license only.)

ochroleuca
ZONES 4–9

(Yellow Scabious) An unusual colour for this genus, with round pincushion flowers in soft primrose yellow. Flowers are held above the foliage on wiry stems, appearing over many weeks. A short-lived perennial, but will often self-seed. Nice in combination with the crimson *Knautia macedonica*.

HEIGHT/SPREAD: 60–75cm (24–34″)/60cm (24″)
LOCATION: Well-drained soil.
BLOOMS: June–September
USES: ✂❦ Borders

SCHIZOSTYLIS
(Kaffir Lily) ☀

coccinea
ZONES 7–9

Vigorous, grassy clumps of sword-shaped leaves, with a fall display of large starry flowers held in a spike well above the foliage. These have been described as looking like a daintier version of a gladiola. Recommended in milder regions, particularly at the West coast, for a burst of colour at the end of the season. Can be wintered in Zone 6 with a deep mulch or brought indoors in pots. Good for cutting. There are a few colour selections in existence, in shades of pink, salmon and white.

> "The silky, cup-shaped blooms of rich crimson with a coppery glint are held in slender spikes in September and October, just when such things are most welcome." —Graham Stuart Thomas, *Perennial Garden Plants*

HEIGHT/SPREAD: 30–60cm (1–2′)/30cm (1′)
LOCATION: Moist, well-drained woodland soil.
BLOOMS: September–December
USES: ✂❦ Borders, Tubs

'Oregon Sunset' Salmon-red flowers.

SCROPHULARIA
(Figwort) ☀◐

aquatica 'Variegata'
ZONES 5–9

A bold foliage perennial, valued for its attractive green and creamy-white variegated leaves. Plants remain evergreen in milder areas. This does best in rich, moist soils, especially at the waterside. Flowers are insignificant and usually trimmed off. Worth trying in containers.

> "It is best in semi-shade and makes a splendid contrast with *Ligularia* 'Desdemona'." —Graham Stuart Thomas, *Perennial Garden Plants*

HEIGHT/SPREAD: 30–45cm (12–18″)/30cm (1′)
LOCATION: Rich, moist to wet soil
BLOOMS: June–July
USES: ❦ Borders, Waterside, Specimen

SEDUM
(Stonecrop) ☀◐

Fleshy, succulent plants, suited to the sunny rock garden or border; many will also tolerate partial shade. These offer the gardener an extensive choice of foliage types with clusters of starry flowers in many shades. Low mat-forming varieties are good ground-covers for hot dry slopes and other difficult sites. Taller cultivars are superb in the late season border.

DWARF VARIETIES
ZONES 2–9

Most of these will form a thick evergreen mat, rooting into the ground as they creep. Fast-spreading types (marked "vigorous and spreading") can easily smother out slow-growing alpines if planted side by side. On the other hand, they might be worth considering as a groundcover or lawn substitute over large areas. The point is to choose varieties carefully to match your landscaping requirements. Extremely drought-tolerant.

SPREAD: 30–45cm (12–18″)
LOCATION: Average to dry to soil.
BLOOMS: See variety description.
USES: ▲◣❦✿ Edging, Slopes, Walls

acre **'Aurea'** (Golden Stonecrop) Ground-hugging carpet, bright golden-yellow in spring, later fading to light green. Yellow flowers June–August. Vigorous and spreading. HEIGHT: 8cm (3″)

album **'Murale'** (Coral Carpet Stonecrop) Rounded green leaves, turning maroon in cold weather. Light pink flowers in summer. Vigorous and spreading. HEIGHT: 10cm (4″)

album **'Murale Cristatum'** (Crested Stonecrop) Tiny, bright green leaves, good mulberry-red colour in cold weather. White flowers in summer. Vigorous and spreading. HEIGHT: 10cm (4″)

anacampseros (Evergreen Orpine) Rounded blue-green leaves, clasping onto trailing stems. Non-spreading. Flowers dusky purple, in July–August. Deciduous. HEIGHT: 15–25cm (6–10″)

cauticola **'Lidakense'** Broad blue-green leaves, with a purple blush, non-spreading. Glistening deep-pink flowers from August–October. Deciduous. HEIGHT: 10cm (4″)

divergens (Old-Man-Bones) Almost globular leaves like green pearls. Yellow flowers in summer. A North American native wildflower. Vigorous and spreading. HEIGHT: 10–15cm (4–6″)

ewersii (Pink Stonecrop) Blue-green rounded leaves, non-spreading. Flowers rose-pink in late summer. Nice for edging. Deciduous. HEIGHT 15cm (6″)

kamtschaticum (Russian Stonecrop) Scalloped green leaves, bright yellow flowers through the summer. One of the best for groundcover use or edging but not considered invasive. Prefers a moist site. Deciduous. HEIGHT: 15cm (6″)

kamtschaticum **'Variegatum'** (Variegated Russian Stonecrop) Light green leaves, edged heavily with cream. Flowers are golden-orange. Very good for edging. Non-spreading. Prefers a moist site. Deciduous. HEIGHT: 15cm (6″)

oreganum (Oregon Stonecrop) Thick shiny green leaves, like a tiny Jade plant. Bright red colour in dry, hot weather. Yellow flowers. A native North American wildflower. Not a fast spreader. HEIGHT: 15cm (6″)

reflexum (Blue Stonecrop) Blue-green spruce-like foliage. Yellow flowers. Vigorous and spreading, outstanding groundcover. HEIGHT: 15cm (6″)

sexangulare (Six-sided Stonecrop) Tiny bright green leaves spiral tightly on the stems. Yellow flowers in

Scabiosa columbaria 'Butterfly Blue'

Schizostylis coccinea 'Oregon Sunset'

Scrophularia aquatica 'Variegata'

Sedum kamtschaticum 'Variegatum'

Sedum spathulifolium 'Capa Blanca'

Sedum spurium 'Red'

Sedum spectabile 'Brilliant'

Sidalcea cultorum × 'Brilliant'

summer. Good winter effect. Vigorous and spreading. HEIGHT: 10cm (4″)

sieboldii **'Medio-variegatum'** (October Daphne) Beautiful blue-green foliage with a creamy-yellow blotch in the centre of each leaf. Large heads of pink flowers appear in very late fall. Slightly tender, dislikes winter wet. Zone 5. Deciduous. HEIGHT: 15–20cm (6–8″)

spathulifolium Tight rosettes of fleshy leaves, taking on bright red colouring during hot dry weather. Yellow flowers in summer. Beautiful groundcover or edging but needs perfect drainage, especially in winter. Zones 5–9. HEIGHT: 10cm (4″)

'Capa Blanca' ('Cape Blanco') Intensely white-grey leaves.

'Purpureum' Unusual purplish-blue foliage. Nice contrast to 'Capa Blanca'.

spurium (Dragon's Blood) An easy and reliable group of Stonecrops. Thick, low mats of leaves and very showy flower clusters in summer. These prefer a warm, moist site and tolerate part shade. Deciduous. HEIGHT: 15cm (6″)

'Pink' Rose-pink flowers, green foliage.

'Red' Ruby-red flowers, beet-red foliage, especially during colder months.

'Tricolor' Leaves variegated green, red and cream. Pinkish flowers. Remove any green shoots immediately or they will take over!

'White' Pure white flowers, green foliage.

BORDER VARIETIES   ZONES 2–9

More upright in habit, these are all late blooming perennials that provide outstanding fall colour with their large clusters of flowers. Suitable for mass planting, especially around shrubs or taller ornamental grasses. For the most part they prefer average to moist conditions but will tolerate short periods of drought. Many of these are excellent for cutting. Attractive to butterflies!

SPREAD:	30–45cm (12–18″)
LOCATION:	Average to moist well-drained soil.
BLOOMS:	See each variety.
USES:	✂ ◁ ♥ ♥ Dried Flower, Borders, Massing

alboroseum **'Medio-variegatum'** Similar to 'Autumn Joy' in stature, the leaves have a creamy-white blotch in the centre. Flowers are greenish-white with a touch of pink. Best in part shade. Any all-green shoots should be rogued out before they take over. Often listed as *S. spectabile* 'Variegatum' Blooms August–September. HEIGHT: 40–50cm (16–20″)

× **'Autumn Joy'** (correctly 'Herbstfreude') Massive heads of salmon-pink flowers, aging to bronzy-red. A favorite of bees and butterflies. Long considered to be one of the top ten perennials. Generally long-lived and trouble free. Flowers September–October. Seed heads remain effective for most of the winter. HEIGHT: 45–60cm (18–24″)

> "The blossoms are creamy ivory at first, but there's a succession of colors that moves to pink, deep cherry-rose, russet, copper, and finally the dark mahogany of the seed heads, which remain handsome in winter, especially against a background of fresh-fallen snow." —
> Allen Lacy, *The Garden in Autumn*

× **'Bertram Anderson'** An outstanding British selection. Low, spreading clumps of deep burgundy-black leaves with bright purple-red flowers in summer. Leaf colour is best in dry, sunny sites. Blooms July–August. HEIGHT: 20cm (8″)

× **'Mohrchen'** A brand new hybrid from Germany. Very deep bronzy-red foliage all season long, turning bright ruby red in late fall. Clusters of pink flowers appear in

August–September. This promises to be an exciting border perennial for foliage contrast. HEIGHT: 45–60cm (18–24″)

spectabile **'Brilliant'** Very similar in appearance to 'Autumn Joy' but with flowers of a brighter mauve-pink. Keep these two away from each other, they clash terribly! Flowers August–October. HEIGHT: 45–60cm (18–24″)

telephium maximum **'Atropurpureum'** Large maroon-purple leaves on an upright clump. Loose clusters of reddish-pink flowers in late summer. Nice contrast to 'Autumn Joy'. Can get floppy unless pinched in mid-June or grown in lean soil. Flowers August–October. HEIGHT: 45–60cm (18–24″)

× **'Vera Jameson'** Mahogany-red foliage, arching stems of dusky pink flowers. Better habit than the older 'Ruby Glow'. Excellent for edging, or in tubs. Flowers August–September. HEIGHT: 20–30cm (9–12″)

SEMPERVIVUM
(Hens and Chicks) ☀ ◐

Well-known succulents, with evergreen rosettes of leaves surrounded by smaller rosettes or "chicks". These are useful for edging borders, in rock gardens, walls, or container gardens. Tolerant of a wide variety of soils, even pure sand, their main requirement is good drainage. Starry flowers rise up on short stems in summer. In Europe these are often seen growing in the gravel on flat rooftops.

HEIGHT/SPREAD:	10–20cm (4–6″)/15–30cm (6–12″)
LOCATION:	Average well-drained soil.
BLOOMS:	June–August
USES:	△ ⋀ ◣ ♥ Edging, Troughs, Walls

Species & Hybrids   ZONES 1–9

The selection of varieties available today is quite astonishing, especially if you are only familiar with the old green-leaved types. They now includes both large and small rosettes, green, blue, red, grey, and multicoloured forms as well various colours of flowers.

Cobweb Types   ZONES 1–9

(*S. arachnoideum*) Fine silvery hairs join together the leaf tips, like a tiny spider's web. A terrific novelty plant for children's gardens!

SIDALCEA
(Prairie Mallow) ☀ ◐

× **cultorum Hybrids**   ZONES 4–9

Elegant long spikes of satiny pink flowers, like small single Hollyhocks. Clumps are upright and narrow, with long stems that are excellent for cutting. Cut back after blooming to encourage a second flush. Best in cool-summer areas. These dislike lime soils. There are several colour selections.

SPREAD:	30cm (12″)
LOCATION:	Rich well-drained soil, preferably acidic.
BLOOMS:	June–August
USES:	✂ ◁ Borders

'Brilliant' Deep rose flowers. HEIGHT: 60–75cm (24–30″)

'Elsie Heugh' Fringed pale pink flowers. HEIGHT: 90–120cm (36–48″)

'Party Girl' A seed mixture of various pink shades. HEIGHT: 60–90cm (2–3′)

'Stark's Hybrids' Shades of rose, red and lilac. Seed strain. HEIGHT: 75–90cm (30–36″)

SILENE
(Campion) ☀

These are similar to *Lychnis*, but the perennial species in cultivation are mostly low plants for rock gardens, walls or edging.

acaulis   ZONES 2–9
(Moss Campion) Flat green cushions are studded with tiny pink flowers through the summer. Not the easiest of alpines, grows best in well-drained, gravelly scree.

HEIGHT/SPREAD: 2.5cm (1")/15–30cm (6–12")
LOCATION: Very well-drained, gravelly soil.
BLOOMS: May–August
USES: ▲▲▼ Screes, Troughs

maritima   ZONES 2–9
(Robin White-breast) Grey-green tufted foliage is similar to *Dianthus* in effect. Inflated flowers appear in summer, white or occasionally pale pink. An easy rock garden plant for midsummer colour, also useful for edging.

HEIGHT/SPREAD: 15–20cm (6–8")/30cm (12")
LOCATION: Average well-drained soil.
BLOOMS: June–August
USES: ▲▼ Edging, Walls

'Swan Lake' Fully double flowers like a ballerina's tutu.

schafta   ZONES 3–9
Starry rose-pink flowers, similar to creeping phlox. Plants form a loose carpet or mound. Good for late-summer colour in the rock garden, when little else is in bloom! Also nice for edging. Easy.

HEIGHT/SPREAD: 10–15cm (4–6")/30cm (12")
LOCATION: Needs very good drainage.
BLOOMS: August–September
USES: ▲▼ Edging, Walls

SISYRINCHIUM
(Blue-eyed Grass) ☀

Dwarf relatives of the *Iris*, forming low tufts of grassy leaves with clusters of small starry flowers. Plants will self-seed if the location suits them. Nice in the rock garden. We find these to be hardier than generally believed.

bellum   ZONES 4–9
Delicate violet-blue flowers in late spring. Neat clumps of grassy leaves are useful for edging. Will grow at the waterside. A pretty little wildflower native to North America.

HEIGHT/SPREAD: 15cm (6")/15–20cm (6–8")
LOCATION: Average to wet well-drained soil.
BLOOMS: May–June
USES: ▲▼ Waterside, Walls

striatum   ZONES 7–9
(Yellow-eyed Grass) Tufts of broad, grassy evergreen leaves resembling an Iris. Flowers are pale creamy-yellow, held in upright spikes that are useful for cutting. Slowly forms a large clump. This species is hardy only in mild areas, appreciating a sunny exposure. Will self-seed.

HEIGHT/SPREAD: 60–75cm (24–30")/30cm (12")
LOCATION: Average to moist well-drained soil.
BLOOMS: June–July
USES: ✂▲ Borders

SOLDANELLA
(Snowbell) ☀●

villosa   ZONES 4–9
(Pyrenean Snowbell) A charming little plant for the woodland garden or shaded rockery. Rounded, glossy evergreen leaves form a small patch. Stems rise above, holding clusters of nodding bell-shaped flowers, magenta pink with fringed petals. Very delicate, usually slow to establish.

HEIGHT/SPREAD: 10cm (4")/20cm (8")
LOCATION: Prefers a moist soil.
BLOOMS: April–May
USES: ▲▲▼ Troughs, Crevices

SOLIDAGO
(Golden-Rod) ☀ ◐

These species and hybrids are much superior to the common wild roadside types. Popular in Europe for years, they are finally gaining acceptance in North American gardens. Their branching clusters of golden flowers combine well with Asters in the fall border. Excellent for cutting. Goldenrod does not cause hay fever but always takes the blame.

brachystachys   ZONES 2–9
(Dwarf Goldenrod) Nice miniature species for edging or rock gardens. Loose sprays of gold flowers.

HEIGHT/SPREAD: 15–20cm (6–8")/30cm (12")
LOCATION: Average to moist soil.
BLOOMS: July–August.
USES: ▲▼ ☙ Borders, Edging

Hybrids   ZONES 2–9
The hybrids have been selected over the years by breeders in Europe, most notably Germany and England. As a group these are very useful to the late summer and autumn border scheme, forming wide leafy clumps that are full of colour for several weeks. They lack the invasive tendencies of our native species, so can be planted in the border with no fear of takeover. Powdery mildew is sometimes a problem, usually a sign that plants are under drought stress. All are excellent for cutting, and will not cause sneezing.

HEIGHT/SPREAD: 90cm (36")/30cm (12")
LOCATION: Average to moist well-drained soil.
BLOOMS: August–October
USES: ✂▼ Borders, Massing, Meadows

'Crown of Rays' ('Strahlenkrone') German selection with golden-yellow flowers held horizontally within the spikes; these have a mop-headed appearance. Bushy, compact habit. Early. HEIGHT: 70cm (28")

'Lemore' Wide-branching panicles of soft primrose-yellow flowers. Late. HEIGHT: 75cm (30")

'Praecox' An early-blooming variety, beginning in July. Flat golden-yellow heads.

sphacelata 'Golden Fleece'   ZONES 4–9
Unusual heart-shaped leaves. A compact-growing selection with flowers quite unlike the more familiar large-headed varieties. Branching wands of little golden flowers are showy in late summer and fall. Especially effective when massed as a groundcover. Recently introduced by the Mt. Cuba Center in Delaware.

HEIGHT/SPREAD: 45cm (18)/30–45cm (12–18")
LOCATION: Average well-drained soil.
BLOOMS: August–October
USES: ✂∿▼ Massing, Borders

× SOLIDASTER
(Solidaster) ☀ ◐

Interesting hybrid between *Aster* and *Solidago*. Useful in the fall border.

luteus   ZONES 4–9
Starry yellow and pale cream flowers arranged in airy sprays. Popular with florists, and sold year-round for cutting. Nice filler in the late summer border. May require staking. Dislikes drying out.

HEIGHT/SPREAD: 60–75cm (24–30")/30cm (12")
LOCATION: Average to moist well-drained soil.
BLOOMS: July–October
USES: ✂ Borders, Meadows

Silene schafta

Sisyrinchium striatum

Soldanella villosa

Solidago × 'Lemore'

Stachys byzantina 'Primrose Heron'

Statice (Limonium latifolium)

Stokesia laevis

Thalictrum aquilegifolium

STACHYS
(Lamb's-Ear) ☀◐

byzantina   **ZONES 3–9**
(= *S. olympica*) A popular edging plant valued for its low
spreading mat of woolly grey leaves. Spikes of pinkish flowers appear in early summer but are often clipped off to
keep plants short and tidy. Evergreen in milder regions.
There are also some named selections, which must be
grown from divisions. Moderately drought-tolerant.

HEIGHT/SPREAD:	30–45cm (12–18")/30cm (12")
LOCATION:	Moist well-drained soil.
BLOOMS:	June
USES:	△∧⋁▲🐝 Massing, Edging, Borders

'**Primrose Heron**' Felty leaves appear golden-yellow in
the spring, becoming light green later in the season.
Magenta flowers.

'**Silver Carpet**' The best for edging and covering large areas.
Plants are much less inclined to flower, so the foliage stays
dense and compact all season. HEIGHT: 15–20cm (6–8")

STATICE
(Perennial Statice) ☀

Now moved into separate genera, we are lumping
these under one common name for convenience
sake but the correct names are indicated below.
Grown mainly for drying, the airy clouds of pale
flowers bloom in the summer on strong, wiry
stems. Effective in the garden as a filler between
other perennials. These are not the same as those
brightly-coloured flat-cluster types, which are
grown as annuals.

Goniolimon tataricum   **ZONES 2–9**
(German Statice, Dumosa) Silvery-white flowers in a
prickly, rounded panicle. Used mainly for cutting and
drying, but also interesting as an edging plant.

HEIGHT/SPREAD:	25–40cm (10–16")/30cm (12")
LOCATION:	Well-drained soil. Dislikes winter wet.
BLOOMS:	July–August
USES:	✂ Edging, Borders

Limonium latifolium   **ZONES 2–9**
(Sea Lavender) Dainty lavender-blue flowers are borne
in large panicles. Plants form a rounded bush, with up
to a dozen flowering stems. This is a showy, attractive
border perennial. Moderately drought-tolerant.

HEIGHT/SPREAD:	60–75cm (24–30")/60cm (24")
LOCATION:	Well-drained soil. Dislikes winter wet.
BLOOMS:	June–August
USES:	✂🐝 Dried Flower, Borders

STOKESIA
(Stoke's Aster) ☀

laevis   **ZONES 4–9**
A native North American wildflower. Flowers are
lavender-blue, something like a double Shasta Daisy, beginning in midsummer and valuable for a late show.
Excellent for cutting. Evergreen in milder regions. Resents
winter wet. A winter mulch is recommended in Zones 4–5.
Named selections exist with white or pale pink flowers.

HEIGHT/SPREAD:	30–60cm (1–2')/30cm (12")
LOCATION:	Moist but well-drained soil.
BLOOMS:	July–September
USES:	✂ Borders

SYMPHYTUM
(Comfrey) ◐●

Rugged, indestructible perennials with the same
tough constitution as the common herb varieties.
These are grown for their attractive clumps of bold,

hairy leaves that quickly form a clump in early
spring. The short spikes of bell-shaped flowers look
similar in appearance to *Pulmonaria*. Best in a
moist, rich soil where they will spread steadily.

× rubrum   **ZONES 3–9**
(Red-flowered Comfrey) Clumps of dark-green foliage,
clusters of dark red bell flowers in early summer.
Excellent for massing as a groundcover among shrubs,
spreads quickly.

HEIGHT/SPREAD:	30–45cm (12–18")/60cm (24")
LOCATION:	Prefers a rich, moist soil.
BLOOMS:	May–July
USES:	∧⋁ Borders, Massing

TANACETUM
(Tansy) ☀

Some members of the *Chrysanthemum* genus
have now been moved here. For convenience sake
we are continuing to list them still under
CHRYSANTHEMUM.

vulgare 'Crispum'   **ZONES 2–9**
(Fernleaf Tansy) Fresh deep green foliage, ruffled and
curled like a parsley. Button-like yellow flowers appear
in late summer and are excellent for cutting. This is a more
ornamental selection of the common roadside variety,
useful as a foliage accent in the border. Spreads quickly
without becoming invasive. A very old plant of European
cottage gardens. Moderately drought-tolerant.

HEIGHT/SPREAD:	75–90cm (30–36")/60cm (24")
LOCATION:	Average well-drained soil.
BLOOMS:	July–September
USES:	✂❮🐝 Borders, Herb gardens

TEUCRIUM
(Germander) ☀◐

Interesting foliage plants, well-suited to formal edging or mass planting. Their short spikes of mint-
like flowers have a delicate effect.

chamaedrys 'Prostratum'   **ZONES 5–9**
(Creeping Germander) Shiny green leaves form a low
mound, spreading to form a patch. Short spikes of rosy-
purple flowers in late summer. Small enough for the rock
garden, excellent for edging. Evergreen in milder areas.
Winter mulch is recommended in Zones 5–6. Reported
to be attractive to cats. Moderately drought-tolerant.
Often listed incorrectly as *T. canadense*.

HEIGHT/SPREAD:	15–25cm (6–10")/30cm (12")
LOCATION:	Well-drained soil.
BLOOMS:	July–August
USES:	△∧⋁▲🐝 Edging, Herb gardens

THALICTRUM
(Meadow-rue) ☀◐

Beautiful woodland perennials from various parts
of the world, all of these have lacy foliage similar to
a columbine or maidenhair fern. The loose cloud-
like sprays of flowers are useful for cutting. Although
these are usually tall their see-through appearance
means they can be moved up toward the front of a
border. All appreciate a cool woodland setting.

aquilegifolium   **ZONES 3–9**
(Columbine Meadow-rue) Very delicate mauve flowers
held in a large spray. Plants form an upright clump of ferny
heat-tolerant foliage. Fairly compact, early blooming.

HEIGHT/SPREAD:	60–90cm (2–3')/60cm (2')
LOCATION:	Rich, moist woodland soil.
BLOOMS:	May–June
USES:	✂ Borders, Woodland gardens

delavayi 'Hewitt's Double'   ZONES 3–9
Large airy clouds of double mauve flowers, similar to Baby's Breath. Foliage is very lacy and fern-like. This variety gets fairly tall and may require staking. Plants increase slowly and are often difficult to obtain. Excellent for cutting, fresh or dried.

HEIGHT/SPREAD:	120–150cm (4–5')/60cm (2')
LOCATION:	Rich, moist woodland soil.
BLOOMS:	June–August
USES:	✄ Borders, Woodland gardens

flavum glaucum   ZONES 4–9
Unusual powdery blue-green foliage, forming a good-size clump. Flowers are yellow, in good-size sprays. An easy and rewarding species for any shady border.

HEIGHT/SPREAD:	1.5–1.8m (5–6')/60cm (2')
LOCATION:	Rich, moist woodland soil.
BLOOMS:	July–August
USES:	✄ Borders, Woodland gardens

THERMOPSIS
(False Lupine) ☀

lupinoides   ZONES 2–9
(= *T. lanceolata*) A North American native wildflower, similar in effect to a dwarf Lupine, with spikes of lemon-yellow flowers in late spring. Plants are long-lived and especially recommended for gardeners who can't seem to succeed with true Lupines. Use towards the front of a border. Resents being disturbed once established. Very drought-tolerant.

HEIGHT/SPREAD:	20–30cm (9–12")/30cm (12")
LOCATION:	Average well-drained soil.
BLOOMS:	May–June
USES:	△✄ Borders, Meadows

THYMUS
(Thyme) ☀
Bushy or mat-forming herbs with small aromatic leaves and short spikes of flowers. Upright forms are good for massing or using as a low hedge. Creeping varieties make an attractive groundcover or lawn substitute for small areas, even tolerating light traffic. All prefer a sunny warm site. All are moderately drought-tolerant. The botanical classification of the thymes is currently in a tangled state, to say the least.

> "The thymes, they are a-changin'…"
> —Bob Dylan

× citriodorus   ZONES 4–9
(Lemon Thyme) A complex group of hybrids, most having extremely fragrant lemon-scented leaves. The habit, foliage colour and hardiness vary considerably between the named cultivars. The upright varieties are excellent cooking herbs.

SPREAD:	30cm (12")
LOCATION:	Lean, well-drained soil.
BLOOMS:	July–August
USES:	△〰▲▼ Edging, Herb gardens, Walls

'Argenteus' (Silver Thyme) Bushy, upright variety. Leaves are light green, variegated with silver. Attractive ornamental, and one of the best for cooking. Lilac flowers. More tender than the others, ZONES 6–9. HEIGHT: 25cm (10")

'Doone Valley' Fairly low creeping type. Dark-green foliage with bright gold tips in fall and spring. Good bronzy-red winter colour. Lavender flowers. HEIGHT: 10–15cm (4–6")

'E. B. Anderson' Dwarf carpeter. Good bright-golden foliage colour all winter and spring. Turns light green in summer. Seldom blooms. HEIGHT: 5cm (2")

'Gold Edge' Delightful strong lemon fragrance. Green and yellow variegated foliage on an upright spreading bush. Pink flowers in summer. HEIGHT: 25cm (10")

doerfleri 'Bressingham'   ZONES 4–9
Low greyish carpeter, covered in a good display of clear pink flowers. Discovered and introduced by Bressingham Gardens. Excellent form for general groundcover purposes, deserves wider use.

HEIGHT/SPREAD:	2cm (1")/30cm (12")
LOCATION:	Lean, well-drained soil.
BLOOMS:	May–June
USES:	△〰▲▼ Edging, Walls

'Moonlight'   ZONES 4–9
A delightful variety, forming a semi-upright bushy mound of grey foliage, with masses of light pink flowers in early summer. For rock gardens or edging. This may be a form of *T. leucotrichus* or *T. nitidus*.

HEIGHT/SPREAD:	10–15cm (4–6")/30cm (12")
LOCATION:	Lean, well-drained soil.
BLOOMS:	May–June
USES:	△〰▲▼ Edging, Walls

× 'Porlock'   ZONES 5–9
A British hybrid. Semi-upright mats covered with bright pink flowers. Good spreader.

HEIGHT/SPREAD:	15–20cm (6–8")/30cm (12")
LOCATION:	Lean, well-drained soil.
BLOOMS:	May–June
USES:	△〰▲▼ Edging, Walls

praecox   ZONES 2–9
(Creeping Thyme, Mother-of-thyme) Very flat mats of tiny leaves, smothered with flowers in summer. Excellent between paving stones and in rock gardens. These form a very dense, long-lived carpet. Some of the varieties listed below are often included under *T. serpyllum*.

> "Collectors enjoy amassing the numerous named forms of garden thymes, but marvelous calico carpets can be woven simply by combining plants of mother of thyme."
> —Ann Lovejoy, *The American Mixed Border*

HEIGHT/SPREAD:	2–5cm (1–2")/30cm (12")
LOCATION:	Lean, well-drained soil.
BLOOMS:	June–July
USES:	△〰▲▼ Edging, Walls

'Albus' (White Moss Thyme) Very flat mat of light green leaves with clear white flowers. Slow to establish.

'Coccineus' (Red Creeping Thyme) Deep scarlet-purple flowers, very small dark green leaves.

'Elfin' A very compact variety for the rock garden. Low buns of tiny leaves bear soft pink flowers in summer. Not a fast spreader.

'Purple Carpet' Similar habit to 'Coccineus', but flowers are a lighter mauve-purple. A chance seedling discovered and introduced by Valleybrook Gardens.

pseudolanuginosus   ZONES 2–9
(Woolly Thyme) (now correctly *T. praecox pseudolanuginosus*.) Fuzzy olive-grey foliage, with sparse pink flowers in summer. Perhaps the best for groundcover use, very vigorous habit.

HEIGHT/SPREAD:	5cm (2")/30cm (12")
LOCATION:	Lean, well-drained soil.
BLOOMS:	June–July
USES:	△〰▲▼ Edging, Walls

Thermopsis lupinoides

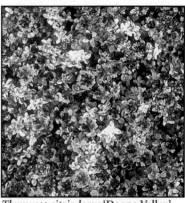
Thymus × citriodorus 'Doone Valley'

Thymus pseudolanuginosus

Thymus praecox

Tiarella var. collina 'Oakleaf'

Tovara virginiana 'Painter's Palette'

Trollius cultorum × 'Lemon Queen'

Trollius cultorum × 'Orange Crest'

serpyllum   **ZONES 2–9**
(Mother-of-Thyme) Vigorous grower, bright green leaves and rose-purple flowers. This is a variable seed-grown variety, not nearly as refined as other creeping types, but very rugged and hardy. This could possibly be *T. pulegoides*.

HEIGHT/SPREAD: 15–20cm (6–8")/30cm (12")
LOCATION: Lean, well-drained soil.
BLOOMS: June–July
USES: ◭⋀•▲▼⛆ Edging, Walls

TIARELLA
(Foamflower) ☼•●

Closely related to Coral Bells, forming similar low clumps of leaves, with airy sprays of light pink or white flowers in early summer. The species are woodland plants native to North America, but several hybrid selections have been developed in recent years and some of these are now becoming widely available. There are both spreading and non-spreading forms.

cordifolia   **ZONES 3–9**
This is a spreading species, best suited for groundcover use or as a low edging in the shady border. Low clumps of hairy green leaves, spikes of white flowers in early summer. Excellent bronzy winter colour. Combines nicely with ferns and other woodland plants. Evergreen.

HEIGHT/SPREAD: 15–30cm (6–12")/30cm (12")
LOCATION: Moist, rich woodland soil.
BLOOMS: May–July
USES: ◭⋀•▲ Edging, Woodland gardens

var. *collina* 'Oakleaf' A recent American selection from the Brandywine Conservancy. Foliage is attractively lobed like an oak leaf. Deep red winter colour. Spikes of flowers are an unusual pale pink shade. A non-spreading clump form, excellent for edging and rock gardens.

HEIGHT/SPREAD: 20–30cm (8–12")/30cm (12")
LOCATION: Moist, rich woodland soil.
BLOOMS: May–July
USES: ◭⋀•▲ Edging, Woodland gardens

TOVARA
(Tovara) ☼☀

virginiana 'Painter's Palette'   **ZONES 5–9**
Sometimes listed under *Polygonum* or *Fallopia*, this is grown for its colourful foliage. The leaves are variegated with cream and green, with an unusual V-shaped chocolate-brown marking. Used as a groundcover for moist areas or as a bushy specimen plant. Sometimes tends to spread, sometimes not. Especially useful among shrubs. Airy sprays of greenish flowers change into deep red seed-heads in late fall.

HEIGHT/SPREAD: 60–120cm (2–4')/60cm (2')
LOCATION: Prefers a rich, moist soil.
BLOOMS: August–September
USES: ⋀•▼ Massing, Waterside

TRADESCANTIA
(Spiderwort) ☼☀

× andersoniana   **ZONES 3–9**
Grassy upright clumps with showy triangular flowers; these open over an exceptionally long season. Plants benefit from good clip after flowering to tidy them up and to encourage a fall bloom. Best in a moist location to keep the foliage from scorching. There are several named cultivars in various shades of light and dark blue, purple, pink, magenta and white.

HEIGHT/SPREAD: 30–60cm (1–2')/45–60cm (18–24")
LOCATION: Average to moist well-drained soil.
BLOOMS: June–September
USES: Borders, Waterside

TRICYRTIS
(Toad-lily) ☀

hirta   **ZONES 4–9**
(Japanese Toad-lily) A unique but easy plant for shady areas. Arching stems produce a fall display of bizarre white star flowers, heavily spotted with dark purple. Deserves a special spot where it can be seen up close. Subtle. Grown commercially as cut flowers.

> "The adjective that seems to be most common in describing the plant's flowers is "weird"; they look almost as though they evolved on some other planet." —Allen Lacy, *The Garden in Autumn*

HEIGHT/SPREAD: 60–90cm (2–3')/30–60cm (1–2')
LOCATION: Prefers a rich, moist soil.
BLOOMS: September–October
USES: ✄◭ Woodland gardens, Borders

TRIFOLIUM
(Clover) ☼●☀

Clover is most familiar as a hay crop or lawn weed, but there are a few ornamental types that are occasionally grown in gardens.

repens 'Atropurpureum'   **ZONES 4–9**
(Black-leaved Clover) A handsome edging or groundcover plant, the foliage is dark purple to black, with a green margin. Lots of lucky four-leaved clovers appear, and plants spread fairly quickly to form a dense patch. White flowers bloom in June. Evergreen in mild areas.

HEIGHT/SPREAD: 10cm (4")/30cm (12")
LOCATION: Average to moist well-drained soil.
BLOOMS: June
USES: ⋀•◭▲▼ Edging, Pots

TRITOMA see KNIPHOFIA

TROLLIUS
(Globeflower) ☼●☀

× cultorum Hybrids   **ZONES 2–9**
(Hybrid Globeflower) Large round buttercup flowers rise above leafy clumps of deeply lobed foliage in late spring. These are popular for the early border, their showy flowers are sometimes used for cutting. Many named selections exist, all are in shades of yellow to orange, including some gorgeous pale forms. Plants can be sheared back in summer if they get tired looking.

HEIGHT/SPREAD: 60–90cm (2–3')/45–60cm (18–24")
LOCATION: Average to moist well-drained soil.
BLOOMS: May–June
USES: ✄ Borders, Meadow gardens

'Canary Bird' Pale yellow flowers. HEIGHT: 75cm (30")

'Lemon Queen' Large clear yellow flowers. Vigorous. HEIGHT: 60cm (24")

'Orange Crest' Deep orange. HEIGHT: 75–90cm (30–36")

'Orange Princess' Orange-yellow. HEIGHT: 75–90cm (30–36")

TUNICA
(Tunic Flower) ☀

saxifraga   ZONES 2–9
(now *Petrorhagia saxifraga*) A low-growing rock garden plant, producing a misty cloud of white or pale pink flowers similar to Baby's Breath. Easy and reliable. Blooms over a long season. Self-seeds prolifically.

HEIGHT/SPREAD: 15–20cm (6–8")/15–30cm (6–12")
LOCATION: Average well-drained soil.
BLOOMS: June–August
USES: ▲△🌱 Walls, Edging

VERATRUM
(False Hellebore) ☀ ◐

nigrum   ZONES 3–9
(Black False Hellebore) Forming exotic upright clumps of pleated leaves, these can be an unusual feature in a partly shaded border. Their stiff, branching spikes of maroon-black flowers are a sight to behold! Although these are often grown in large European gardens they are not often seen here and can be difficult to find. Good for cutting, if you dare.

HEIGHT/SPREAD: 1.5–2.1m (5–7')/60cm (24")
LOCATION: Rich moist soil.
BLOOMS: July–September
USES: ✄ Borders, Waterside

VERBASCUM
(Mullein) ☀
Related to the common roadside Mullein, the garden forms are interesting and showy plants for sunny borders. All have upright spikes of flowers and leaves arranged in a low flat rosette. They are good cut flowers for those with a daring sense of design.

bombyciferum   ZONES 4–9
(Giant Silver Mullein) Silvery-white felted leaves form a large rosette the first year, sending up tall stately spires of yellow flowers the following summer. A spectacular specimen plant, usually treated as a biennial. Will self-seed.

HEIGHT/SPREAD: 1.5–1.8m (5–6')/45cm (18")
LOCATION: Average well-drained soil.
BLOOMS: June–August
USES: ✄🌱 Specimen, Borders, Tubs

× Hybrids   ZONES 5–9
(Hybrid Mullein) Showy, long-blooming varieties suited to the border. Branching spikes of flowers continue blooming all summer if dead-headed regularly. These must be propagated by root cuttings. Foliage forms a low green rosette. Rarely seen in North American gardens.

HEIGHT/SPREAD: 90cm (3')/45cm (18")
LOCATION: Average well-drained soil.
BLOOMS: June–August
USES: ✄🌱 Specimen, Borders, Tubs

'Cotswold Queen' Unique buff, purple and orange flowers.

'Pink Domino' Deep rose spikes.

phoeniceum   ZONES 4–9
(Purple Mullein) Shorter spikes of flowers in a mix of purple, red, pink, or white. Showy when planted in groups towards the front of the border. Short-lived perennial, but self-seeds nicely. Special favorites can be grown from root-cuttings.

HEIGHT/SPREAD: 60–120cm (2–4')/30cm (1')
LOCATION: Average well-drained soil.
BLOOMS: May–July
USES: ✄ Borders

VERBENA
(Verbena) ☀
Most of the perennial species of Verbena are generally on the tender side and are often grown as long-flowering annuals.

bonariensis   ZONES 7–9
(Brazilian Verbena) Stiff, upright branching stems hold clusters of magenta-purple flowers from early summer through late fall. A large grouping makes an unforgettable display. Very heat tolerant. In many areas this is grown as a self-seeding annual.

> "A single plant is curious, three together beautiful, and a large group is a splendid sight." —Graham Stuart Thomas, *Perennial Garden Plants*

HEIGHT/SPREAD: 90–120cm (3–4')/30cm (1')
LOCATION: Average well-drained soil.
BLOOMS: June–October
USES: ✄🌱🦋 Massing, Borders

canadensis 'Homestead Purple' ZONES 6–9
(Clump Verbena) A low trailing perennial species native to the eastern U.S., this selection is a form recently discovered growing in a Georgia garden. Clusters of bright deep-purple flowers cover the plants for weeks on end. This requires good drainage and dislikes winter wet. Excellent in baskets and window boxes, worth considering as an unusual annual. Drought and heat-tolerant.

HEIGHT/SPREAD: 15–20cm (6–8")/45cm (18")
LOCATION: Well-drained soil.
BLOOMS: June–October
USES: ▲△◠🌱🦋🕸 Massing, Walls, Edging

VERONICA
(Speedwell) ☀ ◐
Showy garden perennials, mostly with upright spikes of blue, pink or white flowers from early summer on. Taller varieties are excellent cut flowers. Shorter types put on a bright display in the rock garden.

allionii   ZONES 2–9
(Alpine Speedwell) Very compact spikes of violet-blue flowers on a low mounded clump of evergreen leaves. Excellent edging plant.

HEIGHT/SPREAD: 15cm (6")/30cm (12")
LOCATION: Average well-drained soil.
BLOOMS: June–August
USES: ▲△🌱 Edging

dabneyi   ZONES 2–9
(Pink Speedwell) Bright green foliage forms a low clump, set with short spikes of pale pink flowers in late spring. Used in rock gardens and for edging.

HEIGHT/SPREAD: 15cm (6")/30cm (12")
LOCATION: Average well-drained soil.
BLOOMS: May–June
USES: ▲△ Edging, Walls

filifolia   ZONES 4–9
Quite unlike any of the other species. This is a little gem for the rock garden, and forms a low carpet of ferny green foliage set with large sky blue flowers in late spring. Not to be confused with the lawn weed *V. filiformis*.

HEIGHT/SPREAD: 5–10cm (2–4")/30–45cm (12–18")
LOCATION: Average well-drained soil.
BLOOMS: May–June
USES: ▲△◠▲🌱 Walls, Edging

× 'Goodness Grows'   ZONES 2–9
This recent hybrid flowers for an exceptionally long time. Wands of rich, royal-purple flowers are held above a low

Verbascum bombyciferum

Verbena canadensis 'Homestead Purple'

Veronica allionii

Veronica dabneyi

Veronica incana

Veronica spicata 'Red Fox'

Veronica whitleyi

Viola × 'Black Magic'

clump of green foliage. Recommended for mass planting or edging. Heat tolerant.

HEIGHT/SPREAD: 30cm (12")/30–45cm (12–18")
LOCATION: Average well-drained soil.
BLOOMS: June–August
USES: ✂ Massing, Edging, Borders

incana   ZONES 2–9
(Woolly Speedwell) Compact clumps of silver-grey, woolly foliage. Spikes of violet-blue flowers appear in early summer. Excellent foliage plant for edging or massing. Remove faded flower spikes to maintain foliage interest all season.

HEIGHT/SPREAD: 30–45cm (12–18")/30–45cm (12–18")
LOCATION: Average well-drained soil.
BLOOMS: June–July
USES: ✂〰 Massing, Borders

prostrata   ZONES 4–9
(Creeping Speedwell) Low, creeping mat of grey-green foliage, smothered by flowers in late spring. A showy edging or rockery plant.

HEIGHT/SPREAD: 10cm (4")/30cm (12")
LOCATION: Well-drained soil.
BLOOMS: May–June
USES: △〰 Walls, Edging

'Heavenly Blue' Bright sapphire-blue flowers.

'Mrs. Holt' Bright pink flowers.

repens   ZONES 2–9
(Creeping Speedwell) Makes a completely flat carpet of tiny green leaves, studded with little white flowers in late spring. Nice in the rockery, or between patio stones.

HEIGHT/SPREAD: 1cm (1/2")/15–30cm (6–12")
LOCATION: Average well-drained soil.
BLOOMS: May–June
USES: △〰▲♥ Walls, Between flagstones

spicata   ZONES 2–9
(Spike Speedwell) Bushy border plants, with upright spikes of violet-blue flowers for many weeks. Excellent for cutting. Many selections of this species exist, some with attractive pink or white flowers.

HEIGHT/SPREAD: 30–60cm (1–2')/30cm (12")
LOCATION: Average well-drained soil.
BLOOMS: June–August
USES: ✂ Borders, Massing

'Blue Carpet' ('Blauteppich') Very dwarf, deep blue flowers. HEIGHT: 5–10cm (2–4")

'Icicle' Good clear white spikes. Late.

'Red Fox' Deep rose-pink flowers. Compact habit.

'Rosenrot' Rosy-pink, compact seed strain.

× 'Sunny Border Blue'   ZONES 3–9
This long-blooming hybrid features short spikes of deep violet-blue flowers all summer long. The bright green foliage is unusually crinkled and remains fresh-looking throughout the season, showing excellent mildew resistance. Plants have a dense and compact habit. Useful for massing or edging. A former *Perennial Plant of the Year*.

HEIGHT/SPREAD: 30–45cm (18–24")/30cm (12")
LOCATION: Average well-drained soil.
BLOOMS: July–September
USES: ✂♥ Massing, Edging, Borders

teucrium   ZONES 2–9
(Hungarian Speedwell) An excellent edging plant, with spikes of blue flowers in early summer, plants forming a low clump. Trim back after flowering.

HEIGHT/SPREAD: 20–30cm (8–12")/30cm (12")
LOCATION: Average well-drained soil.
BLOOMS: May–July
USES: △ Edging, Borders

'Crater Lake Blue' Intense gentian-blue flowers.

'Trehane' Bright golden-yellow foliage, compact habit. Unusual!

whitleyi   ZONES 3–9
(Whitley's Speedwell) An outstanding low edging or rockery plant! Forms a spreading mat of small grey-green leaves, absolutely smothered by soft blue flowers in spring with a few continuing all season long. This could also be used as a dense groundcover. This may be an incorrect species name.

HEIGHT/SPREAD: 5–10cm (2–4")/30–45cm (12–18")
LOCATION: Average well-drained soil.
BLOOMS: May–June
USES: △〰▲♥ Edging, Walls

VERONICASTRUM
(Culver's-root) ☀
Very closely related to *Veronica*, and sometimes included with them. These are native North American wildflowers of great garden value. They prefer a sunny location with a rich moist soil.

virginicum   ZONES 3–9
(=*Veronica virginica*) Forming impressive large clumps, these differ from *Veronica* in that the leaves are whorled, arranged on the stem like the spokes of an umbrella. Flowers are held in long wands that arch gracefully, appearing for several weeks in the late summer, excellent for cutting. Lots of moisture is needed for these to do their best.

HEIGHT/SPREAD: 1.2–1.8m (4–6')/90cm (3')
LOCATION: Rich moist soil.
BLOOMS: August–September
USES: ✂ Borders, Meadows

'Album' Clear white flowers, the most impressive.

'Rosea' A very pale pink selection.

VIOLA
(Violet, Pansy) ☽
This group includes the violets of woodlands and meadows as well as the small hardy garden pansies known as violas. All are of easy culture, preferring a cool partly shady location.

× 'Black Magic'   ZONES 4–9
The closest yet to jet black, effective when planted in a large group. Flowers strongly all season where summers are cool, otherwise in spring and fall. This is a bedding viola, likely a variety of *V. cornuta*. Although this form comes from Australia, it could possibly be the same as the British cultivar 'Molly Sanderson'.

HEIGHT/SPREAD: 15cm (6")/15–20cm (6–8")
LOCATION: Average well-drained soil.
BLOOMS: April–October
USES: △▲♥ Edging, Borders, Massing

cornuta   ZONES 4–9
(Perennial Pansy, Horned Violet) Also known as Winter Pansies, these are much hardier than annual pansies, being more tolerant of both summer heat and winter cold. Excellent for bedding, edging, rock gardens or containers. Use a winter mulch in Zones 3–5. These are excellent for massing with tulips and other spring bulbs, in containers or under shrubs. There are several good older seed strains in shades of apricot, yellow, blue, purple, bronzy-red, cream and white. Some of the unique newer varieties are noted below.

> "The horned violet…spills in cascades over the border's edge while lacing shoot after flower laden shoot as much as three feet long through taller plants nearby." —Ann Lovejoy, *The American Mixed Border*

HEIGHT/SPREAD:	10–20cm (4–8″)/15–20cm (6–8″)
LOCATION:	Average to moist well-drained soil.
BLOOMS:	April–October
USES:	⛰▲❦ Massing, Edging, Borders

'Baby Franjo' Bright yellow miniature flowers. Compact.

'Baby Lucia' Small sky-blue flowers. Compact.

'Purple Duet' New. Light and deep purple combination.

'Yellow Frost' Little yellow and blue flowers, whiskered.

cucullata   ZONES 3–9

(Marsh Blue Violet) Lush clumps of heart-shaped leaves are excellent for massing in the shade garden, though they tolerate sun with enough moisture. Large classic violet flowers are held just above the leaves. Flowers have a very slight fragrance. A native to eastern North America, sometimes incorrectly listed as *V. odorata*. There are a few colour selections. Self-seeds prolifically.

HEIGHT/SPREAD:	15cm (6″)/15–30cm (6–12″)
LOCATION:	Average to moist soil.
BLOOMS:	April–June
USES:	ᴧᴧ❦ Woodland gardens, Borders

'Royal Robe' Vibrant purple-blue flowers.

'White Czar' White flowers with a yellow centre.

labradorica   ZONES 4–9

(Purple Labrador Violet) Charming rock garden violet. Low tufts of purple-tinged leaves, with purple wild-violet type flowers. Blooms in spring and fall. Likes a cool, moist spot. A native North American wildflower.

HEIGHT/SPREAD:	10–15cm (4–6″)/15cm (6″)
LOCATION:	Moist, well-drained soil.
BLOOMS:	May–September
USES:	⛰ᴧᴧ❦ Woodland gardens, Borders

pedata   ZONES 3–9

(Bird's Foot Violet) Another wildflower native to eastern North America, grown for its spring display of small violet-blue flowers and interesting divided leaves. Nice addition to a well-drained rock garden in part shade to full sun.

HEIGHT/SPREAD:	10–15cm (4–6″)/20cm (8″)
LOCATION:	Needs a well-drained soil.
BLOOMS:	April–June
USES:	⛰ Borders, Edging

tricolor   ZONES 2–9

(Johnny Jump-Up) Although usually treated as a bedding annual, Jump-ups will often overwinter or at least re-establish by self-seeding. Their tiny pansy flowers appear from early spring through late fall, especially when the nights are cool. Keep these out of the alpine garden to prevent seedlings from taking over.

HEIGHT/SPREAD:	10–15cm (4–6″)/15cm (6″)
LOCATION:	Average to moist soil.
BLOOMS:	April–October
USES:	❦ Massing, Borders, Edging

'Blue Elf' Bright violet-blue flowers. Very different!

'Helen Mount' The more traditional violet, yellow and mauve combination.

WALDSTEINIA
(Barren-strawberry) ◐●

ternata   ZONES 4–9

This makes a low, dense mat of shiny semi-evergreen leaves that somewhat resemble those of a strawberry. A good low-maintenance groundcover, punctuated by little yellow flowers in the spring. Can be used to cover large or small areas, spreading by stolons but not considered invasive. Tolerates summer drought.

HEIGHT/SPREAD:	15cm (6″)/30–45cm (12–18″)
LOCATION:	Average to moist soil.
BLOOMS:	April–May
USES:	ᴧᴧ▲ Massing, Edging

ZANTEDESCHIA
(Calla Lily) ☀◐

aethiopica 'Crowborough'   ZONES 8–9

(White Calla) The hardiest Calla, overwintering outdoors at the West coast. Roots are easily stored indoors for the winter in colder regions, or can even be left in pots and stored in the basement. Tall clumps of broad, leathery leaves give rise to pure white flowers with yellow centres. Easy to grow in containers. Needs a dry period in winter.

HEIGHT/SPREAD:	90cm (3′)/30–60cm (1–2′)
LOCATION:	Moist well-drained soil.
BLOOMS:	June–October
USES:	✂❦ Specimen

ZAUSCHNERIA
(California Fuchsia) ☀◐

californica   ZONES 7–9

A California wildflower, tolerating hot dry sites. Flowers are like scarlet-red hanging bells dangling from arching stems in late summer. This grows best in mild-winter areas, particularly at the West coast. Plants will not thrive without perfect drainage. Very drought-tolerant.

HEIGHT/SPREAD:	30–60cm (12–24″)/30–45cm (12–18″)
LOCATION:	Very well-drained soil.
BLOOMS:	August–October
USES:	⛰ᴧᴧ▲➤❦✦ Walls, Edging

Viola cucullata 'White Czar'

Viola labradorica

Zantedeschia aethiopica 'Crowborough'

Symbols Key

☀ Full Sun

◐ Part Shade

● Full Shade

⛰ Alpine

✂ Good Cut Flower

▲ Evergreen

ᴧᴧ Groundcover

❦ Attracts Butterflies

➤ Attracts Hummingbirds

❦ Suitable for Containers

✦ Drought Tolerant

Ferns ...*some fern facts*

Ferns are valuable garden plants of great dependability and beauty. Their leaves, known as fronds, can be lacy or leathery, plain green or variegated, and provide a long season of interest. Rarely suffering from pests and diseases, they offer trouble-free elegance.

Naturally inhabiting woodland areas, most ferns thrive in the shade and protection provided by trees. They perform best in a moist, well drained soil that is high in organic matter. Ferns were tremendously popular in Victorian times, and many of the British well-to-do had ferneries — shady garden areas or whole greenhouses devoted to fern collections. As we become more aware of the value of foliage texture in modern landscaping, we are re-discovering the refreshing diversity of hardy ferns. Fortunately some of the best ferns have been introduced back into nursery production, so today's selection is much better than what was available even ten years ago.

There are numerous kinds of hardy ferns available in garden centres. While some species are deciduous, dying back to the ground for winter, others are evergreen, providing attractive winter foliage in the garden, especially in mild-winter areas. Ferns vary in texture and

height as well, from low spreading mounds, to bold upright clumps. Even the smallest garden can have a woodland feeling by planting a few ferns along with other shade loving perennials such as Hostas, Primulas and Astilbes.

Try to start with vigorous container-grown plants that have been grown from spores or divisions, and have had a chance to develop a strong healthy root system. A good many of the ferns (and other wildflowers) being sold today have been collected and dug from the wild; buying such plants will only serve to encourage collectors to continue depleting our valuable, limited natural stands of native plants, some of them rare and endangered! When you buy any woodland wildflowers or ferns, be sure to find out whether or not they have been nursery propagated (as opposed to dug from the wild and then nursery grown in pots). All of the ferns listed here can be commercially grown from spores, with no need to obtain stock from the wild.

Tips on Planting and Care

Ferns require moist, humus-rich soil. To improve your soil, dig in 10–15cm (4–6") of well-rotted compost, peat moss or other organic matter to increase its moisture holding ability.

Some ferns can grow well under trees, but tree roots tend to rob the soil of water and nutrients. Also, rain may not penetrate the canopy. You will have to provide regular watering to these areas if you want to grow ferns there, and especially while plants are trying to get established. It is a good idea to mulch deeply around your ferns with compost or leaf litter once a year. This will improve the soil, keep roots cool and help to retain moisture.

If your ferns are forming large patches, or you wish to increase the size of your patch — perhaps even to trade with friends — you might want to tackle dividing your plants. This is very simple to do in early spring, and

is exactly like dividing any other perennial that forms a clump or patch. One word of caution, however; don't try to divide a plant that has only one main crown with no smaller plants surrounding it. Wait a year or two and if you notice secondary shoots (called *offsets*) developing beside the main crown, carefully sneak these away in the spring using a sharp hand trowel.

Where winters are very cold, cover ferns with evergreen boughs or mulch with leaves in the fall to protect them. Any natural leaf-fall that accumulates should be left to decompose; the rich leaf-mould that results over many years is the best possible fertilizer for ferns and other woodland plants. Evergreen ferns may look somewhat tattered by late winter. If so, trim off any unsightly foliage in early spring. Varieties marked EVERGREEN should be so in Zones 7–9, but may become deciduous in colder regions or exposed windy areas.

ADIANTUM
(Maidenhair Fern) ☼•

pedatum   **ZONES 3–9**

(Northern Maidenhair) Very delicate, fan-shaped fronds. Stems are shiny and black, with light green lacy leaves, turning bright gold in fall. Slowly spreads to form a rounded medium-sized clump. This fern is a real gem, and always in demand! Suitable for a rock garden, or among shrubs. Native. DECIDUOUS.

HEIGHT/SPREAD:	30–60cm (12–24″)/30–60cm (12–24″)
LOCATION:	Moist, humusy soil.
USES:	△☂

ASPLENIUM
(Spleenwort) ☼•

Valued for their symmetrical clumps of glossy fronds. This group is quite easy to grow, best suited to a shady rock garden.

× ebenoides   **ZONES 5–9**

(Dragon's-tail Fern) Small, compact plant, best in a shaded rockery or trough garden where it can be seen. Shiny green triangular fronds. EVERGREEN

HEIGHT/SPREAD:	15–30cm (6–12″)/20–30cm (8–12″)
LOCATION:	Moist, rich neutral to alkaline soil.
USES:	△▲☂

scolopendrium   **ZONES 4–9**

(Hart's-tongue Fern) (now correctly *Phyllitus scolopendrium*) A lime-tolerant species, easy to grow. Strap-shaped fronds are not at all divided. Looks like a hardy Bird's-nest fern. Native. EVERGREEN

'Laceratum Kaye' Fronds are curled and crimped, with bizarre forked ends. Very unusual.

HEIGHT/SPREAD:	30–40cm (12–16″)/30–45cm (12–18″)
LOCATION:	Moist, well-drained alkaline soil.
USES:	△▲☂

ATHYRIUM
(Lady Fern) ☼•

Delicate and lacy-looking ferns, their triangular fronds divided into many small leaflets. These mostly form low to medium-sized dense mounds and are excellent for massing or edging. Best in a slightly acid, humus-rich soil.

filix-femina   **ZONES 3–9**

(Lady Fern) Lacy-looking fronds are bright green. Clumps are dense and mounded. An easy variety for any shady corner. Great for massing. Native. DECIDUOUS

'Vernoniae Cristata' (Crested Lady Fern) Fronds have a crisped, tasseled appearance, the ends uniquely forked.

HEIGHT/SPREAD:	60–75cm (24–30″)/60cm (2′)
LOCATION:	Moist, humus-rich soil.
USES:	⋏☂ Massing

nipponicum 'Pictum'   **ZONES 4–9**

(Japanese Painted Fern) (syn. 'Metallicum') Arching fronds are olive green with a handsome metallic-grey and red sheen. Adds a bright touch to the shade garden. Easy to grow and very popular. DECIDUOUS

HEIGHT/SPREAD:	30–60cm (12–24″)/30cm (12″)
LOCATION:	Moist, humus-rich soil.
USES:	△⋏▲☂ Massing, Borders

otophorum   **ZONES 5–9**

(Auriculate Lady Fern) Emerging fronds are a pale silvery colour, turning dark glossy green as they mature. Stems are deep red. DECIDUOUS

HEIGHT/SPREAD:	45cm (18″)/45cm (18″)
LOCATION:	Moist, humus-rich soil.
USES:	▲△⋏☂ Massing

CHEILANTHES
(Lip Fern) ☀•☼

lanosa   **ZONES 6–9**

(Hairy Lip Fern) An exception among ferns, this is one of the few species that prefers a sunny location. Low tufted clumps are made up of very finely divided dark green fronds, covered on both sides with soft rust-brown hairs. Plant this in the rock garden where it can send roots down among the cool stones. EVERGREEN

HEIGHT/SPREAD:	10–15cm (4–6″)/20cm (8″)
LOCATION:	Average well-drained soil.
USES:	△▲☂ Troughs

DRYOPTERIS
(Shield Fern) ☼•

Medium sized ferns, good for massing or groundcover plantings. Their broad, triangular fronds have the classic fern appearance, arranged in a strong-growing clump. Many of these are native to northern regions.

atrata   **ZONES 6–9**

(Shaggy Shield Fern) Light golden-green fronds. Reverse side has interesting black scales. Winter mulching is recommended. EVERGREEN

HEIGHT/SPREAD:	20–60cm (8–24″)/30cm (12″)
LOCATION:	Moist, humus-rich soil.
USES:	△▲ Massing, Borders.

austriaca   **ZONES 4–9**

(Broad Buckler Fern) (= *A. dilitata*) Graceful, wide-spreading dark green fronds. Tolerant of wet sites. Hardier than we first thought, easy. DECIDUOUS

'Lepidota Cristata' Finely cut leaflets with forked tips. Compact and very lacy. HEIGHT: 30–40cm (12–16″)

'Recurvata' Large triangular fronds, quite lacy. HEIGHT: 45–70cm (18–30″)

SPREAD:	60–90cm (2–3′)
LOCATION:	Moist, slightly acid, humus-rich soil.
USES:	△⋏☂ Borders, Massed

carthusiana   **ZONES 2–9**

(Wood Fern) (syn. *D. spinulosa*) Very easy fern. The tall, bright green fronds are widely used by florists for cut foliage. Good for naturalizing. Especially loves wet areas. Native. EVERGREEN

HEIGHT/SPREAD:	60–90cm (2–3′)/30cm (12″)
LOCATION:	Moist to wet humus-rich soil.
USES:	⋏⚡⋏▲☂ Massing

erythrosora   **ZONES 5–9**

(Autumn Fern) Compact habit, nice in the rock garden. New young fronds are coppery-pink, contrasting well against the older green fronds. Can be massed as a groundcover. Easy and adaptable. EVERGREEN

'Prolifica' (Crested Autumn Fern) Feathery, slightly curled fronds. A bit more compact.

HEIGHT/SPREAD:	30–60cm (12–24″)/30–60cm (12–24″)
LOCATION:	Moist, humus-rich soil.
USES:	△⋏▲☂ Borders.

filix-mas   **ZONES 2–9**

(Male Fern) One of the easiest and most common woodland ferns. Elegant fronds of lacy, dark green leaves. Large and robust, excellent for massing. Will tolerate a fair bit of sun if the site is wet. Native. SEMI-EVERGREEN

'Linearis Polydactylon' Lacy, fine-textured fronds, forked or tasseled at the tip.

Adiantum pedatum

Asplenium scolopendrium 'Laceratum Kaye'

Cheilanthes lanosa

Dryopteris erythrosora

Dryopteris filix-mas 'Linearis Polydactylon'

Dryopteris filix-mas 'Undulata Robusta'

Matteucia struthiopteris

'Undulata Robusta' Large leaves, especially vigorous.

HEIGHT/SPREAD: 75–90cm (30–36")/60cm (2')
LOCATION: Moist to wet, humus-rich soil.
USES: ⋔♛ Massing, Borders.

marginalis ZONES 4–9

(Leather Wood Fern) Another native species, recommended for the rock garden. Slowly forms a medium-sized clump of bluish-green fronds. DECIDUOUS

HEIGHT/SPREAD: 45–60cm (18–24")/30–45cm (12–18")
LOCATION: Moist, well-drained gravelly soil.
USES: ▲♛ Specimen

wallichiana ZONES 6–9

(Wallich's Wood Fern) Strongly upright clumps. Large triangular green fronds with a contrasting black stem. New growth is beautiful. Winter mulching recommended. SEMI-EVERGREEN

HEIGHT/SPREAD: 45–75cm (18–30")/60cm (2')
LOCATION: Moist, humus-rich soil.
USES: ▲♛ Massing, Borders.

MATTEUCIA
(Ostrich Fern) ◐●

struthiopteris ZONES 1–9

This is one of the species harvested as edible fiddleheads. Plants will form a wide-spreading patch of upright triangular green fronds. Perhaps the most common fern grown in gardens, easy to the point of becoming invasive! Good groundcover for steep slopes or damp areas. Native. DECIDUOUS

HEIGHT/SPREAD: 90–120cm (3–4')/60cm (2')
LOCATION: Rich moist to wet soil.
USES: ⋔♛ Waterside.

OSMUNDA
(Royal Fern) ☀◐●

regalis 'Purpurascens' ZONES 3–9

A truly unique and spectacular fern. This forms a large crown, sending out a ring of arching leathery green fronds with contrasting red stems. The fertile fronds that emerge from the centre stand boldly upright, and mature to a rich golden-brown. Use this as a specimen plant, or for massing. Lime-tolerant, also sun-tolerant on wet sites. DECIDUOUS

HEIGHT/SPREAD: 90–150cm (3–5')/90cm (3')
LOCATION: Rich, moist to wet soil.
USES: ♛ Specimen, Borders, Waterside.

POLYSTICHUM
(Sword Fern) ◐●

Mostly upright-growing ferns, with leathery fronds that are arranged in a formal-looking clump. Some of our best native ferns are among these.

acrostichoides ZONES 4–9

(Christmas Fern) North American native. Leathery, dark green fronds were once used for decoration at Christmas. One of the most dependable evergreen ferns. Plants form a medium-sized clump. Prefers a lime-free soil, and protection from winter winds. EVERGREEN

HEIGHT/SPREAD: 30–45cm (12–18")/30cm (12")
LOCATION: Moist, humus-rich soil.
USES: ▲♛ Massing, Borders.

braunii ZONES 4–9

(Braun's Holly Fern) Thick, dark green fronds, the stalks covered with contrasting golden-brown scales. A dense, upright grower. Protect from late spring frosts with evergreen boughs or dry leaves. Native. EVERGREEN

HEIGHT/SPREAD: 30–75cm (12–30")/30cm (12")
LOCATION: Moist, humus-rich soil.
USES: ▲♛ Massing, Borders.

munitum ZONES 6–9

(Western Sword Fern, Alaska Fern) Vigorous grower, native to the west coast. The leathery, dark green fronds form a bold clump that gets bigger each year. Excellent for naturalizing. EVERGREEN

HEIGHT/SPREAD: 60–90cm (2–3')/60–90cm (2–3')
LOCATION: Moist, humus-rich soil.
USES: ▲▲⋔♛ Specimen, Massing.

polyblepharum ZONES 5–9

(Tassel Fern) Wide-spreading, glossy dark green fronds with a tassel-like appearance as they emerge. Sensitive to late spring frosts. Medium size. EVERGREEN

HEIGHT/SPREAD: 60–75cm (24–30")/60cm (24")
LOCATION: Moist, humus-rich soil.
USES: ▲⋔♛ Massing, Borders.

tsus-simense ZONES 7–9

(Korean Rock Fern) Neat, compact clumps of dark green, triangular fronds. New leaves have a purplish cast. Heat tolerant. EVERGREEN

HEIGHT/SPREAD: 20–30cm (8–12")/30cm (12")
LOCATION: Moist, humus-rich soil.
USES: ▲▲♛ Edging.

Grasses ...*a unique landscaping opportunity*

GRASSES CAN BE USED IN SO MANY WAYS for landscape design; from bold specimen subjects to large massed plantings waving in the breeze, as a low groundcover or edging, in the border, or growing in containers and tubs.

Some grasses are grown for their colourful foliage in green, gold, red, cream or white; sometimes even attractively striped or banded. Others may be valued more for their showy flower plumes, spikes or seed heads. Several types provide dramatic and lasting interest throughout the winter months. A few varieties can do all of these things!

Ornamental Grasses combine well with almost any kind of plant. Although they can be used in a special border devoted exclusively to grasses, the effect is usually more like a collection rather than a border, and is probably best suited to botanical or demonstration gardens. The most successful way to use grasses, in the smaller residential gardens that most of us have, is to integrate them in a mixed planting along with perennials, annuals, bulbs, deciduous shrubs and evergreens.

Grasses for every garden

The selection of grasses has never been better than it is today, with an astounding range of height, spread, colour and flowering times available. There should be room in every garden for a least one variety of ornamental grass, as they can fill such a variety of functions.

Tall, upright-growing types create linear (up-and-down) interest visually, especially when used towards the back of a border. Their bold lines break up space over a long season, some remaining attractive well into winter.

Medium-sized grasses may be effectively massed together, particularly in gardens with a low-maintenance emphasis. Spring flowering bulbs combine well with these for early season interest. They are often just the perfect size to integrate into a perennial or mixed border design without becoming the centre of attention.

Low-growing grasses are ideal for edging around shrubs or combining with spreading evergreens. When mass-planted, they can often form an attractive low-maintenance groundcover.

There are recommended varieties for every climate zone in North America, so gardeners in most regions can make use of ornamental grasses. Without question, milder climate zones have a larger palette of hardy grasses available, but some of the best grasses are fortunately very hardy and will withstand extremes of cold. There are attractive, worthwhile grasses available for Zones 2–9!

Grasses can be divided into two basic groups, based on their growth cycles:

Cool season grasses. These begin their growth in early spring, reaching their full size before summer heat hits. These are usually low to medium sized plants, and some types tend to brown out in hot summer weather. Clipping or mowing in July encourages lush regrowth for fall. Divide these in late summer or early spring. Several types remain evergreen in mild winter areas.

Warm season grasses. Among these are the stars of the late summer and fall border. Some form tall clumps, often with showy spikes or plumes of flowers. These grasses usually like plenty of light and hot summer weather. They should be pruned back in late winter before new growth begins in the spring. Divide warm-season grasses in early spring only.

Are you grass-shy?

This is not always a user-friendly group of plants. Many of the botanical grass names appear long and complicated at first, and that can be intimidating. Some gardeners remain fearful that all grasses are extremely invasive, which they aren't. And then there's this business of cool-season/warm-season, when to cut them back, when to divide — none of this is of critical importance when you are first becoming familiar with the idea of gardening with grasses.

Perhaps the most important thing is to begin to see what grasses *can* look like when they are used well. Also, to try to understand that some of the best varieties are excellent tools for extending garden interest well into the fall and winter, well beyond the traditional end of the season at the first hard fall frost. Consider visiting botanical gardens or parks in your area that have built up a good collection of grasses so you can see them first hand, and at different seasons.

If you continue to struggle with the grass names and just can't seem to choose from the multitude of varieties available, feel good knowing, at least, that most nursery and garden centre staff are having as hard a time figuring them out as you are.

Grasses for special uses

Showy seed-heads in late summer/fall: Andropogon, Calamagrostis, Chasmanthium, Deschampsia, Erianthus, Miscanthus, Molinia, Panicum, Pennisetum, Stipa.

Grasses native to North America: Andropogon gerardii, Andropogon scoparius, Bouteloua gracilis, Carex grayii, Carex muskingumensis, Chasmanthium latifolium, Panicum virgatum, Stipa tenuissima.

Grasses that spread invasively by underground rhizomes: Arundo donax, Bromus inermis 'Skinner's Golden', Elymus racemosus, Glyceria maxima 'Variegata', Miscanthus sacchariflorus 'Robustus', Phalaris arundinacea, Spartina pectinata 'Aureo-marginata'.

Grasses that may self seed prolifically: (note: removing seed heads before they fully develop will prevent self seeding.) Alopecurus, Andropogon, Bouteloua, Briza, Bromus, Carex (non-variegated types), Chasmanthium, Deschampsia, Festuca, Milium, *Miscanthus, *Pennisetum, Stipa. (* seldom sets seed north of New York City)

Drought-tolerant grasses (once established): Andropogon, Bouteloua, Erianthus, Festuca, Phalaris.

Grasses for moderately dry, well-drained sites: Bouteloua, Elymus racemosus, Festuca, Helictotrichon, Pennisetum orientale, Sesleria caerulea, Stipa.

Grasses for damp or moist soils: Acorus, Carex, Chasmanthium, Deschampsia, Glyceria, Luzula, Milium, Miscanthus, Molinia, Panicum, Pennisetum, Phalaris, Spartina.

Grasses for wet soils (waterside): Acorus, Carex pendula, Chasmanthium, Deschampsia, Erianthus, Glyceria, Miscanthus, Molinia, Phalaris, Typha.

Shade-tolerant grasses: Carex (many), Chasmanthium, Deschampsia, Hakonechloa, Luzula, Milium, Phalaris.

Acorus gramineus 'Variegata'

Alopecurus pratensis 'Aureus'

Arrhenatherum elatius bulbosum 'Variegatum'

Bouteloua gracilis

ACORUS
(Sweet Flag) ☀️ ◐

Not true grasses actually, these are in the Arum or Philodendron family, and form clumps of grassy, sword-shaped leaves. The fragrant roots of certain species have been used for centuries in perfume manufacture. These are happiest growing in wet or boggy sites, especially beside water.

calamus 'Variegatus'   ZONES 4–9

(Variegated Sweet Flag) This is a herbaceous species, dying back to the ground each year. Plants spread slowly to form a sizable clump of sword-shaped leaves, similar to a water Iris, but strongly striped along the length with green and creamy yellow. Effective beside a pond, and will even grow directly in shallow water.

HEIGHT/SPREAD:	60–90cm (2–3')/60cm (24")
LOCATION:	Rich, moist to wet soil.
BLOOMS:	July–August
USES:	✄☙ Waterside

gramineus   ZONES 6–9

(Japanese Sweet Flag) Handsome evergreen clumps, most often seen planted in Japanese gardens. Plants can be effectively massed or used as an edging along paths or water features. As these are slow to establish, space closely at planting time to encourage a quicker fill-in. Foliage is fragrant when bruised. A winter mulch is recommended in Zones 5–6.

SPREAD:	30cm (12")
LOCATION:	Rich, moist to wet soil.
BLOOMS:	July–August
USES:	△〰▲☙ Edging, Waterside

'Ogon' (Golden Variegated Sweet Flag) Golden-yellow leaves with a narrow green stripe. One of the brightest forms. Excellent in pots. HEIGHT: 25cm (9").

'Pusillus Minimus Aureus' (Miniature Variegated Sweet Flag) Very dwarf form with all-gold leaves. Very slow growing. HEIGHT: 7cm (3").

'Variegatus' (Variegated Japanese Sweet Flag) Leaves are striped along their length with green and creamy-white. Best in part shade. Good for massing. HEIGHT: 20–30cm (8–12").

ALOPECURUS
(Meadow Foxtail) ☀️ ◐

pratensis 'Aureus'   ZONES 4–9

(Golden Meadow Foxtail) Medium-sized clumps of yellow and green striped leaves, slowly forming a wide clump. Good for massing towards the front of a border. Short tan-coloured spikes in late spring. Remove seed heads to prevent self-sowing. Cool-season.

HEIGHT/SPREAD:	45–60cm (18–24")/30–60cm (1–2')
LOCATION:	Rich, average to moist soil.
BLOOMS:	May–June
USES:	〰 Borders, Massing

ANDROPOGON
(Blue Stem) ☀️

Native North American grasses, originally covering large areas of the continent as a component of the prairie community, which has now largely disappeared. These are valuable grasses for late-season interest, developing warm rich foliage colours in the fall, as well as having beautiful seedheads. Warm-season.

gerardii   ZONES 2–9

(Big Bluestem) Strongly upright clumps of blue-green foliage, leaf tips often tinged with red. Distinctive seedheads are shaped like a turkey's foot and useful for floral design. Fall colour is coppery red. The best tall grass for colder zones.

HEIGHT/SPREAD:	120–180cm (4–6')/30cm (12")
LOCATION:	Average well-drained soil.
BLOOMS:	August–September
USES:	✄ Specimen, Borders, Meadow.

scoparius   ZONES 3–9

(Little Bluestem) (= *Shizachyrium scoparium*) A clumping grass native to the eastern half of the continent, this has a good compact habit that makes it well-suited for use in the border. Also effective for mass plantings or naturalizing. The ripening plumes develop a dark coppery-brown colour, an excellent contrast to the foliage as it turns from green to bronzy-orange in the fall.

HEIGHT/SPREAD:	75–90cm (30–36")/30cm (12")
LOCATION:	Average well-drained soil.
BLOOMS:	August–September
USES:	✄🌾 Borders, Meadow.

ARRHENATHERUM
(Bulbous Oat Grass) ☀️ ◐

elatius bulbosum 'Variegatum'   ZONES 2–9

Bushy, low clumps of cream and green striped leaves. Tan-coloured spikes in early summer. Combines nicely with bulbs in the spring garden. Plants usually brown out in July and should be clipped back to regrow for an attractive fall display. Drought tolerant once established. Cool-season.

HEIGHT/SPREAD:	30–45cm (12–18")/30cm (12")
LOCATION:	Average well-drained soil.
BLOOMS:	June
USES:	△🌾 Massing, Borders

ARUNDO
(Giant Reed) ☀️

donax   ZONES 7–9

Truly imposing and enormous plants, in habit these fall somewhere in between herbaceous grasses and bamboos. Clumps spread underground from woody rhizomes to form a tall patch of stout, hollow canes. Leaves are blue-green, arching gracefully out in a layered manner. In colder climates these are most often used as a foliage focal point in annual bedding schemes, and potted up to winter indoors. Where hardy, they can be used as a fast-growing screen or windbreak. Heat tolerant. Warm-season.

'Variegatus' (Variegated Giant Reed) Leaves of this form are strongly striped with creamy-yellow and green. Popular specimen plant in large parks.

HEIGHT/SPREAD:	1.8–3.5m (6–12')/90cm (3')
LOCATION:	Rich, moist soil.
BLOOMS:	September–October
USES:	Specimen, Waterside, Screen

AVENA see Helictotrichon

BOUTELOUA
(Mosquito Grass) ☀️

gracilis   ZONES 3–9

Another important native North American grass, this was a common component of the short-grass prairie plant community in the western plains. Mosquito Grass makes a low tuft of olive green leaves, with unusual spikes of bristly flowers that are held at an odd angle, somewhat resembling a flying insect. Well-behaved in the sunny border or rock garden. Drought-tolerant. Warm-season.

HEIGHT/SPREAD: 30–60cm (12–24")/30cm (12")
LOCATION: Lean to average well-drained soil.
BLOOMS: July–September
USES: △✂🏵 Borders, Massing

BRIZA
(Quaking Grass) ☀

media   ZONES 5–9
Loose clusters of delicate heart-shaped flowers are used for fresh or dried arranging. Plants form a low green tuft of leaves. Effective when combined with heaths and heathers in a moor planting. Evergreen in milder areas. Cool-season.

HEIGHT/SPREAD: 25–45cm (10–18")/30cm (12")
LOCATION: Lean well-drained soil.
BLOOMS: July–September
USES: △✂◣ Massing, Borders

BROMUS
(Brome Grass) ☀

inermis 'Skinner's Golden'   ZONES 1–9
Gold and green striped leaves make this a bright feature in the landscape. A fast spreader, best used on slopes or other difficult sites. Also excellent in containers. Remove ruthlessly any sections that turn plain green. Benefits from a mid-summer trim. Cool-season.

HEIGHT/SPREAD: 60–90cm (2–3')/60–90cm (2–3')
LOCATION: Average well-drained soil.
BLOOMS: June–July
USES: 〰🏵 Massing

CALAMAGROSTIS
(Feather Reed Grass) ☀◐

These are favorite grasses of landscape designers, who value the stiff, upright linear effect that Feather Reed Grass provides. Plants are often massed in great numbers, their wands of flowers waving in the breeze. They are equally effective used within a border in smaller groupings, remaining attractive well into the winter. Cool-season, but heat-tolerant.

SPREAD: 60cm (2')
LOCATION: Average well-drained soil.
BLOOMS: June–September
USES: ✂🏵 Accent, Massing, Borders.

× acutiflora 'Karl Foerster'   ZONES 4–9
(Foerster's Reed Grass) With its stiffly upright habit, this can be one of the most effective vertical elements in the summer and fall border. Narrow clumps of green foliage bear spikes of white flowers, first fading to rose then followed by tan seedheads. They begin blooming in early summer, remaining attractive well into the winter. Can be used as a specimen but most effective when planted in groups. HEIGHT: 120–150cm (4–5')

arundinacea 'Overdam'   ZONES 5–9
(Variegated Reed Grass) A newer selection with foliage boldly striped in white and green. Spikes of gold flowers are a nice contrast. This is one of the most exciting grasses to come along in years! Excellent as a specimen. HEIGHT: 90–120cm (3–4')

CAREX
(Sedge) ☀◐●
Though not true grasses, the Sedges are similar in appearance. Forming low to medium-sized tufts, they are frequently used for groundcover plantings, performing especially well in moist or wet areas. Flowers are usually insignificant. Most varieties benefit from a light clipping in early spring.

buchananii   ZONES 6–9
(Leatherleaf Sedge) Creates an arching, tufted clump of coppery-brown, hairlike foliage. Excellent for contrasting with dwarf conifers or other evergreens, especially in the winter garden. Also nice beside water. Everbrown.

HEIGHT/SPREAD: 45cm (18")/30cm (12")
LOCATION: Prefers a rich, moist soil.
BLOOMS: June–July
USES: △▲🏵 Borders, Massing, Waterside

comans 'Bronze'   ZONES 6–9
(Bronze Hair Sedge) Darker in colour than *C. buchananii*, this variety is otherwise fairly similar, but more compact and mounded. Effective year round. Everbrown.

HEIGHT/SPREAD: 20–30cm (9–12")/30cm (12")
LOCATION: Prefers a rich, moist soil.
BLOOMS: June–July
USES: △▲🏵 Borders, Massing, Waterside

conica 'Variegata'   ZONES 5–9
(Miniature Variegated Sedge, Hime-Kan-suge) Hardier than first expected, this little sedge is a rock garden gem. Leaves are dark green with a silver edge. Best in part shade. Evergreen.

HEIGHT/SPREAD: 15cm (6")/15–30cm (6–12")
LOCATION: Prefers a rich, moist soil.
BLOOMS: May–June
USES: △▲🏵 Edging

flagellifera   ZONES 6–9
(Orange Hair Sedge) Similar to the other Hair Sedges, but this species is much taller, more stiffly upright, with leaves of a lighter orange-rust shade. Evergreen.

HEIGHT/SPREAD: 60–90cm (2–3')/60cm (2')
LOCATION: Prefers a rich, moist soil.
BLOOMS: June–July
USES: ▲🏵 Borders, Massing, Waterside

glauca   ZONES 5–9
(Blue Sedge) Leaves are steel blue, in a low tufted clump. An adaptable sedge, growing in most garden situations. Good groundcover. Mow or clip back hard in early spring. Evergreen.

HEIGHT/SPREAD: 15cm (6")/15–30cm (6–12")
LOCATION: Prefers a rich, moist soil.
BLOOMS: May–June
USES: △〰▲🏵 Massing, Edging

grayii   ZONES 3–9
(Morning Star Sedge) A native North American species, growing best beside water. Fresh green leaves are narrow and leathery, forming an upright clump. Insignificant flowers are followed by attractive, spiky star-shaped seed pods which are interesting to use in floral arranging.

HEIGHT/SPREAD: 60cm (2')/30cm (12")
LOCATION: Prefers a rich, moist soil.
BLOOMS: May–June
USES: ✂ Massing, Waterside

morrowii 'Aureo-variegata'   ZONES 6–9
(Variegated Japanese Sedge) (= *C. hachioensis* 'Evergold') Compact, cascading tufts of creamy-yellow

Briza media

Calamagrostis arundinacea 'Overdam'

Carex comans 'Bronze'

Carex glauca

Carex morrowii 'Aureo-variegata'

Chasmanthium latifolium

Deschampsia caespitosa 'Bronzeschleier'

Elymus racemosus

and green striped leaves. Excellent plant for brightening up damp shady areas. Terrific in containers. Try underplanting with masses of purple crocus. Evergreen.

HEIGHT/SPREAD: 30cm (12")/15–30cm (6–12")
LOCATION: Prefers a rich, moist soil.
BLOOMS: May–June
USES: ⌂⋌⋏⋎⋏ Edging, Massing

muskingumensis   ZONES 4–9
(Palm Sedge) Another native North American species, though with an unusual tropical appearance. Plants form graceful clumps of divided leaves similar in effect to papyrus. Equally at home beside water or in a moist border. Best in part shade.

HEIGHT/SPREAD: 40–60cm (16–24")/30–45cm (12–18")
LOCATION: Prefers a rich, moist soil.
BLOOMS: July
USES: ⋌ Massing, Waterside

nigra   ZONES 4–9
(Black-flowered Sedge) Compact tufts of dark green foliage, black flower spikes. Recommended as a groundcover or rock garden plant in shaded areas. Evergreen.

HEIGHT/SPREAD: 15–25cm (6–10")/15–30cm (6–12")
LOCATION: Prefers a rich, moist soil.
BLOOMS: May–June
USES: ⌂⋌⋏⋎⋏ Edging, Massing

pendula   ZONES 5–9
(Drooping Sedge) Evergreen in mild winter areas, this species forms an arching clump of bright green leaves with interesting spikes of flowers held well above in summer. Useful for floral arranging, and a nice waterside feature in the garden. Shade tolerant.

HEIGHT/SPREAD: 60–120cm (2–4')/30–60cm (12–24")
LOCATION: Prefers a rich, moist soil.
BLOOMS: May–June
USES: ⋌ Massing, Borders, Waterside

siderostica 'Variegata'   ZONES 4–9
(Variegated Broad-leaved Sedge) On first viewing this is often mistaken for a narrow-leaved Hosta. The broad, sword-shaped leaves are bright green with a wide margin of creamy-white. Plants spread underground to form a loose clump or patch, so it can be used as a groundcover among taller woodland plants. Although the foliage is deciduous, the fresh spring growth is reported to emerge bright pink. Prefers dappled shade.

HEIGHT/SPREAD: 30–40cm (12–16")/30–60cm (12–24")
LOCATION: Prefers a rich, moist soil.
BLOOMS: June
USES: ⌂⋌⋎ Borders, Woodland

CHASMANTHIUM
(Sea Oats) ☀☽●

latifolium   ZONES 5–9
(Northern Sea Oats) One of the best grasses for shady sites. Upright clumps resemble a dwarf green bamboo. Gracefully arching stems hold dangling flower spikes that look like little fishes. Good for cutting. May self-seed prolifically. Native wildflower. Warm-season.

HEIGHT/SPREAD: 75–90cm (30–36")/30cm (12")
LOCATION: Prefers a rich moist soil.
BLOOMS: July–August
USES: ⋌ Specimen, Massing, Borders

DESCHAMPSIA
(Tufted Hair Grass) ☀☽

caespitosa   ZONES 4–9
Clump-forming evergreen grass with symmetrical, tufted foliage. Airy sprays of delicate green flowers

appear in early summer, maturing to deeper colours as summer goes on, and in such great numbers that the leaves become totally hidden below. Most effective when massed or allowed to drape over more substantial plants. Clip back hard in early spring. Fairly shade tolerant. Cool-season.

HEIGHT/SPREAD: 75–90cm (30–36")/30–45cm (12–18")
LOCATION: Prefers a moist, rich soil.
BLOOMS: May–August
USES: ⋌ Massing, Borders, Meadows

'Bronzeschleier' (Bronzeveil Hair Grass) Flowers mature to a mass of bronzy-mustard. Early-blooming.

'Goldstaub' (Gold-dust Hair Grass) Sprays of bright golden-yellow flowers. Late-blooming.

ELYMUS
(Lyme Grass) ☀☽

(= *Leymus*) The various garden forms of Lyme Grass are almost all grown for their exceptionally beautiful steel-blue foliage. Most of them are invasive to the extreme, so some extra consideration in placing them is advised. Control the spread by planting inside a tile or concrete drain sunk two feet down in the ground, or take advantage of the spreading nature to stabilize steep slopes. Also, use to fill in areas with poor soil where nothing else will grow. Large tubs or pots of Lyme Grass are very decorative. Warm-season.

racemosus   ZONES 4–9
(Siberian Blue Lyme Grass) Outstanding blue colour; foliage is beautiful in the garden or can be used for flower arranging. Quickly forms a large patch. Spikes of tan flowers appear in summer. Tolerant of salt spray.

HEIGHT/SPREAD: 90–120cm (3–4')/60–90cm (2–3')
LOCATION: Poor to average well-drained soil.
BLOOMS: July–August
USES: ⋌⋏⋎ Massing, Naturalizing

ERIANTHUS
(Plume Grass) ☀

ravennae   ZONES 6–9
(Northern Pampas Grass) Large, stout clumps of grey-green leaves. Silvery plumes of flowers rise on very tall stems in late summer, lasting into the winter. Almost as dramatic in the landscape as true Pampas Grass, but much hardier.

HEIGHT/SPREAD: 2.4–3.6m (8–12')/90cm (3')
LOCATION: Prefers a moist well-drained soil.
BLOOMS: August–October
USES: ⋌ Specimen, Massing, Borders

FESTUCA
(Fescue) ☀☽

Low tufted clump-formers, with fine-textured foliage from silver-blue to green. Fescues are widely planted as an edging, or massed to create a low, hummocky groundcover. All are cool-season grasses, at their best in spring and early summer. Most remain evergreen in all but the coldest regions. Removing the faded flower heads will prevent self seeding.

ovina glauca   ZONES 3–9
(Blue Fescue) (= *F. cinerea*) Valued for their low tufts of steely-blue foliage. Tan-coloured spikes rise on short stems in late spring. Clip seed heads off by mid-summer to tidy plants up. Nice in containers. Best in full sun.

SPREAD: 20–30cm (8–12")
LOCATION: Average well-drained soil.
BLOOMS: May–June
USES: ⌂▲☗ Borders, Edging, Massing

'Elijah Blue' This is the best and brightest blue selection we have ever seen! Maintains its colour throughout the season. HEIGHT: 20–25cm (8–10")

'Sea Urchin' ('Seeigel') Fairly compact form, good metallic blue-grey colour. HEIGHT: 15cm (6")

'Solling' Good steel-blue throughout the season, this selection rarely blooms, so remains fresh-looking all season long. Highly recommended for hot summer areas. HEIGHT: 20cm (8")

'Skinner's Blue' Very hardy variety, selected in Manitoba. Colour is turquoise-green, not as intense as some, but better in cold winter areas where other varieties are short-lived. HEIGHT: 30cm (12")

scoparia 'Pic Carlit'   **ZONES 5–9**
(Dwarf Bearskin Fescue) Bizarre little mounds of evergreen leaves, stiff and sharp like a spruce needle. Flower spikes are held just above the leaves. A true alpine species, this appreciates a sunny location with the sort of cool, moist root-run that rocks can easily provide. Excellent in troughs.
HEIGHT/SPREAD: 5–10cm (2–4")/20–30cm (8–12")
LOCATION: Cool, moist well-drained soil.
BLOOMS: May–June
USES: ⌂▲☗ Troughs, Edging

tenuifolia   **ZONES 3–9**
(Fine-leaved Green Fescue) Low tufts of leaves like bright green hair. Effective on its own or in combination with Blue Fescue. Nice fresh colour in early spring, excellent cover for small bulbs. Also good in troughs.
HEIGHT/SPREAD: 15–20cm (6–8")/20–30cm (8–12")
LOCATION: Average well-drained soil.
BLOOMS: May–June
USES: ⌂▲☗ Borders, Edging, Massing

GLYCERIA
(Manna Grass) ☀

maxima 'Variegata'   **ZONES 4–9**
(Variegated Manna Grass) Similar in appearance to Ribbon Grass, with leaves striped green and creamy yellow. A spreading grass best planted at the waterside, or contained in the border. Insignificant flower spikes.
HEIGHT/SPREAD: 75–90cm (30–36")/20–30cm (8–12")
LOCATION: Moist to wet soil.
BLOOMS: June–July
USES: ☗∿ Waterside

HAKONECHLOA
(Hakonechloa) ☽

macra 'Aureola'   **ZONES 6–9**
(Golden Variegated Hakonechloa) One of the slowest grasses to establish, but well worth the extra effort to grow. Leaves are bright golden-yellow with narrow green stripes, arching all to one side like a waterfall. Airy flowers appear in late summer but are mostly hidden in the foliage. Fall colour is buff. This makes a fine specimen plant, especially near a patio or water garden, with a distinctly Oriental flavour. Excellent in large tubs.
HEIGHT/SPREAD: 45–60cm (18–24")/60cm (24")
LOCATION: Rich, moist well-drained soil.
USES: ⌂☗ Specimen, Woodland, Border

HELICTOTRICHON
(Blue Oat Grass) ☀

sempervirens   **ZONES 4–9**
Incredibly popular for its perfect, dome-shaped clumps of intensely blue leaves. This non-spreader is the best blue grass for general purpose border use. Tan spikes appear above on graceful arching stems. Evergreen. Cool-season.
HEIGHT/SPREAD: 60–90cm (2–3'/60cm (2')
LOCATION: Average well-drained soil.
BLOOMS: May–July
USES: ☗ Border, Accent, Massing

HOLCUS
(Velvet Grass) ☀☽

lanatus 'Albo-variegatus'   **ZONES 4–9**
Somewhat similar to *Arrhenatherum* in appearance, this forms a compact creeping patch of fine green and white striped leaves. Good for edging along the front of a border, or beside a water feature. At its best in the cooler months, expect Velvet Grass to brown out in summer heat.
HEIGHT/SPREAD: 20–30cm (8–12")/30cm (12")
LOCATION: Prefers a rich, moist soil.
USES: ∿ Edging, Winter garden

IMPERATA
(Japanese Blood Grass) ☀☽

cylindrica 'Red Baron'   **ZONES 5–9**
Unusual and dramatic grass that slowly forms a medium-sized clump. Leaves are green at the base, and blood red at the top. Excellent for massing, and particularly effective with some clever backlighting. This can be slow to establish, and may not always predictably take to the site you have in mind; it seems to regard both hot, dry soils and heavy, wet soils with equal disdain. Warm-season.
HEIGHT/SPREAD: 45cm (18")/30cm (12")
LOCATION: Moist but well-drained soil.
USES: ⌂∿☗ Massing, Borders

LIRIOPE see Perennial chapter

LUZULA
(Wood Rush) ☽●

Grasslike plants, native to moist woodland sites, but tolerant of dry shade. They spread to form a low, dense ground cover of flat, softly hairy leaves. Although evergreen, these will need a light trim in early spring.

nivea   **ZONES 4–9**
(Snowy Wood Rush) Upright, arching clumps of grey-green leaves. Clusters of white flowers are showy in summer, good for cutting. Nice accent plant for the shade.
HEIGHT/SPREAD: 60cm (2')/30cm (1')
LOCATION: Rich, average to moist soil, preferably on the acid side.
BLOOMS: May–July
USES: ✂◁∿▲ Accent, Massing, Borders

sylvatica   **ZONES 4–9**
(Greater Wood Rush) Dense clumps of shiny, tousled green leaves. Makes a thick spreading groundcover, but isn't invasive. Small clusters of brownish flowers. Grows well beneath trees and shrubs, even tolerating dry shade.

Festuca ovina glauca 'Elijah Blue'

Glyceria maxima 'Variegata'

Hakonechloa macra 'Aureola'

Imperata cylindrica 'Red Baron'

Miscanthus floridulus

Miscanthus sinensis 'Silberfeder'

Miscanthus sinensis purpurascens

Miscanthus sinensis 'Strictus'

HEIGHT/SPREAD:	30cm (12")/30cm (12")
LOCATION:	Average to moist soil, preferably on the acid side.
BLOOMS:	May–June
USES:	△Μ·▲❦ Massing, Naturalizing

MILIUM
(Golden Grass) ☼•

effusum 'Aureum'   ZONES 5–9

A colourful little grass to lighten up a shady corner with its bright golden-yellow new growth in spring. Plants form a low clump of foliage mingled with delicate sprays of flowers. Most effective when mass planted in a cool moist location. Can be short-lived but will usually self seed. Cool-season.

HEIGHT/SPREAD:	30–40cm (12–16")/30cm (12")
LOCATION:	Prefers a rich, moist soil.
USES:	Μ· Borders, Waterside

MISCANTHUS
(Miscanthus, Eulalia) ☼☼

Large, bold grasses suited to massed plantings in the low-maintenance garden, and integrating into the perennial or mixed border. These are all warm-season grasses, tolerating heat and humidity very well. Flowers are in fan-shaped panicles, showy in the fall border, and sometimes used for cutting.

floridulus   ZONES 4–9

(Giant Chinese Silver Grass) Very tall clumps of green leaves, their tips arching gracefully in layers. Sometimes used to create a living screen or fence. Corn-like stalks remain upright through the winter. Reddish-pink flower spikes turn to silvery plumes as they mature. Tolerates shade and poor soils.

HEIGHT/SPREAD:	3m (10')/90cm (3')
LOCATION:	Prefers a moist but well-drained soil.
BLOOMS:	September–October
USES:	Specimen, Screen, Living Fence

sacchariflorus 'Robustus'   ZONES 4–9

(Giant Silver Grass) Quickly forms a patch of tall, stout corn-like stems, clothed by gracefully arching foliage with a bamboo-like, tropical appearance. Silvery plumes turn reddish as they mature, and the foliage also has good red-orange fall colour. This plant may need to be contained to keep it in bounds as the roots have a tendency to run.

HEIGHT/SPREAD:	1.8m (6')/90cm (3')
LOCATION:	Prefers a rich, moist to wet soil.
BLOOMS:	August–September
USES:	Specimen, Screen, Waterside

sinensis   ZONES 5–9

(Japanese Silver Grass) A superb group of grasses, versatile both as specimens or in mass plantings. All bloom in the fall, and hold their shape well into the winter, fading to shades of tan or cream and contrasting nicely with evergreens. Selections vary widely in leaf color, height, form and hardiness.

SPREAD:	90cm (3')
LOCATION:	Prefers a moist but well-drained soil.
BLOOMS:	August–October
USES:	✂❦ Borders, Specimen, Massing

'Autumn Light' One of the hardiest cultivars, a vigorous variety that resembles the species, with creamy plumes in late summer. Zones 4–9. HEIGHT: 1.8–2.4m (6–8')

'Cosmopolitan' Similar to 'Variegatus' but leaves are twice as wide, creating a very bold white-and-green striped effect. Plants are self-supporting. Hardiness

range is not yet fully determined, but probably Zones 6–9. HEIGHT: 1.8–2.4m (6–8')

'Gracillimus' (Maiden Grass) Long, arching narrow green leaves, forming a large symmetrical clump. The best for formal plantings. Does not flower reliably in cool-summer areas. HEIGHT: 1.2–1.8m (4–6')

'Malepartus' Very hardy variety, with showy purple-pink plumes in late summer. Green foliage, becoming bronze in fall. Zones 4–9. HEIGHT: 1.5–1.8m (5–6')

'Morning Light' (Variegated Maiden Grass) Very narrow rolled leaves similar to 'Gracillimus', but with a narrow band of white on the margin. The effect from several feet away is silvery and shimmering. Very late to flower with bronzy-red spikes. A recent introduction that is quickly becoming very popular. HEIGHT: 1.5–1.8m (5–6')

'Nippon' Compact variety with fine-textured leaves, better suited to smaller gardens or containers. Fall colour is bronzy-red. HEIGHT: 1.2m (4')

purpurascens (Flame Grass) Early-blooming variety with spikes of rose flowers in August. Strongly upright clumps of green leaves, turning flame-orange and rust for the fall. Hardy to Zone 4. HEIGHT: 120–150cm (4–5')

'Rotsilber' (Red-Silver Maiden Grass) Compact German selection with outstanding large deep red plumes. Silvery foliage develops good fall colour as well. HEIGHT: 90–150cm (3–5')

'Silberfeder' (Silver Feather Grass) A older selection, a refined version of the species, with shimmering silvery-white plumes appearing in late August, held up high above the foliage. Hardy to Zone 4. HEIGHT: 150–180cm (5–6')

'Silberpfeil' (Silver Arrow Miscanthus) Similar in appearance to 'Variegatus', with brighter variegation and a more upright habit. HEIGHT: 1.8–2.4m (6–8')

'Strictus' (Porcupine Grass) Bright green leaves with golden horizontal banding. Stiff, upright clumps that never require staking. Unique specimen plant. HEIGHT: 150–180cm (5–6')

'Undine' Selected for its low foliage, the showy silver-white plumes held well above in early fall. Good compact form that is in scale with smaller gardens. HEIGHT: 1.2–1.5m (4–5')

'Variegatus' (Variegated Silver Grass) Distinct green and white striped leaves in an arching clump. Creamy-pink plumes in September in warm-summer regions. Very bright and showy. ZONES 6–9. HEIGHT: 1.5–1.8m (5–6')

'Yaku Jima' (Dwarf Maiden Grass) A newer, compact selection from Japan. Foliage is narrow, silvery green, similar to 'Gracillimus'. Silver plumes appear in August. Zones 6–9. HEIGHT: 90–120cm (3–4')

'Zebrinus' (Zebra Grass) Exactly like 'Strictus', but the plant habit is not quite as upright. May need support in shady exposures. HEIGHT: 1.5–2.1m (5–7')

MOLINIA
(Moor Grass) ☼☼

caerulea   ZONES 3–9

A variable species that has given a number of excellent cultivars. Native to moist, acid moors in northern Europe but readily adapts to garden conditions. Plants form a non-spreading mound of grassy leaves at the base, with tall branching stems of delicate flowers rising above in summer. Warm-season.

SPREAD: 30–60cm (1–2')
LOCATION: Prefers a rich, moist soil.
BLOOMS: July–October
USES: ✂❀ Specimen, Massing, Borders

***arundinacea* 'Transparent'** A tall-growing selection, which has been described as a "kinetic sculpture". Heads of flowers are in constant motion from the slightest breeze. Excellent in front of a dark backdrop. HEIGHT: 1.5–1.8m (5–6'). Another very similar selection is called 'Skyracer'.

'Moorhexe' (Moor-witch) Compact habit. Leaves are dark green with some red tones in fall, with airy sprays of purple flowers. HEIGHT: 45–75cm (18–30")

'Variegata' An older selection, but still one of the best variegated grasses. Bright yellow-and-green striped leaves, medium-tall stems of purplish flowers. HEIGHT: 60–75cm (24–30")

OPHIOPOGON see Perennial chapter

PANICUM
(Switch Grass) ☀◐

Switch grass has made great strides in recent years, some of the newer selections becoming valued additions to perennial and mixed borders all over Europe and North America.

***virgatum* 'Rehbraun'**   ZONES 3–9
(Red Switch Grass) One of the best grasses for multi-season interest, particularly for winter display. Plants form a wide clump of narrow green leaves, with airy clouds of flowers in July giving way to red seed heads in late summer. Outstanding yellow and red fall foliage colour, fading to tan in the winter. An important component of the original tallgrass prairie which once covered large areas of the North American plains. Drought and salt tolerant. Warm-season.

SPREAD: 60–90cm (2–3')
LOCATION: Average to moist fertile soil.
BLOOMS: July–September
USES: ✂❀❈ Borders, Massing

'Haense Herms' Compact variety. Orange-red fall colour. HEIGHT: 90cm (3')

'Heavy Metal' Excellent new selection. Bright metallic-blue foliage all season, developing yellow and red fall highlights. HEIGHT: 90–120cm (3–4')

'Rehbraun' Reddish-brown tinged leaves. HEIGHT: 90–120cm (3–4')

'Rotstrahlbusch' The best variety for deep red fall colour. HEIGHT: 90–120cm (3–4'

'Strictum' Tall-growing seed strain. Good blue-green foliage, stiff upright habit. HEIGHT: 120–180cm (4–6')

PENNISETUM
(Fountain Grass) ☀

A well-named grass, as the hundreds of soft bottlebrush flower spikes that arch out and move in the breeze do indeed resemble the spray of a fountain. The different species and selections now available vary greatly in hardiness, but most are quite effective even when treated as annuals in colder regions, especially in container plantings. Warm season.

alopecuroides   ZONES 5–9
Medium-sized clumps of cascading green leaves. Flowers are buff-coloured feathery spikes, held just above the leaves, followed by similar seed-heads.

Excellent fall and early winter effect, foliage turns bright almond. Blooms best in a hot location. The species itself varies somewhat in height, flower colour and hardiness.

HEIGHT/SPREAD: 90–120cm (3–4')/60–75cm (24–30")
LOCATION: Average well-drained soil.
BLOOMS: August–October
USES: ✂❀❈ Borders, Massing, Specimen

'Hameln' (Dwarf Fountain Grass) Compact, earlier flowering selection. Excellent for massing and in containers. Reported to be the most reliably hardy variety in Zones 5–6. HEIGHT: 60–75cm (24–30")

'Little Bunny' A new miniature form, ideal for edging borders or in the rock garden. Also the perfect plant for children's gardens! HEIGHT: 30cm (12")

'Moudry' (Black-flowered Fountain Grass) Dark, near-black bottlebrush spikes in early fall. Late to flower. Zone 6. HEIGHT: 75–90cm (30–36")

'Burgundy Giant'   ZONE 9
(Burgundy Giant Fountain Grass) Newer selection with similar uses to *P. setaceum* 'Rubrum', but quite distinct in appearance. The wide, arching leaves are deep beet-red in colour, and held in layers that give an exotic tropical feel to the plant. Rosy-purple flower plumes are held above in late summer. Plants will reach a large size in warm summer regions. Best used in containers so it can be wintered indoors. Protect from wind.

HEIGHT/SPREAD: 120–160cm (4–6')/60–90cm (24–36")
LOCATION: Moist, well-drained soil.
BLOOMS: August–October
USES: ✂❀ Massing, Specimen, Borders

orientale   ZONES 7–9
(Oriental Fountain Grass) Unusual for its showy display of rose-pink flowers, blooming earlier and longer than other types as well. Great numbers of plumes are held well above the dense clump of grey-green foliage. Excellent medium-sized grass for the border.

HEIGHT/SPREAD: 60–75cm (24–30")/60–75cm (24–30")
LOCATION: Average to moist well-drained soil.
BLOOMS: August–October
USES: ✂❀❈ Borders, Massing, Specimen

setaceum 'Rubrum'   ZONE 9
(Purple-leaved Fountain Grass) Outstanding burgundy-red foliage. Showy rosy-red plumes arch from the clump in late summer and fall. Though not hardy in most areas, this grass is widely used as a specimen or accent plant for summer bedding, in containers and tubs. Remains effective into late fall.

HEIGHT/SPREAD: 90–120cm (3–4')/60–75cm (24–30")
LOCATION: Average to moist soil.
BLOOMS: August–October
USES: ✂❀ Massing, Specimen, Borders

PHALARIS
(Ribbon Grass) ☀◐

arundinacea   ZONES 2–9
Fast-spreading clumps of semi-evergreen leaves, brightly striped with various colours. Flowers are tan-coloured spikes. Useful groundcover, especially in wet areas, but spreads too quickly for the border unless contained. Excellent in pots and tubs. Cool-season.

HEIGHT/SPREAD: 60–90cm (2–3')/60–90cm (2–3')
LOCATION: Average to wet soil.
BLOOMS: June–July
USES: ✂∿❀ Massing, Waterside

'Feesey's Form' (= 'Tricolor') Attractive stripes of pink, green and cream, most effective in the spring. Reported to be an improvement on 'Picta', standing up better to summer heat and humidity, and remaining attractive

Molinia caerulea 'Variegata'

Panicum virgatum 'Heavy Metal'

Pennisetum orientale

Pennisetum setaceum 'Rubrum'

Stipa tenuissima

Stipa capillata

Typha minima

all season long. Foliage is excellent for floral arranging.
HEIGHT: 45–70cm (18–30")

'Picta' (Gardener's Garters) The old-fashioned form, green and creamy white stripes.

SESLERIA
(Moor Grass) ☀ ◔

caerulea   ZONES 5–9
(Blue Moor Grass) A clump-forming grass with metallic blue-grey foliage. Spikes of purplish flowers appear in early spring. Compact clumps can be used as an accent or for massing. Tolerates wet sites.

HEIGHT/SPREAD:	20–45cm (8–18")/30cm (12")
LOCATION:	Average to moist soil.
BLOOMS:	April–May
USES:	△ ⋀⋅ Massing, Borders, Meadows

SPARTINA
(Cord Grass) ☀ ◔

pectinata 'Aureo-marginata'   ZONES 5–9
(Variegated Cord Grass) An upright grass, spreading quickly to form a patch or open clump. Stems are tall, the strongly arching foliage is bright green with a wide yellow margin. Most effective for massing, especially beside a pond or stream. Also nice at the back of the border. Good foliage for flower arranging. Drought-resistant once established.

HEIGHT/SPREAD:	1.5–2.1m (5–7')/90cm (3')
LOCATION:	Average to moist soil.
BLOOMS:	August–September
USES:	✂ ⋔ Massing, Borders, Waterside

STIPA
(Feather Grass) ☀

Quite unique among grasses, Stipa are valued for their whiskered panicles or flower-heads. These are usually airy open sprays of tiny individual flowers held well above the leaves on the ends of graceful arching stems. Some types are especially valuable in hot, dry climates as they readily withstand drought. Warm-season.

capillata   ZONES 5–9
(Needle-and-thread) Especially beautiful flower panicles with long, straight silky awns or whiskers in mid-summer. These are loved by floral designers for fresh or dry use. This dislikes heavy wet soils but adapts very well to summer drought conditions. Excellent when massed on a slope or hill, but also nice in a sunny border.

HEIGHT/SPREAD:	75–120cm (30–48")/45cm (18")
LOCATION:	Fertile, well-drained soil.
BLOOMS:	July–August
USES:	✂ ⋔ ⋫ Massing, Borders

tenuissima   ZONES 6–9
(Mexican Feather Grass) (= *S. tenuifolia*) Beautiful compact species, the fine hair-like bright green leaves forming a low clump. Spikes of bearded green flowers begin to appear in mid-summer, soon changing into handsome, golden-blond plumes. Even just a few plants will constantly be in motion from the slightest breeze. A unique flower for cutting, either fresh or dried. This may prove to be far hardier than first thought as long as plants have excellent drainage.

HEIGHT/SPREAD:	45–60cm (18–24")/30cm (12")
LOCATION:	Average to dry well-drained soil.
BLOOMS:	June–September
USES:	✂ ⋔ ⋫ Massing, Borders

TYPHA
(Cattail) ☀

minima   ZONES 4–9
(Dwarf Japanese Cattail) This is like a miniature version of our native Cattail, on a scale more suited to the smaller garden. Narrow grassy leaves form a clump or small patch. Short, dark brown cattails appear in early summer. These can be cut for flower arranging. Prefers a wet to moist site, and is best at the waterside. Also worth trying in tubs.

HEIGHT/SPREAD:	45–70cm (18–30")/30–60cm (1–2')
LOCATION:	Moist to wet soil.
BLOOMS:	June–July
USES:	✂ ⋔ Waterside, Specimen

Symbols Key

☀	Full Sun
◔	Part Shade
●	Full Shade
△	Alpine
✂	Good Cut Flower
▲	Evergreen
⋀⋅	Groundcover
⋩	Attracts Butterflies
⋌	Attracts Hummingbirds
⋔	Suitable for Containers
⋫	Drought Tolerant

Groundcovers *...a low–maintenance alternative*

GROUNDCOVERS HAVE BECOME VERY important elements within the context of contemporary landscape design. For one thing, their ability to cover large areas quickly can significantly reduce the time, energy and cost that would otherwise be required to remove weeds. But there are other benefits to consider; dense groundcovers can act as a living mulch, helping to conserve water. For difficult sites, such as dense shade or steep slopes, there are groundcovers that will happily thrive where turf might fail or be too hazardous to maintain.

Also, there is more and more concern lately over the long-term environmental effects of maintaining huge areas of lawn. Certain groundcovers may be used effectively as alternatives to lawn monoculture, hopefully reducing the need for heavy doses of fertilizers and pesticides.

Planning & planting

From a design point of view, there are many interesting textural choices available among the various types of groundcovers. Some are evergreen, others deciduous. A few have showy fall or winter colour, some have bright berries that attract birds and other wildlife. Different regions of the country have their own ubiquitous, overused groundcover plants (Japanese Spurge, Periwinkle, Hypericum), but recently we are noticing a swing towards alternatives to these old standbys, and again this varies from region to region.

Whatever plants you select, if carefully chosen and properly installed, can last for many years with a minimum of care and attention. However, when badly chosen or poorly

established, groundcover plantings can be a real eyesore, getting patchy and full of weeds. The extra time and cost involved in planning and preparing your site will pay off many times over the long term.

1. Eradicate all perennial weeds with a systemic, non-selective herbicide, or smother them out by using a black plastic mulch or thick layers of newspaper for a full year.

2. Look carefully at light, soil and moisture conditions first, and then try to find a plant that will tolerate what the site has to offer.

3. Modify the soil, if necessary, by adding plenty of weed-free organic matter. A loose, open soil is ideal for plants to get rooted and establish quickly. Steep slopes may require stabilizing with wire mesh before planting.

4. Space plants closely enough to fill in completely within two or three growing seasons. Spacing them too far apart will allow weeds to become established. Each variety listed has a recommended number of plants per square metre (e.g. 5–9 plants/m²). Roughly the same number per square yard should be used. Note that the cost of installation increases proportionately when you use more plants. In other words, certain groundcovers can be darned expensive to install!

5. Use an organic mulch, such as bark chips, to minimize future weed problems, but don't go more than about two inches thick if the plants you have chosen send out runners that want to root into the ground. In any case, hand weeding will still be required, especially in the first two years.

6. Water new plantings regularly for the first year. An oscillating sprinkler or soaker hose is ideal for this. Deep waterings every two weeks or so will help to encourage strong healthy roots. In subsequent years, groundcovers that have been well-chosen for the site should need watering only during extended periods of drought.

7. Fertilizing yearly in the spring will help to keep your groundcover thick and vigorous; a thin or patchy groundcover lets in weeds! Choose from the many organic or inorganic fertilizers available at your garden centre. Avoid lawn formulations with high nitrogen, and never use a Weed-and-Feed as it will kill or severely damage all groundcovers. Compost or composted manure is also excellent as an annual top dressing in the spring.

Check out these varieties…

These varieties, sometimes considered to be groundcovers, may be found listed under Perennials. In order to save space we have chosen not to list them twice: Aegopodium, Ajuga, Alchemilla, Artemisia, Cerastium, Ceratostigma, Chrysogonum, Convallaria, Coronilla, Dianthus, Epimedium, Fragaria, Galium, Geranium, Helianthemum, Hemerocallis, Hosta, Lamiastrum, Lamium, Liriope, Lysimachia, Mazus, Ophiopogon, Phlox, Saxifraga, Sedum, Stachys, Thymus, Tiarella, Waldtsteinia.

Andromeda polifolia 'Nana'

Cornus canadensis

Gaultheria procumbens

Genista pilosa 'Vancouver Gold'

ANDROMEDA
(Bog Rosemary) ☀ ◐

polifolia 'Nana'   ZONES 1–9
(Dwarf Bog Rosemary) Low, evergreen shrub with narrow grey-green leaves similar to Rosemary. Clusters of light pink bell-flowers make a nice display in spring. Does well in difficult wet sites. Needs acidic conditions, so makes a good companion plant beneath Rhododendrons or Azaleas. Best used to cover small areas only.

HEIGHT:	15–20cm (6–8")
SPACING:	30cm (1'); 7–12 plants/m²
LOCATION:	Moist to wet acid soil.
BLOOMS:	April–June
USES:	△∿▲🐦 Wildflower, Woodland

ARCTOSTAPHYLOS
(Bearberry, Kinnikinnick) ☀ ◐

uva-ursi   ZONES 2–9
Despite it being a native plant from coast to coast, Bearberry in not yet widely known and grown across the country. This will form a mat of glossy, evergreen foliage on low trailing stems. Pink bell-shaped flowers appear in spring, followed by bright red berries that remain showy for months. Foliage turns bronzy-red in cold winter areas. Fairly drought tolerant once established. Plantings seem to do best in sandy, acid soils with plenty of humus. Dislikes heavy wet soils.
'Vancouver Jade' An especially vigorous and disease-resistant selection from the west coast. Effective as a lawn substitute over large areas. Introduced by the U.B.C. Botanical Garden and registered with the Canadian Ornamental Plant Foundation. Recommended for Zones 4–9.

HEIGHT:	10–15cm (4–6")
SPACING:	30–60cm (1–2'); 5–9 plants/m²
LOCATION:	Prefers an acid, well-drained soil.
BLOOMS:	April–June
USES:	△∿▲🐦🦌 Wildflower

CORNUS
(Dogwood) ◐

canadensis   ZONES 1–9
(Bunchberry) Native all across northern Canada, usually seen growing in bright, open deciduous or mixed woods. Plants creep to make a loose mat of pointed green leaves, developing deep bronze-red tones in the fall. Miniature greenish-white dogwood flowers appear in spring, later bearing showy clusters of scarlet-red berries. Plants dug directly from the wild seldom survive transplanting; look for strong container-grown plants to get off to a vigorous start. A slow-growing gem for neutral or acidic conditions. Best used to cover small areas only.

HEIGHT:	10–15cm (4–6")
SPACING:	20–30cm (8–12"); 9–16 plants/m²
LOCATION:	Moist, sandy or peaty acidic soil.
BLOOMS:	May–June
USES:	△∿ Woodland garden

COTONEASTER
(Cotoneaster) ☀ ◐

dammeri   ZONES 5–9
(Bearberry Cotoneaster) Fast-growing creeping shrub, excellent choice for slopes, walls or containers. Effective as a lawn substitute over large areas. Rounded leathery green leaves are evergreen in mild winter areas, other-wise deciduous. White flowers in early summer, followed by bright red berries that remain showy all winter.

HEIGHT:	15–30cm (6–12")
SPACING:	60–90cm (2–3'); 3–8 plants/m²
LOCATION:	Average well-drained soil.
BLOOMS:	May–June
USES:	△∿▲🐦 Lawn substitute.

EUONYMUS
(Winter Creeper) ☀◐●

fortunei 'Colorata'   ZONES 3–9
(Purple-Leaf Wintercreeper) The hardiest of the Winter Creepers, with spreading stems of leathery evergreen leaves of a coarse to medium texture. Foliage turns dusky purple in the fall, and may go deciduous in cold winter areas. Widely used for mass planting, especially in the eastern part of the country. Plants will also climb walls, trees or rough fences.

HEIGHT:	30–45cm (12–18")
SPACING:	60–75cm (24–30"); 3–4 plants/m²
LOCATION:	Average well-drained soil.
USES:	∿▲🐦 Climbing Vine

GAULTHERIA
(Wintergreen) ◐

procumbens   ZONES 3–9
(Wintergreen, Checkerberry) Beautiful little native North American groundcover flourishing in acidic peaty areas across northern Canada. Plants form a low mat of glossy dark green leaves, bearing pink bell-shaped flowers in early summer, followed by a crop of fat red edible berries in fall and winter. Widely planted as a groundcover at the west coast, but worth a try elsewhere in neutral to acidic conditions such as might be found beneath Rhododendrons. Slow spreading. Best used to cover small areas only.

HEIGHT:	15cm (6")
SPACING:	20–30cm (8–12"); 9–16 plants/m²
LOCATION:	Moist, sandy or peaty acidic soil.
BLOOMS:	June–August
USES:	△∿▲ Wildflower, Edible fruit

GENISTA
(Broom) ☀

pilosa 'Vancouver Gold'   ZONES 4–9
Fast-spreading evergreen shrub, forming a dense carpet of grey-green stems, smothered by golden-yellow pea flowers in late spring. Good choice for slopes and effective over large areas as a lawn substitute. Fairly drought resistant. Introduced by the U.B.C. Botanical Garden and registered with the Canadian Ornamental Plant Foundation.

HEIGHT:	15–20cm (6–8")
SPACING:	60–75cm (24–30"); 3–5 plants/m²
LOCATION:	Prefers a light well-drained soil.
BLOOMS:	May–June
USES:	△∿▲🦌 Lawn substitute

HEDERA
(Ivy) ☀◐●

A very well-known, popular group of evergreen vines. Of the hundreds of varieties in existence only a few are used outdoors as hardy groundcovers or climbers. Plants are generally vigorous, quickly spreading to form a dense patch, with the stems rooting where they touch the ground or forming aerial roots to climb up verticle surfaces. Cold dry winds or full sun may cause scorching in winter, so choose a sheltered site in colder regions.

HEIGHT: 10–15cm (4–6″)
SPACING: 30–60cm (1–2′); 5–16 plants/m²
LOCATION: Prefers a rich, moist soil.
USES: 〰▲ﾈ Climbing vine, Lawn substitute

colchica 'Dentata Variegata'   ZONES 7–9
(Variegated Persian Ivy) A rather large-leaved Ivy, the unlobed leathery foliage is light green overlaid with grey-green and creamy-yellow blotches. Widely grown at the west coast.

helix   ZONES 5–9
(English Ivy) Vigorous evergreen groundcover or climbing vine. Creeping stems form a dense mat of dark-green leathery leaves. Very tolerant of shady sites. All varieties will either creep along the ground or climb by aerial roots, given some initial support. The various cultivars of English Ivy are currently in a rather mixed-up state within the trade, and sometimes even the descriptions in reference books disagree.
'Baltica' (Baltic Ivy) Medium-sized leaves, bright green in summer, dark green in winter or bronzy in colder areas. New growth is glossy. An excellent groundcover or climbing vine.
'Glacier' Leaves are small, dark green with grey-green and creamy-yellow margins. Freely branching, with a low, compact habit. Not a fast spreader. Beautiful with spring flowering bulbs. Also easily grown in pots to take inside for the winter. Zones 6–9.
'Hahn's' Bright green medium-sized leaves, the self-branching habit makes this a good groundcover selection. Zones 6–9.
'Little Diamond' Interesting diamond-shaped leaves without the usual ivy points at first. Habit is dense and bushy, colour is grey-green with a creamy-white edge. Zones 6–9.
'Needlepoint' A bushy, well-branched variety forming a dense mat of dark green birdsfoot-shaped leaves. Zones 6–9.
'Thorndale' Leaves are small, leathery, dark green with prominent white veins. This variety is often recommended as the hardiest type. Bronzy-red winter colour. Zones 5–9.

HYPERICUM
(St. John's-wort) ☀☼●

calycinum   ZONES 5–9
Large golden-yellow flowers appear throughout the summer and fall, blooming more reliably in sunny exposures. Plants have upright stems of bright green leaves, forming a dense weed-proof patch. Tolerant of poor soils and moderately drought-tolerant. Especially good for stabilizing slopes. Widely used at the west coast. Evergreen in Zones 7–9.

HEIGHT: 30–45cm (12–18″)
SPACING: 30–45cm (12–18″); 5–9 plants/m²
LOCATION: Average well-drained soil.
BLOOMS: May–October
USES: 〰▲ﾈﾉ

MAIANTHEMUM
(False Lily-of-the-Valley) ☼●

dilatatum   ZONES 5–9
(= *M. kamtschaticum*) A west-coast native wildflower, similar in effect to the true Lily-of-the-Valley. Plants slowly spread to form a patch of rounded green leaves, bearing short spikes of delicate white flowers in spring. Prefers a moist woodland setting. Best used to cover small areas only.

HEIGHT: 15–30cm (6–12″)
SPACING: 20–30cm (8–12″); 9–16 plants/m²
LOCATION: Moist, sandy or peaty acidic soil.
BLOOMS: April–June
USES: ◿〰 Woodland garden

PACHYSANDRA
(Japanese Spurge) ☼●

terminalis   ZONES 3–9
Dark green, glossy foliage forms a dense, spreading patch. White flowers appear briefly in spring. Very tolerant of poor soils and deep shade. One of the most reliable evergreen groundcovers, but notoriously slow to establish.

HEIGHT: 20cm (8″)
SPACING: 15–30cm (6–12″); 9–16 plants/m²
LOCATION: Prefers a rich, moist soil.
BLOOMS: April–May
USES: 〰▲ Lawn substitute

PAXISTIMA
(Cliff Green, Ratstripper) ☀☼

canbyi   ZONES 2–9
Native North American evergreen shrub with small, glossy dark-green leaves, turning bronze in fall and winter. Fine-textured plant deserving of wider use. Excellent for underplanting trees and shrubs. Will spread slowly to form a dense patch. Best used to cover small areas only.

HEIGHT: 30cm (12″)
SPACING: 30–45cm (12–18″); 6–9 plants/m²
LOCATION: Average well-drained soil.
USES: ◿〰▲

POTENTILLA
(Cinquefoil) ☀☼

fruticosa 'Yellow Gem'   ZONES 2–9
An outstanding groundcover selection introduced by the U.B.C. Botanical Garden. Large yellow flowers appear over many months on this low, spreading shrub. Excellent for edging, containers, or in mass plantings. Deciduous. Registered with the Canadian Ornamental Plant Foundation.

HEIGHT: 30–40cm (12–16″)
SPACING: 45–60cm (18–24″); 4–9 plants/m²
LOCATION: Average well-drained soil.
BLOOMS: May–October
USES: ◿〰ﾈ Mixed borders

RUBUS
(Raspberry) ☀☼

calycinoides 'Emerald Carpet'   ZONES 7–9
(Taiwan Creeper) Low spreading, fast-growing evergreen groundcover. Rounded leaves are rough-textured and attractively scalloped. Edible golden berries appear in late summer. Effective as a lawn substitute over large areas. Fairly drought-tolerant. Introduced by the U.B.C. Botanical Garden and registered with the Canadian Ornamental Plant Foundation.

HEIGHT: 10–15cm (4–6″)
SPACING: 60–90cm (2–3′); 4–9 plants/m²
LOCATION: Average well-drained soil.
USES: ◿〰▲ﾉ Lawn substitute.

Hedera helix 'Baltica'

Hedera helix 'Glacier'

Pachysandra terminalis

Rubus calycinoides 'Emerald Carpet'

Vaccinium vitis-idaea 'Minus'

Vinca minor 'Atropurpurea'

VACCINIUM
(Cranberry) ☀ ◔

vitis-idaea 'Minus'   ZONES 2–9
(Cowberry, Lingonberry) Low spreading bushes of rounded, shiny green leaves. Pale-pink bell flowers in late spring, followed by bright red edible berries. Very popular in Scandinavia for making jams and jellies. Also native to North America. Nice in cool, shady areas; good companion to Rhododendrons or Azaleas. Best used to cover small areas only.

HEIGHT:	20cm (8")
SPACING:	30cm (12"); 9–12 plants/m²
LOCATION:	Prefers a moist, acid soil.
BLOOMS:	May–June
USES:	◭〰▲ Edible berries

VINCA
(Periwinkle, Myrtle) ☀ ◔ ●

These are low, mat-forming plants, with creeping stems that root as they touch the ground. Flowers appear in spring, contrasting nicely with the glossy leaves.

herbacea   ZONES 2–9
(Deciduous Periwinkle) More vigorous than *Vinca minor* and much better in sunny areas. Clear blue, starry flowers appear over a trailing mat of narrow, bright green leaves. Excellent groundcover for cold winter areas, but not really dense enough to suppress weeds without a mulch.

HEIGHT:	10–15cm (4–6")
SPACING:	30–45cm (12–18"); 9–12 plants/m²
LOCATION:	Average well-drained soil.
BLOOMS:	May–June
USES:	◭〰 Sunny banks and slopes.

minor   ZONES 3–9
Extremely popular groundcover, valued for its thick mat of glossy evergreen leaves, studded with periwinkle-blue flowers in spring. Very shade tolerant, even of dry shade, but tends to burn in full sun. Good reliable cover for large or small areas.
'Alba' Green leaves, white flowers.
'Atropurpurea' Deep wine-red flowers, green leaves.
'Aureo-variegata' Green and golden-yellow leaves, blue flowers.
'Sterling Silver' Leaves green, edged in silver. White flowers.
'Variegata' Roundish leaves, green with white edge. Blue flowers.

HEIGHT:	10–15cm (4–6")
SPACING:	30–45cm (12–18"); 6–12 plants/m²
LOCATION:	Average to moist well-drained soil.
BLOOMS:	April–June
USES:	◭〰▲ Lawn substitute

Hardiness Zones

Use this table to help determine which plants are suitable for your winter conditions. Any plant with your zone number or lower should be suitable. **If you are in doubt be sure to ask your local garden centre staff.**

	Minimum Winter Temp.	
Zone	°F	°C
1	Below -50	Below -46
2	-50 to -40	-46 to -40
3	-40 to -30	-40 to -34
4	-30 to -20	-34 to -29
5	-20 to -10	-29 to -23
6	-10 to 0	-23 to -18
7	0 to 10	-18 to -12
8	10 to 20	-12 to -7
9	20 to 30	-7 to -1
10	30 to 40	-1 to 4

Use this information as a general guide for selecting suitable plants for your area. Many other factors affect overwintering of perennials. Some of these factors include: reliability and depth of snow cover, soil moisture levels, and site-specific micro-climates.

Calculating groundcover requirements

First, calculate the Area (either Metric or U.S.) of the site. Look at the plant description to determine recommended spacings. These spacings should allow for a solid fill in two or three growing seasons if you begin with vigorous, healthy plants grown in 9cm (3") pots. Then use the chart below to figure out approximately how many plants will be required.

Spacing	Plants/m²	Plants/ft²	Area per 100 plants
10cm (4")	96.8	9	1.0m² (11ft²)
15cm (6")	43	4	2.3m² (25ft²)
20cm (8")	24.2	2.25	4.1m² (45ft²)
25cm (10")	15	1.4	6.7m² (72ft²)
30cm (12")	10.8	1	9.3m² (100ft²)
40cm (16")	6.1	.57	16.5m² (176ft²)
45cm (18")	4.7	.44	21.3m² (227ft²)
60cm (24")	2.7	.25	37.0m² (400ft²)

Multiply:	By:	To Calculate:
Square metres	10.76	Square feet
Square metres	1.20	Square yards
Square feet	.09	Square metres
Square yards	.84	Square metres

Herbs …*packed full of flavour & goodness*

THE WORD *HERB* HAS HAD MANY DIFFERENT meanings over time. Nowadays the definition has been broadened to include all plants that are of use to man for such diverse purposes as flavouring foods and beverages, for medicinal purposes, as pest repellents, room deodorizers, in perfumes and cosmetics, or for dying cloth and fibres.

Most of our common cooking herbs, like basil or parsley, have flavourful leaves. With chicory we can roast and grind the root as a coffee substitute. In the case of lovage and Florence fennel the stems may be eaten as a vegetable. The seeds of caraway and coriander are ground and used as a spice. Spices are usually dried parts of plants that can be stored for a long time. Some herbs, therefore, are also spices when they are used dried: oregano, rosemary, sage, and marjoram for example.

Growing Herbs

Any sunny garden that can successfully grow vegetables or geraniums should be an excellent site for most herbs. Direct sun all day long is recommended, but a site with full sun for only 3 to 4 hours, or even filtered sunlight all day should still give good results.

Growing herbs indoors is also possible with a sunny south window, or fluorescent lights; they can be grown in pots of soil or even hydroponically. Good candidates for the house include basil, chives, dill, lemon balm, marjoram, mint, oregano, parsley, rosemary, sage, tarragon and thyme.

Almost all herbs prefer a warm site with excellent drainage. For general soil and site preparation please refer to the steps outlined in the front sections of this Gardening Guide; what works for a wide range of perennials will be ideal for herbs.

If you use fresh herbs a lot for cooking, try to choose a site that is convenient to the kitchen door so they can be picked just before using, insuring optimum flavour and freshness. Raised beds are an excellent place for growing herbs, making them especially easy to harvest. Herbs with attractive foliage and flowers won't look out of place planted in a mixed border with annuals, perennials, bulbs, and even flowering shrubs.

Container gardening with herbs is especially successful. All kinds of pots, tubs, and baskets can be pressed into use as herbal containers, just make sure they have a drainage hole or two. Large half-barrels are especially good for containing various types of mint, to keep them from spreading all over the garden.

Planting & Maintenance

Please see the section near the front of this Gardening Guide for some basics on planting and maintenance.

Annual herb varieties will need to be replanted every year, or allowed to seed themselves. Sometimes they will self-seed in such numbers that they will need to be thinned. Just throw any unwanted seedlings on to the compost heap or pot up to give to friends.

Biennial varieties, such as caraway, will not set seed until the second year. If you want a crop every year, be sure to do a new planting each spring or allow them to self seed.

Perennial herbs may need to be lifted every few years and divided to keep them vigorous and healthy. Spring is the best time to do this, before they get more than a few inches tall. In

colder areas, some of the more tender perennial herbs will need a thick mulch in late fall in order to protect the plants for the winter. In the listing that follows, perennial varieties are indicated by the presence of hardiness zones.

Tender perennial herbs, like Pineapple Sage and Lemon Verbena, are best grown in a container so they can be easily moved indoors for the winter. Some people prefer to just take cuttings in late summer to start fresh plants indoors. This will help to avoid bringing in unwanted insect pests to your house plants.

Anise-hyssop

Lettuce-Leaf Basil

Bay Laurel

Borage

ANISE-HYSSOP

(Agastache foeniculum)   **ZONES 2–9**

Long spikes of lavender flowers are attractive to bees and excellent for cutting. Whole plant is strongly licorice scented and flavored. Leaves may be used in teas and herbal jellies, flowers in salads. Mingles nicely with other summer-blooming perennials in the border. North American native wildflower. Anise-hyssop is not the same as Anise, an annual grown for its licorice-flavored seeds. HEIGHT: 90–120cm (3–4′) USES: ✕ ❦ Borders

BALM, LEMON see LEMON BALM

BASIL

(Ocimum spp.)   **ANNUAL**

One of the most widely-used herbs in all of its various forms. Especially valued in Italy and other Mediterranean countries for flavouring sauces, soups, pasta and tomato dishes, and vegetable salads, as well as meats and poultry. All Basils are very cold-sensitive, and should never be planted outside until late spring. Pinching off the flowers will encourage plants to keep producing leaves. Can also be grown successfully indoors over the winter in a sunny window. Basil is best used fresh; home-dried basil loses most of its flavour and is far inferior to fresh. Preserve or freeze it instead for winter use. HEIGHT: 30–45cm (12–18″) USES: ❦ Borders

Anise Basil (O. basilicum) A variety used in Asia, particularly in Thai and Vietnamese cooking. Sweet, exotic flavour with a hint of anise, purplish foliage. Worth experimenting with as you would use regular Sweet Basil.

Bush Basil (O. basilicum minimum) A compact, tiny-leaved dwarf basil, excellent for container growing or using as an edging. Very strong, spicy smell reminiscent of cloves. Good flavor, but no match for Sweet Basil.

Cinnamon Basil (O. basilicum) Interesting cinnamon scent and flavour. Although this variety comes from Mexico, it seems to have an affinity for Middle Eastern and Italian meat dishes. Similar in appearance to Sweet Basil.

Holy Basil (O. sanctum) Very different from the other basils in appearance, taste and flavour. Leaves are downy, gray-green in colour. Very spicy taste and strong fragrance of cloves. Has religious uses in India, and is occasionally added to cold vegetable dishes or salads. Makes an unusual tea.

Lettuce-Leaf Basil (O. basilicum 'Crispum') A selected form of Sweet Basil with extra-large leaves. Good flavour. Produces the maximum amount of leaves in the smallest amount of space, with the least amount of effort!

Licorice Basil (O. basilicum) A form of Sweet Basil with a slightly stronger licorice scent and flavour, purplish foliage.

Purple Ruffles Basil (O. basilicum 'Purple Ruffles') Very ornamental selection, the dark-purple leaves have a ruffled and crimped texture. Not always a vigorous grower, seems especially sensitive to cold spring weather. Used to make bright pink Basil vinegar. The leaves turn green when added to hot foods.

Sweet Basil (O. basilicum) The traditional large-leaved variety. Still the most popular variety, grown for its pungent, slightly licorice flavour. The major ingredient in classic Italian pesto sauce.

BAY LAUREL

(Laurus nobilis)   **ZONE 9**

Evergreen shrub or small tree. Bay is best grown in a large pot or tub so it can be moved indoors to overwinter in a sunny window. The large, leathery leaves are used fresh or dried as a flavoring in soups, stews and meat dishes, especially in French cooking. Prune plants in spring to keep them compact. Can be trained as a bush or standard. HEIGHT: 90–180cm (3–6′) USES: ❦▲

BEEBALM

(Monarda didyma)   **ZONES 2–9**

Also known as Bergamot or Oswego Tea. Popular flowering perennial wildflower, the leaves and flowers may be used to make a delicious fragrant tea, or sparingly in salads. Fragrant and colourful ingredient for potpourri mixtures. Also listed in the PERENNIAL section under *Monarda*. HEIGHT: 90cm (3′) USES: ✕ 🦋 ➤ Borders

BORAGE

(Borago officinalis)   **ANNUAL**

Young cucumber-flavored leaves are used in salads. The star-shaped bright blue flowers are also fun to put in salads, or float in cold drinks. Adventurous bakers may like to have candied flowers on hand to decorate cakes and desserts. Older leaves are sometimes cooked as greens. An excellent plant for children's gardens, as it is fast to grow and practically foolproof. Borage usually self-seeds, so you only need to plant it once. Loved by bees. HEIGHT: 75cm (30″) USES: ❦ Borders

BURNET, SALAD

(Poterium sanguisorba)   **ZONES 2–9**

Known in Europe as *Pimpinella*. The lacy blue-green leaves are occasionally added to salads and sauces when young, lending a mild cool-cucumber taste. Sometimes minced with other *fines herbes* (chervil, parsley, tarragon, chives) and mixed into mayonnaise, sour cream, or quark cheese as a topping for boiled new potatoes. Also nice for flavoring vinegars, or floating as a garnish in cool drinks. Useful edging plant, remaining evergreen most winters. Crimson-red ball-shaped flowers rise up on stems in early summer. 30cm (12″) USES: ✕▲❦ Edging, Borders

CARAWAY

(Carum carvi)   **BIENNIAL**

Grown for its pungent seeds. These are commonly incorporated into breads (especially rye) and cheeses, and added to various foods as an important flavouring ingredient in several Northern European countries; sauerkraut, noodles, soups, cabbage and pork, to name a few. A few finely-chopped leaves can be added to salads or sandwiches. Plants have tall stems of lacy white flowers in their second year, followed by a heavy crop of seeds. These should be allowed to turn light brown before being harvested. HEIGHT: 90cm (3′) USES: ✕ Borders

CATNIP

(Nepeta cataria)   ZONES 2–9

Most cats love this plant fresh or dried, and a couple of plants in your garden will attract every cat in the neighbourhood. The leaves can also be used to make into a soothing bedtime tea for humans. Plants have a tendency to self-seed prolifically, and are not especially attractive in the border. HEIGHT: 90cm (3′) USES: Herb gardens, Back lanes

CHAMOMILE

German   ANNUAL

(Matricaria recutita) Grown for their pretty little white daisies, which are used fresh or dried to make a calming tea. Save any cold leftover tea; you can use it as a hair-rinse to bring out blonde highlights. Readily self-seeds. HEIGHT: 30cm (1′) USES: Herb gardens

Roman   ZONES 4–9

(Anthemis nobilis) Flowers are used exactly the same as German Chamomile. The fragrant foliage is very dense, forming a fine-textured bright green mat. Sometimes been used as a lawn substitute in hot, dry sites; will tolerate light foot traffic. HEIGHT: 15cm (6″) USES: Edging, Lawn substitute

CHERVIL

(Anthriscus cerefolium)   ANNUAL

Has feathery green leaves that are used much the same way as parsley. One of the classic French *fines herbes*, and a favorite flavoring for tomato, egg and fish dishes. Often added to mayonnaise, butter, various sauces, soups and salads. Leaves must be used while young, as they turn very bitter with maturity. Best to grow this in part shade. HEIGHT: 30cm (12″) USES: Herb gardens

CHICORY

(Cichorium intybus)   ZONES 2–9

Very young leaves may be used as a salad green. The roots of this variety are roasted until thoroughly dried, then ground as a coffee additive or substitute. Plants produce sky-blue daisy flowers all summer long in their second year, commonly seen on roadsides across the country, but pretty in the garden too. HEIGHT: 75cm (3′) USES: Borders

CHIVES

Common Chives   ZONES 1–9

(Allium schoenoprasum) One of the classic French *fines herbes*, and a good plant to have growing close to the kitchen door, handy for last-minute snipping into salads and sauces. A favorite addition to soups, egg or vegetable dishes, and as a topping on baked potatoes, imparting a mild onion flavour. Attractive purple flowers appear in late spring, and these also can be eaten in salads or used as an edible garnish. HEIGHT: 30cm (12″) USES: ✂✽❦ Borders

Garlic Chives   ZONES 2–9

(Allium tuberosum) Similar uses to Common Chives, and just as handy to have nearby the kitchen. Leaves are strongly flavoured with garlic, so use sparingly. Beautiful heads of white flowers appear in late summer and these are also edible. Remove faded flower heads to prevent self seeding everywhere. HEIGHT: 30–60cm (1–2′) USES: ✂✽❦ Borders

COMFREY

(Symphytum officinale)   ZONES 2–9

Bold-leaved, showy plants that fit well into the perennial border where their clusters of sky-blue or pinkish flowers are much appreciated. Comfrey was once used extensively in poultices on cuts, bruises, and broken bones, which explains one of its common names, Boneset. Plants are very tough and will survive for years without any attention. Cut plants right back to the ground in mid-summer as soon as you think they look a bit tired; fresh new growth will appear in no time. Bees love Comfrey flowers! Because of their extensive root system, plants are difficult to eradicate once established. HEIGHT: 90cm (3′) USES: Borders

CORIANDER, CILANTRO

(Coriandrum sativum)   ANNUAL

Also called Chinese Parsley. Said to be the most widely-grown herb in the world. This is showing up in every green grocer and supermarket lately, so North Americans are quickly developing a taste for it. The fresh young leaves resemble parsley, and are used extensively as both a flavouring and garnish in foods from many diverse regions, including Asia, India, Latin America, Thailand, Mexico and Morocco. Its pungent flavour is truly international! Pick the leaves before plants begin to flower. Later the seeds can be harvested and dried when they begin to turn brown. HEIGHT: 90cm (3′) USES: ❦ Herb gardens

CURRY PLANT

(Helichrysum angustifolium)   ANNUAL

Woolly silver-grey foliage with a distinctive scent of curry powder. Grown commercially for its distilled oil, used as a flavour-enhancer in the food industry, and in perfume manufacture. Not used as a flavouring ingredient in Indian cooking. HEIGHT: 30cm (1′) USES: Fragrance gardens, Herb gardens

DILL

(Anethum graveolens)   ANNUAL

Commonly used in Eastern and Northern European cooking, both the leaves and seeds contribute their unique flavour to a variety of foods including pickles, marinated cucumbers, soups, sauces, fish dishes, and salad dressings. Dill will usually self-seed after the first year. HEIGHT: 90cm (3′) USES: ✂ Herb gardens.

ECHINACEA

(Echinacea angustifolia)   ZONES 3–9

(Narrowleaf Coneflower, Western Coneflower) Being widely promoted lately for strengthening the human immune system, and as an all-round tonic and blood purifier. Most health-food stores have reams of information and products containing Echinacea. This species is said to be the most medicinally active. Flowers are very similar in appearance to the Purple Coneflower (see Perennial section), but with paler, narrower petals. HEIGHT: 60–120cm (2–4′) USES: ✂✽❦ Borders, Herb gardens

Catnip

Chives

Cilantro, Coriander

Dill

Fennel

Hyssop

Lavender

Lemon Balm

FENNEL
(Foeniculum vulgare)
If you aren't familiar with fennel, try to imagine a dill plant that tastes mildly of black licorice. The leaves of all varieties are very graceful and ferny, and can be used fresh or dried to impart their special flavour to fish or egg dishes, soups, salads, and stuffings. The seed is also dried and used in similar ways to Caraway or Dillseed. USES: ✂❦ Borders

Bronze Fennel   ZONES 5–9
('Purpureum') The most versatile Fennel, forming a large clump of ferny foliage that starts out dark purple then matures to metallic bronze. An outstanding ornamental perennial, and useful kitchen herb as well. Self-seeds vigorously, if permitted. HEIGHT: 120–180cm (4–6')

Florence Fennel   ANNUAL
(var. azoricum) As well as the leaves, this variety forms a swollen bulb of celery-like stems that are popular as a vegetable in Italy (known as *Finocchio*), where they are sliced and added to salads, baked with butter and garlic, or added to soups and stews. Harvest in late fall. HEIGHT: 90cm (3')

Sweet Fennel   ZONES 5–9
(var. dulce) Common ingredient in German cooking, this is the variety generally grown for its seeds. Ferny foliage is attractive in the flower border. HEIGHT: 120cm (4')

FEVERFEW
(Chrysanthemum parthenium) ZONES 4–9
(Also known as *Matricaria*) Recently shown by British researchers to prevent migraine headaches in about thirty percent of sufferers. One to four leaves per day are recommended, either just chewed, made into a tea or hidden in a sandwich. Some pharmacies even sell matricaria capsules. For those without migraines, consider growing Feverfew just for its pretty heads of white or yellow flowers, resembling a dwarf fall chrysanthemum. Plants are short-lived perennials that will self-seed year after year. HEIGHT: 30–45cm (12–18") USES: ✂❦ Borders

GARLIC
(Allium sativum)   ANNUAL
Very well-known flavouring ingredient, used by nearly every cuisine of the world. Most often garlic is added to savory foods, including meat and vegetable dishes, soups, salads sauces and breads. Onion-like plants form a bulb which should be harvested in late summer. HEIGHT: 30cm (12") USES: Herb or vegetable gardens

GARLIC CHIVES see CHIVES, GARLIC

GARLIC, ELEPHANT
(Allium ampeloprasum)   ANNUAL
Forms a monstrous bulb, but with a much milder flavour than regular garlic. Especially good roasted or grilled as a vegetable, developing a sweet, nutty taste. Children love this novelty! Attractive mauve flower heads appear in late summer. HEIGHT: 30–45cm (12–18") USES: ✂ Herb or vegetable garden

GARLIC, TRICOLOR SOCIETY
(Tulbaghia violacea 'Tricolor')   TENDER
Related to *Agapanthus*, this forms a clump of grassy leaves, strongly striped with green, pink and cream. Umbels of lilac-pink flowers are produced in the summer. Smells and tastes of garlic, but supposedly does not leave you with garlic breath after eating. Best grown in a pot and brought indoors for the winter. HEIGHT: 30–45cm (12–18"). USES: ❦ Indoor/outdoor plant

HYSSOP
(Hyssopus officinalis)   ZONES 4–9
An ancient, bitter herb that was once used extensively in Europe to mask the flavour of strong meat or game. Small amounts are said to aid digestion. The leaves taste slightly of pine needles, and can be finely chopped and added to salads, soups or stew in small quantities. Plants send up spikes of pretty blue flowers in summer, and these too are edible in salads. An excellent cut flower, pretty in the border. HEIGHT: 60–75cm (24–30"). USES: ✂❦ Borders

LAVENDER
(Lavandula spp.)
The various kinds of Lavender all share the same sweet fragrance of both leaves and pretty spikes of flowers. In parts of Europe fields of it are still grown and harvested for the fragrant oil, an important ingredient in many fine perfumes. Fragrant potpourri, sachets, tussie-mussies and other gifts from the garden can be made if you have a good supply of Lavender handy. All varieties thrive in a warm sunny location and are moderately drought-tolerant. For a more complete listing of cultivars look under *Lavandula* in the Perennial section. USES: ▲▲❦✂❦

English Lavender   ZONES 4–9
(Lavandula angustifolium) The hardiest and most popular type grown. Compact bushy plants with the classic deep-blue flowers and good strong fragrance. Sometimes used to make a low clipped herbal hedge or knot garden. In cold regions this can be grown in a container and wintered indoors in a bright south window. HEIGHT: 30–60cm (1–2')

French Lavender   ZONES 8–9
(Lavandula dentata) Uses are similar to English Lavender. Foliage is finer, silvery-grey in colour, with spikes of purple flowers. Not nearly as hardy, best grown in a pot and overwintered in a sunny window. Add a few sprigs to your bath! HEIGHT: 30–90cm (1–3')

LEMON BALM
(Melissa officinalis)   ZONES 4–9
With its shiny bright green foliage, Lemon Balm is an attractive low-maintenance groundcover as well as a useful kitchen herb. Easy to grow in shade or sun, preferring a rich, moist soil. The fresh leaves can be used to brew a deliciously lemon-flavoured and scented tea that is said to have a calming effect. Some cooks substitute finely chopped Lemon Balm leaves for the lemon in certain recipes or use whole sprigs as a garnish. Try a little scattered in a fruit salad or throw in a handful when poaching fish. Bees love the tiny nectar-filled flowers. HEIGHT: 30–60cm (1–2') USES: ☜❦ Edging

LEMON VERBENA

(Aloysia triphylla)   ZONES 9–10

Grown as a tender perennial or sub-tropical shrub in most regions. An intensely lemon-scented and flavored plant, just a few leaves will add zest to hot or cold desserts, sauces, rice, fish dishes, cold drinks and anything else you might use lemon with. Combines well with other tea herbs, and is a fragrant addition to potpourri. Grow Lemon Verbena in a container and take indoors for the winter. Needs full sun. HEIGHT: 30–90cm (1–3′) USES: ♥ Herb Gardens

LOVAGE

(Levisticum officinale)   ZONES 2–9

Having been grown there for hundreds of years, in Europe it is as common in gardens as rhubarb is here. The entire plant smells and tastes strongly of celery, the leaves and stems used (sparingly) to add their pleasant flavour to soups, stew and various meat, poultry or fish dishes, in stir-fries or vegetable salads. The seeds are also sometimes dried and ground, then sprinkled over biscuits, breads, roasting meats or added to cheese dishes. Once Lovage settles in, it can be expected to be the giant of the herb garden, looking somewhat like a monstrous celery plant, but handsome enough to use in the back of a perennial border. Appreciates a rich, moist soil in part shade or full sun. HEIGHT: 1.5m (5′) USES: ✕ ♥ Borders

MARJORAM

(Origanum spp.)

These are closely related to Oregano, and sorting out the differences can be confusing. They have a preference for sunny sites, and would not look out of place in a rock garden or edging a border. Marjorams have a fairly strong flavour that has sometimes been described as "perfumy," though it lacks the bite that makes Oregano the pizza herb. The various types can be used interchangeably for flavouring meats, poultry, sausages, stuffings, soup and stews, or in vegetable dishes, especially with tomatoes, squash or dried beans. Can be used to make a tea. USES: ♥ Edging, Rock gardens

Sweet Marjoram   ANNUAL

(O. marjorana) The strongest-flavored marjoram, and the one commonly sold in dried form. Definitely a tender annual, but also easily grown indoors for the winter. HEIGHT: 30cm (12″)

Pot Marjoram   ZONES 6–9

(O. onites) Hardier species with a slightly milder flavor, said to be inferior to Sweet Marjoram. Mild enough to use in salads. HEIGHT: 20–30cm (8–12″)

Variegated Marjoram   ZONES 7–9

(O. onites 'Variegatum') Mild flavor. Very attractive, heavily variegated green and white leaves. An excellent edging plant for the herb garden or border, also attractive in containers. HEIGHT: 20cm (8″)

MINT

(Mentha spp.)

Possibly the easiest of all the herbs to grow; in fact, mints are often accused of growing a little *too* well. Most varieties have a determined tendency to spread by sneaky underground stems or stolons. Mints can be easily controlled by planting in large tubs or containers — large square clay drain tiles, half-barrels, or deep plastic pots, for instance. Containers can be either free-standing or sunk into the ground, the method advised for cold winter areas. All varieties prefer a rich, moist soil in sun or partial shade. Divide plants every other year to maintain a good thick patch. Clip plants back when they flower to maintain a constant harvest until winter. One word of caution: don't unleash mint into the perennial border or anywhere else that you may regret in a few years time. HEIGHT: Most types grow 30–60cm (1–2′) USES: ♥ Herb gardens

Spearmint is the variety most commonly used for cooking, but since all types share the same base menthol flavour, they can be used somewhat interchangeably. Mint adds a cool, refreshing flavour to fruit salads. Sprinkle finely chopped mint on cooked vegetables, peas, carrots, beets, or onions. Mint sauce is a classic finish to roast lamb. Used extensively in Indian, Thai, Vietnamese, Moroccan and Middle Eastern cuisines.

Apple Mint   ZONES 4–9

(M. suaveolens) Good flavor and strong green-apple fragrance; rounded, downy leaves. Excellent for cooking, especially fragrant in tea.

Corsican Mint   ZONES 7–9

(M. requienii) Low, creeping variety mostly used as a groundcover. The tiny leaves smell and taste of creme de menthe, but are really too small to be of any culinary use. Excellent container plant, and grows well indoors. HEIGHT: 2cm (1″)

Orange Mint   ZONES 2–9

(M. × piperita citrata) Especially pleasant for tea. Also used in cooking, and for potpourri. Fruity citrus scent.

Peppermint   ZONES 1–9

(M. × piperita) A strong-flavored variety, used mostly for tea, a bit overpowering for most foods. True peppermint has reddish stems, smells and tastes exactly like a candy cane, and must be grown from divisions or cuttings as plants do not set seed. Watch out for impostors!

Spearmint   ZONES 1–9

(M. spicata) Pebbled, pointed leaves, and that familiar classic mint fragrance. This is the type most widely used for cooking. Also the key ingredient for a tall, cool Mint Julep.

Variegated Pineapplemint   ZONES 5–9

(M. suaveolens 'Variegata') Woolly leaves, with showy white and green variegation. The most attractive of the mints. Good flavour and a definite pineapple fragrance. Said to be less aggressive than other varieties.

ONION

(Allium fistulosum)

Welsh Onion   ZONES 2–9

Primarily used for early green onions, these are one of the first things to come up in the spring. A hardy perennial, slowly forming a clump of hollow green leaves, topped with showy heads of white flowers in early summer. Use the same as you would any regular green onion. Does not form a bulb. HEIGHT: 30–60cm (1–2′) USES: ✕ Borders, Herb garden.

Sweet Marjoram

Apple Mint

Orange Mint

Spearmint

Oregano

Curled Parsley

Perilla

Rosemary

OREGANO
(Origanum spp.)

Closely related to the Marjorams, but with a spicier flavour. Commonly used as an ingredient in pizza and pasta sauces. Used in Italy for a variety of stews and bean soups. Greek cooks add Oregano to marinades for meats, poultry and grilled vegetables, and to salad dressings. Also added to certain Mexican bean dishes, soups, meat and fish.

Oregano prefers a warm sunny site and a well-drained soil. The clusters of pretty pink flowers that appear in mid-summer make them suitable candidates for the perennial border. Bees and butterflies love the flowers. USES: ✂✿🐝 Borders, Herb garden

Dwarf Greek   ZONES 4–9
(O. vulgare 'Compacta') Full-flavored form with a bushy, compact habit. Best choice for containers and indoors. Could be used as a low edging. HEIGHT: 15cm (6")

Greek   ZONES 4–9
(O. spp.) Excellent strong oregano flavor, dark green leaves. HEIGHT: 30–45cm (12–18")

Golden   ZONES 4–9
(O. vulgare 'Aureum') Forms a mat of bright golden-yellow leaves. Poor flavour, but really nice for edging or growing in tubs. Clip back hard in mid-summer to keep plants colourful and compact. HEIGHT: 30cm (12")

PARSLEY
(Petroselinum crispum)

North Americans have finally taken a bite of the garnish and realized that parsley tastes good! There is such a multitude of uses for fresh parsley; it is commonly added to stews, soups, casseroles, egg and cheese dishes, chopped and sprinkled on cooked vegetables, meats, pasta, and many other savory foods. Different cuisines from all over the world make use of the fresh, somewhat peppery flavour.

Although biennial, parsley should be treated as an annual and planted each year, otherwise the plants bolt and go to seed in their second year and are of no culinary use anyway. The plants are fresh green and compact, and look right at home as an edging plant for general border use; no need to restrict parsley to the vegetable garden. Plants grown in pots may be brought indoors in the late fall for an indoor supply of parsley all winter. HEIGHT: 20–30cm (8–12") USES: ✿ Edging, Herb garden

Curled   BIENNIAL
(var. crispum) The extra-curled type so familiar as a garnish. Perhaps the best general-purpose parsley. Especially attractive edging plant.

Italian   BIENNIAL
(var. neopolitanum) Many gourmet chefs swear that this plain-leaved type has a superior flavour, a bit stronger than regular curled parsley. Especially recommended for Italian and Middle Eastern cooking. Plants are not quite so compact.

PENNYROYAL
(Mentha pulegium)   ZONES 5–9

Closely related to mint, with a very strong wild-mint fragrance. The leaves were once used in small quantities to flavour puddings and sauces, however pregnant women should avoid eating it. Pennyroyal is now more commonly used to repel fleas and other flying insects, by simply rubbing some bruised leaves on the skin and clothing or on pets. Plants will make a dense spreading groundcover for a moist partly shaded location. HEIGHT: 20–30cm (8–12") USES: ⋌⋋ Edging, Herb garden

PERILLA
(Perilla frutescens)   ANNUAL

Also called Beefsteak Plant. Known in Japan as *Shiso*, where both the red and green-leaved forms are used for a variety of things; garnishing, battered and fried as tempura, chopped finely to use in sushi, and to colour *umeboshi*, a salty plum pickle. The purple-leaved form is especially handsome in the border, in effect similar to Coleus, but tolerating full sun. Excellent in containers, or massed for summer bedding. This is bound to catch on quickly as a multi-purpose garden plant. HEIGHT: 45–60cm (18–24") USES: ✂✿ Massing, Borders

PINEAPPLE SAGE see SAGE, PINEAPPLE

ROSEMARY
(Rosmarinus officinalis)

Native to Mediterranean regions, Rosemary is an important flavouring herb, especially in Italy, France and Greece. The leaves are used to flavour a wide variety of foods, especially chicken, lamb, pork, potato and other vegetable dishes, as well as many soups. The plants are evergreen, with needle-like leaves and pretty mauve flowers in early spring. Because they are tender in most parts of the country, a good solution is to grow in pots that may be taken indoors for the winter. Rosemary is actually a woody shrub and can be easily clipped or formed into various shapes or allowed to grow in a natural way. Plants appreciate full sun and a well-drained soil. USES: ▲✿🌿 Mixed borders, Herb gardens

Bush   ZONES 8–9
The more popular upright form, easily maintained as a dense bush with a yearly clipping in late spring. Plants are sometimes trained as a standard or wreath. HEIGHT: 60cm (2') or more

Trailing   ZONES 8–9
('Prostratum') Excellent rosemary for containers and hanging baskets, with a prostrate to cascading habit. HEIGHT: 15cm (6")

RUE
(Ruta graveolens)   ZONES 4–9

An ancient bitter herb, this once had great importance as a medicinal herb and as protection from witchcraft and evil in general. Although poisonous in large quantities, the leaves are used sparingly in salads or to flavour soft cheeses. It should not be eaten by pregnant women. Nowadays Rue is mostly grown in the border for its attractive blue-green foliage, or clipped as a hedge in formal knot gardens. The sap may cause skin irritation in sensitive individuals. HEIGHT: 30–90cm (1–3') USES: ▲🌿✿ Borders, Herb gardens

SAGE
(Salvia spp.)
Some of the best garden flowers can be found among the ranks of this enormous group of plants, including several listed under *Salvia* in the Perennial section. The herbal varieties of Sage bear fragrant leaves as well as showy flowers.

Common Sage   ZONES 4–9
(Salvia officinalis) A favorite flavouring for poultry stuffings, Sage can be easily grown in a sunny border where both its grey-green leaves and short spikes of violet-purple flowers are valued. The leaves are used sparingly, either fresh or dried, to flavour rich meats and stews, dried-bean dishes, in sausages and in cream cheese. Sage was an important medicinal herb, and many people still drink a cup of sage tea to ward off a sore throat. Plants should be pruned back to 15cm (6″) in early spring so they stay compact. Flowers are attractive to bees and hummingbirds. HEIGHT: 45–75cm (18–30″) USES: ✂▲♥➤♣ Borders, Herb gardens

The unique selections of Common Sage listed below are well worth seeking. In addition to being useful kitchen herbs, they are extremely ornamental. All are slightly tender and should be planted in a protected area, mulched for the winter or carried over in a coldframe.

Dwarf Sage
('Compacta') A very bushy and compact form, reaching only 30cm (12″) tall. The best for containers.

Golden Sage   ZONES 6–9
('Icterina' or 'Variegata') Leaves are strongly variegated with green and gold. Makes a nice edging. A favorite for containers.

Purple Sage   ZONES 6–9
('Purpurascens') Leaves are overlaid with a violet-purple caste, purple stems. Handsome.

Tricolor Sage   ZONES 7–9
('Tricolor') Foliage is boldly splashed with purple, pink, cream and green. Also useful for edging. The most tender cultivar.

Pineapple Sage   TENDER PERENNIAL
(Salvia elegans) Tropical variety, grown as an annual or indoor/outdoor container plant. The hairy, bright green leaves smell strongly of pineapple with a mild, fruity flavour. Used finely chopped in salads, whole in jams, jellies, and cold drinks, or as a garnish for nearly anything. Also makes a refreshing hot tea. Over the course of one season this will form a substantial plant in a sunny site. Large, edible scarlet flowers appear very late in the fall, if at all, in the northern states and most of Canada. HEIGHT: 90–120cm (3–4″) USES: ✂♥➤ Borders, Herb gardens

SAVORY
(Satureja spp.)
Often added as a flavouring for recipes made with dried legumes, and sometimes referred to as "the bean herb". The fresh or dried leaves have a rich peppery flavour that can be overpowering in the wrong hands.

Summer Savory   ANNUAL
(S. hortensis) The milder-flavoured type, and favored by many cooks for this reason. Can subtly flavour egg dishes, tender summer vegetables, soups and stews, and a wide variety of other foods. Excellent used either fresh or dried. Summer Savory is an easy annual, growing in any average garden soil with a sunny exposure. HEIGHT: 30-60cm (1–2′) USES: ♥ Herb gardens

Winter Savory   ZONES 4–9
(S. montana) With a more pungent, stronger taste than Summer Savory, this is best used to flavour rich meats or stews, bean soups, casseroles and stuffings. Plants form a low evergreen bush that does not look out of place as either an edging or in the rock garden. Pale mauve flowers appear in late summer. HEIGHT: 25cm (10″) USES: ▲△∧▸▲♥ Borders

SORREL, FRENCH
(Rumex acetosa)   ZONES 2–9
Also known as sour grass in Europe, where the leaves are widely used to make a delicious, tangy soup. The spinach-like leaves of Sorrel have a sharp sour-lemon flavour that is refreshing when added to other greens in a salad. Excellent cooked and pureed in sauces for broiled or poached fish. Tender young leaves will be produced all season long if flower spikes are faithfully removed. HEIGHT: 30cm (12″). USES: Herb gardens.

SOUTHERNWOOD
(Artemisia abrotanum)   ZONES 2–9
Also known as Old Man or Lad's Love. Plants form an upright bush of ferny grey-green leaves, with a spicy pine-orange fragrance. Has been used for centuries to repel moths from stored clothing, and as a popular ingredient of sachets and potpourri. Dried boughs add a nice aroma to a burning fire. Has been used medicinally. Try to locate this in a spot where passers-by will brush against it, releasing its fragrance into the air. Foliage is excellent for flower arranging. HEIGHT: 60–90cm (2–3′) USES: ✂◂♥♣ Borders, Herb gardens

STRAWBERRY
(Fragaria vesca)   ZONES 2–9
Picking wild strawberries is a distant childhood memory for many people. Growing them in your own garden, however, can easily be an adult reality! Selected forms of wild strawberry offer larger fruit, easily twice the size of their wild cousins, but with that same special flavour that is definitely lacking in the larger commercial varieties. In addition, the plants are runnerless, forming compact clumps that don't spread all over. An excellent size for edging purposes. Leaves of wild strawberry can be steeped into a soothing tea. HEIGHT: 20–30cm (8–12″) USES: ♥ Edging, Borders

Alpine
('Rügen') Superb flavour. Showy, bright-red conical fruits. Everbearing.

Yellow Fruited
('Yellow Wonder') Pale creamy-yellow fruit, distinctive strawberry flavour with a hint of something else… apricot? A real novelty, especially nice growing next to the red-fruited form. Everbearing. An added feature of this variety is that birds won't steal the fruit because of the unusual colour.

Common Sage

Southernwood

Winter Savory

Yellow Fruited Strawberry

Sweet Woodruff

French Tarragon

Lemon Thyme

Water Cress

SWEET WOODRUFF

(Galium odoratum)   ZONES 4–9

Becoming exceedingly popular as a groundcover for shady areas. Plants form a low mat of bright green leaves, studded with tiny white flowers in late spring. The stems and leaves, when dried, develop a wonderful aroma that is similar to vanilla or fresh-mown hay. A common use is in sachets, scented pillows and potpourri, where it also acts as a fixative. Sweet Woodruff is also the key ingredient for making German May-wine (*Waldmeister-Bowle*). HEIGHT: 20cm (8″) USES: ⋀⋏ Woodland gardens

TARRAGON, FRENCH

(Artemisia dranunculus sativa) ZONES 4–9

True French Tarragon is unmistakable once you know the clue; a couple of fresh leaves when chewed should develop a strong licorice flavour. If not, you are dealing with the impostor, Russian Tarragon, a plant of no culinary value whatsoever! It is of the utmost importance in fine French cooking, being included among the four essential *fines herbes* (Chervil, Parsley, Chives and Tarragon). Tarragon is added to a wide variety of dishes, especially fish, shellfish, chicken, eggs, fresh tomatoes, and in green salads and dressings. Tarragon vinegar can easily be made at home.

The plant, for the most part, is rather unimpressive in appearance, with slender stems of narrow green leaves, forming a loose bush of medium height. Lacking vigour, it should be given a special spot with rich, well-drained soil, full sun, and a good supply of moisture. Divide plants every year or two to keep them young and healthy. HEIGHT: 45–60cm (18–24″) USES: ⋏ Herb gardens

THYME
(Thymus spp.)

There are a great many different kinds of Thyme, varying remarkably in their foliage and flower colour, habit, fragrance and flavour. See under *Thymus* in the Perennial section for a more complete listing. The culinary varieties form semi-upright bushes of spicy fragrant evergreen leaves. They prefer a well-drained, sunny location and are tolerant of hot, dry conditions once established. HEIGHT: 15–20cm (6–12″) USES: ⋀⋏ Edging, Borders

Common Thyme   ZONES 5–9

(T. vulgaris) This is the standard cooking thyme, the one dried and sold in packages at the supermarket. The grey-green foliage is pleasantly aromatic, and can be used fresh or dried to flavour meats, poultry, stews and soups, as well as a whole range of vegetable and dried-bean dishes. Common Thyme needs excellent drainage, particularly through the winter months. It can also be grown in pots to bring indoors for the winter.

Lemon Thyme   ZONES 4–9

(T. × citriodorus) Delicious strong lemon fragrance, mild spicy thyme-citrus flavour. There are several forms of this around, the most ornamental kinds having bright gold-and-green variegated leaves. Before buying plants, be sure to test the fragrance first; don't settle for less than a big burst of fresh honey-lemon. Lemon Thyme can be used the same way as regular Thyme. Add a few sprigs to a pot of tea, or chop finely and sprinkle over baked fish, chicken or veal. Lemon Thyme should only be used fresh, and always added at the last minute or its fragrance will be lost.

VALERIAN

(Valeriana officinalis)   ZONES 2–9

Also known as Garden Heliotrope, which describes the intensely fragrant clusters of white or pale-pink flowers. Plants form a tall upright clump of lacy leaves, blooming in the summer months. Said to attract cats. The dried, powdered roots of Valerian were formerly very important in relieving pain, calming nerves, and as a sedative. Nice in the back of a perennial border, the flowers are good for cutting. HEIGHT: 1.2–1.5m (4–5′) USES: ✄ Borders

VERBENA, LEMON see LEMON VERBENA

WATER CRESS

(Nasturtium officinale)   ZONES 4–9

Not such an easy plant to grow in the average home garden, demanding a constant supply of moisture in a sunny or partly shaded location. In the wild it grows along the edges of slow-moving streams. It might be possible to succeed in growing Watercress if you have a pond, water garden, or even a large tub that is well aerated; plant in pots first, then submerge up to the rims. The peppery-flavoured leaves are a favorite spring salad green, also sometimes put in sandwiches or made into a French cream and potato soup. HEIGHT: 15cm (6″) USES: ⋏ Water gardens, Naturalizing

WOODRUFF see SWEET WOODRUFF

WORMWOOD

(Artemisia absinthium)   ZONES 2–9

An ancient bitter herb, used medicinally for hundreds of years to treat intestinal worms, and in soothing liniments. Also was once used as a flavoring ingredient in Absinthe, Vermouth, aperitifs and herbal wines. The leaves are occasionally used today in small quantities to flavour stuffings for goose or duck. Plants form a fairly large bush of silvery-green ferny foliage, with a pleasant spicy fragrance. Sometimes included in sachets or potpourri. Trim back to 15cm (6″) in late fall or early spring. HEIGHT: 90cm (3′) USES: ✄⋔ Borders, Herb gardens

Preserving the harvest

Most of the common kitchen herbs can be preserved at home, in one way or another, for using all the year round. There are four basic methods commonly used: drying, freezing, preserving in oil, or making herbal vinegars.

Drying herbs

Drying your own herbs is easy to do. The resulting harvest, packed into airtight bags or jars, can be kept handy to add all kinds of interesting and exotic flavours to your cooking. Bunches of dried herbs are also attractive decorations for the kitchen, and can be turned into easy, inexpensive gifts from the garden.

Leaves: When harvesting the leaves, most herbs achieve their maximum flavour just before the plants flower, and first thing in the morning, so choose this time to pick the herbs whenever possible. Using garden shears or sharp scissors, cut nice long whole stems; flowers, leaves and all. Rinse them quickly in cold water to remove any dirt or insects, then shake dry. Tie the stems together in bunches of five to ten, and hang upside-down in a warm, dry place. A dark room is ideal, so long as there is good air circulation, but a brighter room will do so long as the herbs are kept out of direct sun. Some people prefer to tie a paper bag around the bunches to keep off dust and insects. Let the bundle hang for about two weeks to dry thoroughly. Then untie them, and separate the whole leaves from the stems. Pack leaves whole into jars or heavy zip-top freezer bags and store in a dark, dry place. For the best possible flavour, wait until you need to use the dried herbs before crumbling or crushing just enough for the recipe.

Seeds: Wait until the seeds begin to change colour from green to shades of medium brown, a sure sign of ripening. Gather the seeds by hand and put them into paper bags; this is a great job for kids! Don't worry about any stems or leaves that might fall in. Store the bags in a warm, dark room for at least a couple of weeks so they can finish ripening and drying. When dry, empty the contents onto a pie plate or cookie sheet. Pick out any stems, leaves or dirt. To get rid of small chaff, take the pie plate outside, shaking it back and forth while blowing gently across the seeds. The chaff should blow away, leaving a clean plate of seeds that are ready to store in clean jars or zip-top bags.

Herbs for home drying: Bay Laurel, Caraway (seeds), Coriander (seeds), Dill (leaves & seeds), Fennel (leaves & seeds), Lovage (leaves & seeds), Marjoram, Mint, Oregano, Parsley, Rosemary, Sage, Summer Savory, Thyme.

Freezing herbs

Certain herbs will lose their unique flavour when dried at home. Some of these are commercially freeze-dried (Chives, Tarragon), but for home use plain freezing is the best alternative. For maximum flavour gather the herbs just before the plants flower, and first thing in the morning if possible. Rinse them quickly in cold water and shake dry. Simply pick off the leaves and chop coarsely on a cutting board, using a large sharp knife. Then place them in heavy zip-top bags and throw into the freezer. Some cooks like to freeze the herbs first on cookie sheets before packing, to keep the leaves separate. Use the same amount of frozen herbs as you would fresh. Herbs will usually freeze well for only four to six months before they dry out and lose their flavour.

Herbs that are better frozen than dried (tend to lose their flavour when home-dried): Basil, Chives, Garlic (whole cloves), Lemon Balm, Lemon Verbena, Parsley, Tarragon.

Preserving herbs in oil

Certain herbs, most notably Basil and Tarragon, do not lend themselves well to drying because the flavours all but disappear. An alternative to freezing is this method of preserving in oil. Finely chop the herbs by hand, or use a food processor or blender, and put into a glass bowl. For every cup of chopped herbs add about two tablespoons of Extra-virgin olive oil, two teaspoons of salt, and mix well. Pack this into fairly small jars, leaving about an inch of headspace. Pour more oil in each jar, right to the top, and cover. Leave at room temperature for a few hours, top off the jars with more oil as needed, and refrigerate.

To use herbs, dig down below the oil with a spoon, pull out what you need, smooth the oil back over the top (adding a little more to cover if necessary) and put back in the fridge. The idea here is that the oil keeps out air, which helps to prevent the herbs from spoiling, but for a maximum of two months in the refrigerator. Discard immediately if there are signs of surface mould, an off smell, or discoloration. Herbs in oil will keep very nicely in the freezer for a year or more.

Herbs that can be preserved in oil: Basil, Chervil, Coriander (Cilantro), Dill, Fennel, Garlic, Parsley, Sage, Sorrel, Tarragon.

Herbal vinegars

These flavoured vinegars are very handy for splashing over salad greens or adding to salad dressings and marinades. They are easy to make at home, and make attractive gifts, packed with the flavours of summer.

Begin with a good quality vinegar; apple cider and white wine vinegar are the best choices, but even regular white vinegar will do. Select the herb or combination of herbs that you wish to use, rinse in cold water, bruise with a kitchen mallet and place them whole (or coarsely chopped) into the bottom of a clean glass jar, bottle or crock. Pour the vinegar over, seal the top and leave to steep in a warm place (like on top of the fridge) for two to three weeks, shaking every once in awhile if you think of it. Taste the vinegar; if it seems strong enough continue on to the next step, otherwise leave to steep for another week. Strain the vinegar into a stainless steel or enamel pot, heat to boiling, pour into hot, sterilized bottles or jars, seal the tops and store in a cool, dark place. Some cooks skip this last step, but unpasteurized herb vinegar may not keep for as long.

The amount of herbs to vinegar can vary according to your taste, but a good ratio to begin with is ¼ to ½ cup (60–125ml) of fresh herbs to 2 cups (500ml) vinegar (or about a handful per pint). Choose single herbs or try a combination of different ones you like. To tint your vinegar deep pink use a generous amount of Purple Ruffles basil, chive blossoms or purple perilla leaves. Certain fruits might combine well with herbs to make vinegars; try raspberries, blackberries, blueberries or sour cherries. Some other potential garden or kitchen ingredients: nasturtium flowers and leaves, rose petals, calendula petals, violet flowers, fresh or dried chili peppers, ginger root, juniper berries, black pepper, chopped shallots.

Herbs for flavoured vinegars: Basil, Bay, Borage, Burnet, Chervil, Chives, Dill, Fennel, Garlic, Lemon Balm, Lemon Verbena, Lovage, Marjoram, Mint, Parsley, Perilla, Rosemary, Sage, Thyme, Tarragon.

Herbal tea

A refreshing alternative to regular tea or coffee, limited in flavour only by your imagination. Serve them fresh-brewed and piping hot or chilled over ice, depending on your mood and the time of year. Certain herbal teas are considered to have medicinal uses, but that sort of natural treatment should only be carried out under the guidance of a certified trained Homeopath, Naturopath, or Herbalist. Fortunately, many herbal teas are quite harmless, in moderation, and can be made easily with your own home-grown herbs.

To make tea from fresh herbs, simply throw a couple of handfuls of chopped leaves and flowers into a tea pot, pour boiling water over and steep for five or ten minutes. Tasting part way through steeping is a good idea at first, until you get a feel for how much time is required, how many leaves to use, and which herbs you like. Frozen herbs will make acceptable herbal teas.

Dried herbs can also be used, but in much smaller quantities because of their concentrated flavour. The rule of thumb is one teaspoon dried herbs per cup of water, increase to taste for milder-flavoured varieties. Honey, sugar, or lemon compliment the flavours of most herbal teas, but milk is not recommended.

Certain spices can be interesting in combination with fresh or dried herbs: try anise, cinnamon, cloves, coriander, ginger, lemon or orange peel. Commercial herbal teas often include dried hibiscus flowers, strawberry, raspberry, blackberry or black currant leaves, rosehips, lemon grass, dried apples and other dried fruits; these can usually be found in bulk at health food stores if you want to try making you own personal blends.

Herbs for tea: Anise-hyssop, Beebalm, Catnip, Chamomile, Lavender (flowers), Lemon Balm, Lemon Verbena, Marjoram, Mint (all types), Peppermint, Sage (especially Pineapple Sage), Thyme.

References

The quotes used throughout this book are taken from the following publications:

Hobhouse, Penelope; *Color In Your Garden*; 1989; Little, Brown & Company, Boston; ISBN 0-316-36748-6

Jekyll, Gertrude (editor Penelope Hobhouse); *Gertrude Jekyll on Gardening*; 1985; Vintage Books/Random House, NY; ISBN 0-394-72924-2

Lacy, Allen; *The Garden in Autumn*; 1990; The Atlantic Monthly Press; ISBN 0-87113-347-4

Lima, Patrick; *The Harrowsmith Perennial Garden*; 1987; Camden House Publishing; ISBN 0-920656-74-9

Lloyd, Christopher; *Christopher Lloyd's Flower Garden*; 1993; Dorling Kindersley, London; ISBN 0-7513-0023-3

Lloyd, Christopher; *Foliage Plants*; 1985; Viking/Penguin Books, Markham ON; ISBN 0-670-80197-6

Lovejoy, Ann; *The American Mixed Border*; 1993; MacMillan Publishing Company, NY; ISBN 0-02-575580-3

Mitchell, Henry; *One Man's Garden*; 1992; Houghton Mifflin Company, NY; ISBN 0-395-63319-2

Thomas, Graham Stuart; *Perennial Garden Plants*; 1982; J.M. Dent & Sons, Toronto; ISBN 0-460-04575-X

Wilson, Helen Van Pelt; *Helen Van Pelt Wilson's Own Garden and Landscape Book*; 1973; Weathervane Books, NY; ISBN 0-517-191458

C O L O P H O N

Published by:

Valleybrook Gardens Ltd.
Abbotsford, British Columbia, Canada
March, 1995

Printed in Canada by Mitchell Press Ltd.

Book design and production by Edward Kehler, Valleybrook Gardens Ltd.

Cover design by Alfred Siemens.

This entire book was produced on an Apple Power Macintosh® 6100 using Quark Xpress®, Adobe Photoshop™ and Adobe Illustrator® software. Photographs were digitized using Kodak PhotoCD.™ Text was edited with Microsoft® Word.

Type is set in Adobe's Minion™ and Myriad™ typefaces.

Perennial pest problems & remedies

Cultural approaches to pest prevention

Growing strong, healthy plants to begin with can do much towards preventing a buildup of pests. Unhealthy plants seem to give off visual signals of stress that attract a wide range of insect predators.

Siting and spacing

Proper siting alone will meet the basic needs of many plants. Assess what kind of conditions exist in your garden before choosing the appropriate perennials. Getting a soil analysis done might be very helpful, any good garden centre will know how to go about this. A wider initial spacing of plants means that they will take much longer to become congested; when plants are packed closely together they have to compete for available moisture, nutrients and light, which leads to stress.

Maintenance

Regular fertilizing, watering and division of perennials, particularly in a closely-spaced border setting, will help them to stay healthy. See the Introduction for more details about these activities, and for initial soil preparation tips.

Good Hygiene

General garden hygiene is the key to preventing fungal and bacterial disease problems. Remove and dispose of diseased plant material promptly by putting it in the garbage; don't put it in the compost heap or the problem may eventually spread all over the garden. Clean up the dead tops of perennials in late fall or early spring and put them on the compost. This activity does for the border what flossing does for your teeth: it removes the opportunity for insects and diseases to hide and possibly spread to living plants.

Monitor

Throughout the season, keep an eye out for plants that don't look quite right. Examine them for signs of insects or disease and remove the affected part immediately or treat as required before the problem spreads. If you know of certain plants that are particularly prone to aphids or mildew, for example, develop a regular routine of checking them every week or two for signs of trouble. Usually the worst problems develop as weather warms up, especially in humid regions. Early June is an excellent opportunity to prevent a disaster from happening in early July.

Diseases

Much more mysterious than insects, fungal diseases often seem to suddenly appear from nowhere. They are a problem on certain perennials in some years yet don't seem to appear in others. We can blame some of this on the weather conditions that promote the germination and growth of spores that happen to land on the appropriate host plants. Cleaning up garden debris and weeds will help to eliminate many of the fungus spores and bacteria that might be lurking around your healthy plants.

LEAFSPOT: Brown or black spots on leaves. Leaves may drop off.

Damage: Unsightly. May slightly weaken plant.

Recommended controls: Sanitation; remove infected leaves, clean up around plants in fall. Usually worse in warm humid weather. Good air circulation may help in prevention.

Plant hosts: Wide range of perennials and other plants. Peonies, Foxglove.

POWDERY MILDEW: White powdery-looking coating on the upper surface of leaves. Usually apparent in late summer or fall.

Damage: Leaves may drop or be unsightly. Severe, recurrent infestation can weaken and kill plant.

Recommended controls: Increase air circulation. Use a preventative fungicidal spray. Select a resistant variety.

Plant hosts: Wide range of perennials, especially Asters, Phlox, Delphinium, Monarda, Solidago.

RUST: Orange or red spots, usually on the underside of leaves.

Damage: Unsightly. Can weaken plant if severe.

Recommended controls: Sanitation; remove infected leaves. Clear weeds in the vicinity. Use a recommended fungicide.

Plant hosts: Wide range of perennials, especially Hollyhocks, Sidalcea, Lavatera, Heuchera, Helenium, Helianthus, Monarda.

VIRUSES: Wide range of symptoms. Look for stunted, unhealthy-looking plants. Most plant viruses are spread by insect pests.

Damage: Yellowing or mottling leaf colour, crinkled, twisted or distorted leaves, flattened and weird-looking multiple stems (especially lilies).

Recommended controls: Destroy and discard all infected plants. Control insect infestations. No cure. Plants usually wane and die.

Plant hosts: Wide range of perennials, especially Chrysanthemum, Primula, Delphinium.

WILTS: Arching or withered shoots and leaves. Sudden collapsing of infected plants, not due to lack of water. Rather mysterious.

Damage: Shoot or whole plant usually dies.

Recommended controls: May be caused by a fungal or bacterial wilt infection. Destroy and discard infected plants. Wilts are soil-borne so avoid putting another plant of the same kind in the vicinity.

Plant hosts: Wide range of perennials, Asters, Chrysanthemum, Helianthus, Peony Foxglove.